Youth Justice and Child Protection

of related interest

Child Welfare Policy and Practice
Issues and Lessons Emerging from Current Research
Edited by Dorota Iwaniec and Malcolm Hill
ISBN 1 85302 812 6

Effective Ways of Working with Children and their Families
Edited by Malcolm Hill
ISBN 1 85302 619 0
Research Highlights in Social Work 35

Residential Child Care
International Perspectives on Links with Families and Peers
Edited by Mono Chakrabarti and Malcolm Hill
ISBN 1 85302 687 5

Family Support as Reflective Practice
Edited by Pat Dolan, John Canavan and John Pinkerton
Foreword by Neil Thompson
ISBN 1 84310 320 6

Culture and Child Protection: Reflexive Responses
Marie Connolly, Yvonne Crichton-Hill and Tony Ward
ISBN 1 84310 270 6

Working with Gangs and Young People
A Toolkit for Resolving Group Conflict
Jessie Feinstein and Nia Imani Kuumba
ISBN 1 84310 447 4

Young People in Care and Criminal Behaviour
Claire Taylor
Foreword by David Smith
ISBN 1 84310 169 6

Constructive Work with Offenders
Edited by Kevin Gorman, Marilyn Gregory, Michelle Hayles and Nigel Parton
ISBN 1 84310 345 1

Fostering Now
Messages from Research
Ian Sinclair
Foreword by Tom Jeffreys
ISBN 1 84310 362 1

Children Who Commit Acts of Serious Interpersonal Violence
Messages for Best Practice
Edited by Ann Hagell and Renuka Jeyarajah-Dent
ISBN 1 84310 384 2

Youth Justice and Child Protection

*Edited by Malcolm Hill, Andrew Lockyer
and Fred Stone*

Jessica Kingsley Publishers
London and Philadelphia

First published in 2007
by Jessica Kingsley Publishers
116 Pentonville Road
London N1 9JB, UK
and
400 Market Street, Suite 400
Philadelphia, PA 19106, USA

www.jkp.com

Library of Congress Cataloging in Publication Data
Youth justice and child protection / edited by Malcolm Hill, Andrew Lockyer and Fred Stone.
   p. cm.
Includes bibliographical references and index.
ISBN-13: 978-1-84310-279-3 (pbk. : alk. paper)
ISBN-10: 1-84310-279-X (pbk. : alk. paper) 1. Juvenile justice, Administration of. 2. Children--Legal status, laws, etc. 3. Child welfare. 4. Juvenile delinquency. I. Hill, Malcolm. II. Lockyer, Andrew. III. Stone, Frederick H.
   K5575.Y68 2007
   364.36--dc22

                           2006026592

British Library Cataloguing in Publication Data
A CIP catalogue record for this book is available from the British Library

ISBN-13: 978 1 84310 279 3
ISBN-10: 1 84310 279 X

Printed and bound in Great Britain by
Athenaeum Press, Gateshead, Tyne and Wear

Contents

Preface

This book arose out of a conference held in Scotland in September 2003, under the auspices of the University of Glasgow, entitled 'The Scottish Children's Hearings at a Crossroads'. This conference reviewed the Children's Hearings System in the light of developments in other jurisdictions.

The Children's Hearings were first convened in April 1971. They resulted from the recommendations of a working party chaired by a distinguished judge, Lord Kilbrandon, whose report was published in 1964. The remit of this committee was 'to consider the provisions of the law of Scotland relating to the treatment of juvenile delinquents and juveniles in need of care and protection or beyond parental control'. The 'Kilbrandon Report', as it came to be known, aimed to remove children under the age of 16 years from adult criminal procedures. The report proved to be an unexpectedly radical document with its central proposal to replace court attendance by appearance of child and parents before a lay panel of three members: the 'Children's Hearing'.

In the 35 years of their existence these informal panels, comprising and chaired by lay volunteers, have established themselves as a significant contribution to child welfare and juvenile justice in Scotland with only minor modifications of procedures. The decision to bring a child to the Hearing is the responsibility of an official, the Children's Reporter, guided by two considerations: that the grounds for so doing are accepted by the child and parent or can be proved, and that compulsory measures of 'treatment' are required. This separates judgment of innocence or guilt from measures in the interests of the welfare of the child.

Whereas in the early decades of the system, the majority of children were referred because of adolescent behavioural problems, the age range has steadily lowered and the concerns are increasingly those associated with child neglect and abuse. More recently, issues have emerged, social and political, with both national and international implications. Within the United Kingdom, legislative power was devolved to the recreated Scottish Parliament and Executive. In 2004 the Scottish Executive initiated a review of the Scottish Children's Hearings System, partly in response to growing public and political concerns about the care and control of young people.

The European Convention on Human Rights 1950 was incorporated in UK law in 1998. This raised issues on the legal representation of children, the status of lay decision-making, and whether the protection of very young children as well as measures dealing with offences by adolescents could effectively and appropriately belong in a single welfare approach.

The aforementioned conference was held in order to review such matters. Having taken soundings from colleagues who had an intimate knowledge of the Scottish scene and the Hearings, there was strong support for a conference, and while the Scottish dimension was central, there was much to be gained by a broader perspective with participation from abroad. So it came about that the conference proceedings were enriched by participants not only from different parts of the UK but also from Ireland, the Channel Islands, the USA, Finland, Spain and Sweden. It seemed a useful idea, moreover, to produce a book that went beyond the focus of the conference by including accounts of other countries' approaches to similar problems.

The chapters that follow are mainly the work of the conference plenary speakers, augmented by invited contributions. The editors have provided the introductory and concluding sections. Special thanks are due to the enthusiastic and energetic Conference Planning Committee, and the Scottish Executive for timely financial support.

The Conference Planning Committee consisted of the three editors plus Brian Kearney, Sally Kuenssberg, Rita Ray and Barbara Reid.

We are most grateful to our contributors for all their work. Thanks are due to the publishers for their support. We have valued highly the extensive assistance we have received throughout from Ian Gillan, and the hard work and patience of Elaine Cross in referencing and producing the final text.

Introduction: The Principles and Practice of Compulsory Intervention when Children are 'At Risk' or Engage in Criminal Behaviour

Malcolm Hill, Andrew Lockyer and Fred Stone

This book is concerned with the interactions between state responses to offences committed by young people and to 'inadequate care' or 'harm' to children within their families. In other words it deals with the interface between policies and practices in the realms of what are usually designated youth justice or juvenile justice, on the one hand, and child care or child welfare, on the other.

The emphasis is on the ways in which decisions are reached by judicial or quasi-judicial bodies when compulsory action by state agencies is being considered. However, it is recognised that there is a complex relationship between the decision-making framework and the providers of services and alternative care, since the experience and outcomes of sentences or disposals made by courts or other decision-making bodies are crucially affected by the nature of the subsequent measures taken.

Reflecting the origins of the material for the book in an international conference held in Scotland, it concentrates on developments in the UK (particularly Scotland and England), but with a strong comparative focus embracing systems elsewhere in western Europe and in North America. In many countries the media, the public and politicians have recurrently expressed concern about failures both to tackle criminal activity by young people and to protect children from serious harm. The former, for the most part, derives from chronic concerns about threats to the property, peace of mind and safety of adults, although children and young people are themselves also often victims. In contrast, concern about ill-treatment of children has episodically been prompted by extreme incidents, usually involving the death of one or more children (e.g. the Du Troux case in Belgium, and various 'avoidable' child deaths in Britain and North America). These often entail degrees of cruelty that seriously offend normative concepts of childhood.

The central focus of the book will be on whether the ends of justice and effective intervention are better served by treating young people according to the grounds upon which they come to public attention as offenders, victims or both, or on the basis of their individual needs in the context of family support. In the first section of this Introduction we outline important trends in youth justice and child care and protection policy, and the extent to which there has been divergence or convergence. Then we discuss some of the principles that underlie compulsory state intervention in relation to children and families, whether arising from young people's offending behaviour or from the conduct of others towards them. Finally arguments are presented concerning the basis for integrated or separate responses.

Policy trends

In many parts of western Europe and North America, the past 20–30 years have witnessed a tendency towards differentiation of responses to criminal offences committed by children from mechanisms for handling serious concerns about the care of children. This section first examines the extent to which divergence has taken place and why, then considers persistent and new ways in which similar trends have occurred.

Divergence between youth justice and child care and protection

For the last 100 years or more most western countries have accepted that children who break the law should be treated differently from adults on account of their relative immaturity, vulnerability and diminished responsibility, so that special account should be taken of their welfare both in the nature of any proceedings and in decisions about compulsory measures (Goldson

2002). Also 'it is believed that young offenders can, more than adults, be influenced positively' (Walgrave and Mehlbye 1998, p.23).

A somewhat different point from this global distinction between adults and children has been a common assumption that the particular children who engage in crime in a substantial way tend also to have welfare needs related to deficiencies in their upbringing, which partly or wholly account for their criminal activity. Hence, from this point of view, it is necessary to redress those deficiencies and needs in order to tackle crime. This viewpoint was strong in the UK and USA during the 1950s and 1960s when policies and decisions in particular cases often paid little attention to the offence, but were based more on the associated welfare needs (Asquith and Hill 1994; Pitts 1988). Dissatisfaction with this approach grew as it was seen to be ineffective, to ignore formal procedures and lead to interventions that were longer, and possibly more liberty invasive, than other measures (Crawford and Newburn 2003). Governments have also been influenced by recurrent concerns that welfare-based responses to youth crime were too 'soft' (Pitts 2001).

Subsequently, in many jurisdictions changes in approaches to youth crime occurred, which have prioritised specialist attention to offending behaviour, attitudes and beliefs (Bala *et al.* 2002; Buist and Whyte 2004). At the same time, some countries also separated the legal and service processes for dealing with youth crime from those dealing with other protection or 'welfare' matters, such as ill-treatment or family conflict. This divergence has sometimes, though not always, been accompanied by more punishment-orientated measures (Muncie 2004). Most US states have dismantled special court procedures for young people, widened the types of charge and extended the age range for trying young people as adults. Canada's Youth Criminal Justice Act 2001 'prioritised punishment and accountability' (Muncie 2004, p.157). After 1989, New Zealand law separated child welfare and juvenile offending cases, and stressed responsibility and accountability, tempered by an emphasis on diversion and use of least restrictive alternatives wherever possible (Maxwell and Morris 2002). In Australia the 1980s and 1990s witnessed 'a clear shift from the welfare approach', with a greater emphasis on retribution and imprisonment of young offenders (Omaji 2003, p.69).

In England, according to Crawford and Newburn (2003) the move away from 'welfarism' was rapid. During the late 1980s and early 1990s government policy encouraged a shift in practice 'from the provision of generic help and support to offenders to a much more specific focus on offending as the target for change' (Stewart *et al.* 1994, p.3). Juvenile courts had previously dealt with a wide range of concerns about children, but were now replaced by separate youth courts for offending, and family courts for care and protection issues. Also youth justice services have been separated from social work services for children and families (Bottoms and Dignan 2004). However, more welfare, supportive approaches often remain at ground level, cohabiting with more recent top-down changes (Muncie 2004). In Germany, separate courts had existed for many years, but in the 1980s efforts to establish a unitary youth protection system reached the draft law stage. In the end a bipartite system was retained (Weitekamp, Kerner and Herberger 1998).

Such segregation has been contrasted with the situation in Scotland (e.g. Asquith 1998; King 1994b), where for the most part all serious concerns about children and young people that invoke the possibility of compulsory intervention, whether on the basis of their behaviour or of how they are treated, continue to be dealt with by the same decision-making forum, with the child's interests the primary consideration. Decisions about the need for compulsory measures are taken not by courts but by Children's Hearings, which are informal though structured meetings where three lay representatives of the community decide what should be done (Lockyer and Stone 1998).

However, the use of this bipolar distinction between two sharply distinct approaches can be misleading and is often exaggerated. Although many countries have shifted towards offences as primary determinants of outcomes, nearly all do take some account of children's welfare as required by the Beijing Rules of 1985 and the UN Convention on the Rights of the Child (UNCRC). Furthermore, in many countries of Europe the move to separate court systems for young offenders from those dealing with care and protection has largely been confined to an older age group (typically 15 years plus), so that younger children who offend continue to be dealt with by welfare-orientated courts and agencies (Booth 1991; Buist and Whyte 2004). In countries such as Belgium, France and Italy, although there have been times of greater emphasis on punishment, the same court has retained concurrent jurisdiction to deal with child protection matters and crime (Walgrave 1996; Waterhouse and McGhee 2004), while in the Netherlands juvenile justice has remained 'embedded in the more encompassing childcare and protection system' (Junger-Tas 1998, p.392). Decisions are usually based on assessment of family circumstances and the child's needs, and the same types of services are brought into play for offending as for care and protection.

Some countries have recently sought to reconcile welfare and offence considerations in a new way. For instance, Zermatten (2004) describes Swiss legislation introduced in 2003 for dealing with youth crime as reviving an orientation to child protection, while retaining formal processes. Key features include: clear procedural guarantees for young people in conflict with the law; requirements for courts and others to consider all the personal and family cir-cumstances of the child; and a favouring of out-of-court measures, with detention and custody to be used as a last resort. In the Netherlands and England, increasingly services have focused on the 'causes' of youth crime, which usually correspond with meeting individual and family needs (Haines and Drakeford 1998; van der Laan 2003).

Within child care and protection policy and service organisation, there has also been a tendency towards internal division. In the USA, Canada, the UK and Australia methods and staff dealing with child abuse have often become specialist and separated from other kinds of work with children and families, particularly family support but also sometimes arrangements for children in foster and residential care. Child protection in the 1990s came to focus largely on the investigation of child abuse allegations and on associated decisions about whether or not compulsory intervention was needed. Many have criticised this trend as overly bureaucratic and legalised, neglecting issues of prevention and giving low priority to help or treatment for the children affected (Parton 1991; Waldfogel 2001; Waterhouse 1993). By contrast, countries like France, Germany and the Netherlands have main-tained a more holistic approach based more on assessment and meeting of needs than on the identification and minimisation of risk (Cooper 2005; Hetherington and Stanley-Hagan 1999).

Commonalities in trends

Although there has been increased segregation in many countries in responses to youth crime and children's welfare and safety, shared features are also evident. In current *theorising* much common ground exists with regard to the importance of early emotional attachment for both phenomena (Hirschi and Gottfredson 1991; Howe *et al.* 1999), as well as the wider social environment

(Jack 2000; Smith 1995). Similarly, the ideas of resilience in child care and desistance with regard to youth crime each emphasise strengths and choices in the individual or social network that can help them recover from a poor start (Bottoms *et al.* 2004; Luthar 2003).

A parallel organisational development has been a strong emphasis on *inter-professional and inter-agency co-operation.* Many child abuse inquiries have for years highlighted the need to improve communication and planning at both case and strategic levels (Munro 2002). More recently the British government has promoted service collaboration in relation to youth crime, for instance by multi-agency partnerships (Smith 2003).

A strong development in the UK across a range of policy areas, including child and family policy, has been the growth of accountability mechanisms, including more widespread agency inspections, government targets and standards, and the proliferation of performance indicators. Among the aims have been to improve quality of services and ensure that these are delivered in line with government targets (Flynn 2002), but these policy mechanisms have also been perceived as ways of extending state control over professionals and have been criticised for unintended negative consequences (Garrett 2003; Goldson, Lavalette and McKechnie 2002). Examples have been the priority given to speeding up the time taken to deal with crime (Hill *et al.* 2005; van der Laan 2003) and adoption (Lowe *et al.* 1999).

Both youth justice and child protection have been influenced by the aspiration of *quantifying* 'risk' and then tailoring responses to the level of risk. This can be seen as part of the project of late modernity, which seeks to minimise threats to well-being by applying scientific or insurance-based principles (Beck 1992). In child protection, the move towards formal risk assessment has been especially strong in the USA, Canada and Australia, where in many states and provinces it has become a mandatory case allocation and management tool. Standard scales are used to assess risk of abuse or re-abuse, based on formal research into factors associated with different kinds of abuse, usually physical injury and neglect. This is regarded as a means of targeting resources where they are most needed and also avoiding un-necessary interventions in 'low risk' cases. However, risk assessment has been criticised for the crude basis of the factor analysis, neglect of environmental influences and for producing a form of rationing, whereby families in need get little or no help if they have a low risk level (Kufeldt and McKenzie 2003;

Tomison 2002). In parts of Europe such as Sweden, Belgium and the Netherlands, much greater reliance is placed on professional skill and discretion to determine the allocation of services (Hill, Stafford and Green Lister 2003).

Similarly in American and British youth justice a marked trend has been apparent towards what Muncie (2004) terms actuarial justice, through the use of performance targets and standardised risk assessment tools like ASSET and Youth Level of Service (YLS) (Baker 2004). Several of the dimensions covered are similar to those in child abuse risk assessment, but with less focus on parenting and more on peers and the external environment. Naturally the pattern of offending is of critical importance, while in child protection it is the history of care and ill-treatment that is central: both the frequency and severity of past behaviour (offending or abusive) are strong indicators of future risk (Beckett 2003; Farrington 1992). Risk assessment scales in youth justice work have been criticised for subjective application, being ill suited to deal with the dynamic interaction of risk factors and for translating structural issues like unemployment into an individual issue (Kemshall 2005).

As in social policy more generally, both child protection and youth justice have been affected by the popularity among many professionals and politicians of *evidence-based policy and practice* (Fullwood and Powell 2004; Jonkman, Junger-Tas and van Dijk 2005; Newman 2004). The idea that policies and interventions should be based on 'robust' evaluations showing they are effective seems to offer both certainty of good outcomes and an avoidance of prejudice or taken-for-granted assumptions in determining how to respond. However, evidence can be conflicting or open to interpretation (Hill 1999; Trinder 2000) and may be invoked selectively to fit with pre-existing values.

Despite these qualifications, a fair degree of consensus has emerged in the field of youth justice about effective intervention (Lipsey 1995; Utting and Vennard 2000). Among the key conclusions are that structured, focused work with individuals and families, often having a cognitive-behavioural component, tends to be most effective. While this supports very specific interventions, research also shows that success in reducing problems comes from multi-dimensional and multi-level comprehensive programmes (Burnett and Roberts 2004; Lipsey 1995). Interestingly, more diffuse evidence in the care and protection field has often reached similar conclusions (Cameron 2003; Corby 2000).

Finally there has been a trend to include *community and family members* in decision-making. By contrast with traditional societies, in many countries nowadays decisions about societal responses to family problems and threats to social order have become increasingly specialist, professionalised and detached from ordinary people. Recently attempts have been made to re-connect official action with the community, both with regard to those directly affected as perpetrators or victims and to those who in some way represent the community as a whole. In this context, 'community' is roughly equivalent to those living in the area where problems occur.

There is a long tradition of lay involvement in judicial decision-making that dates back to classical Greece where citizen 'juries' sat in judgment of their fellow citizens and office holders. In modern times the appointment of juries and lay judges as decision-makers has been linked with varied concepts of community, represented for instance by elite members or peers. The justification for lay involvement is that a public interest exists in the decision to be made. This is particularly so when dealing with young people since the community beyond the household is thought to share some responsibility for their well-being.

Community-based strategies for preventing youth crime, such as community safety and situational crime prevention measures, are now common (Muncie *et al.* 1995), but such approaches are less developed in child protection (though see Fuchs 1995; Gilligan 1999). One interesting initiative has been Communities that Care, which is based on neighbourhood risk assessments and actions tailored to the local area in order to reduce crime, in part through tackling social and environmental problems that affect family well-being. The aim is to reduce local risk factors and enhance protective factors (France and Crow 2005). Developed in North America, this model has been applied in the UK and the Netherlands, the latter building on existing preventive programmes (Jonkman *et al.* 2005). Pitts and Hope (1998) contrast the British approach, focusing on community safety and risk management, with the French emphasis on social inclusion by offering positive education, employment and housing services to alienated young people.

Family Group Conferences and restorative justice are two developments initiated in New Zealand and Australia that have had a major impact in many parts of the world. The adaptation of these traditional Maori approaches within the statutory system in New Zealand has been associated with large reductions in the 'numbers of children and young people both in care and custody' (Jackson and Nixon 1999, p.133). In the field of child protection Family Group Conferences blend the idea of extended kin gatherings, which have long dealt with local problems in many non-western societies, and the more modern practice of case conferences (i.e. inter-agency meetings aimed at improving communication and shared decision-making). They represent an attempt to hand back power to key figures in a child's social network (normally relatives, but including friends, neighbours and others) and to enable the child to benefit from the resources available in that network, while incorporating mechanisms to ensure the child's safety. In situations of serious actual or potential abuse, the professionals retain the right to veto plans they think do not safeguard the child's welfare (Jackson and Nixon 1999; Lupton 2000; Marsh and Crow 1998).

Family Group Conferences have also been used to deal with young people who offend, and in Australia and New Zealand their widespread use is associated with low rates of formal processing by courts of youth offences (Muncie 2004). In the UK, use of family group conferences by youth justice workers has been slower to develop than in the child protection field, but some schemes have been introduced (Marsh and Crow 1998; McKenzie 2000).

Restorative justice ideas have come to prominence even more recently, prompting many systems to place greater emphasis on the interests of victims. (Edwards 2004; Miers 2001). Both principles and mechanisms are diverse, but the two key ideas are, first, that offenders should in some way make amends for their crime to those affected, whether by way of apology or compensation to victims, or making reparation to the community at large and, second, this should have a positive impact on the offender's self-regard, having a rehabilitative or reintegrative affect (Braithwaite 1989). The growing use of restorative justice has been criticised for being imposed on victims who may not want it, placing pressures on young people who may not be able to handle it and providing an individualised response to a public problem. Also 'private and parochial interests' may skew public decisions (Crawford and Newburn 2003, p.50).

In principle, restorative justice is also relevant to child abuse, since the abusers are usually offenders. However, the power imbalance and in many instances the family relationships often make it difficult to apply reparation without potentially distressing the children involved or exposing them to further harm. Sometimes it can be part of a family reunification plan for parents or other abusers to apologise and make amends.

Having discussed divergent and convergent trends in policy and practice, we now take a step back to review the principles that underpin state intervention with respect to children, whatever the ground for action. This leads on to consideration of arguments concerning the extent to which integrated or separate decision-making systems are desirable for handling child crime, care and protection issues.

Compulsory state intervention: general principles and concepts

When there is compulsory intervention in the lives of children and their families by agencies of the state, there is some loss of liberty and potential for inequity. The intervention must therefore accord with principles that are justifiable. Of particular importance for the central theme of this book is to examine whether essentially the same or different considerations apply when the intervention is precipitated by young people committing offences as when they are being harmed or are at risk of harm. This may not settle the further question as to whether 'systems' of juvenile justice and care and protection are best integrated, separated or overlapping, but this has a bearing on the conceptual coherence of their integration or distinctness.

Justice and welfare

Since the 1960s, a central thread in discussion on this matter has been the appeal to two contrasted concepts of justice and welfare. These terms both have multiple meanings. They are used to describe, first, a set of institutional arrangements (i.e. 'justice' or 'welfare' systems) and, second, a set of ideals carrying evaluative or prescriptive force. To lessen confusion, we have decided where possible in this book to employ the phrase 'child care and protection system' instead of 'welfare system'. Welfare is commonly used to summarise children's well-being, needs and interests. Systems that prioritise the child's interests whatever the reason for public intervention have therefore been characterised as having a 'welfare' approach. Likewise, besides referring descriptively to formal organisations that deal with crime, justice has a long-standing sense of embracing a cluster of ideas about fairness and equity. However, it has also been used in recent decades to refer to an approach to youth crime that contrasted with the welfare approach. In that context, the 'justice approach' might more accurately have been described as a 'due process and outcome approach' since it emphasises that responses to youth crime should follow due process (e.g. presumption of innocence; rights to answer allegations, have legal representation, appeal) (van der Laan 2003) and have dispositions that are proportionate to the offence (Crawford and Newburn 2003). These matters, it is said, have often been ignored when the child's welfare has been a primary consideration in decision-making.

We suggest that the presumed opposition of these two approaches can be challenged not only by unpacking their ambiguous labels, but also more substantively their rationales and implications. In particular, state actions on the grounds of fundamental need may be expressed according to the requirements of justice as well as the recipient's welfare (Miller 1976; Campbell 1988).

The concept of welfare has long been associated with the idea that the state has the ultimate responsibility of ensuring that the most basic needs of its citizens are met (Pinker 1979). The idea of the 'welfare state' had its origin in the nineteenth century with the endeavour to mitigate the worst effects of unregulated market capitalism (Macpherson1977; Polanyi 1968). The nature and role of the state has long been highly contested, but it has been recognised across the political spectrum that producing the next generation of citizens cannot be left entirely to the resources of households, neither in terms of doing justice to individuals, nor in the interests of preserving the social order (O'Neill 1994). The provision of compulsory schooling, in addition to child welfare services and family support, is grounded in the belief that, whatever the differences in family circumstances, children deserve as equal a chance as possible (Fishkin 1983; Gutmann 1987). This links the idea of welfare with a conception of justice, albeit one which presumes that some social goods are entitlements that do not necessarily have to be 'earned' or merited by the actions of the individual recipient.

Justice in its most general sense, as Aristotle put it, is 'treating equals equally and unequals unequally' (*Ethics*, Book V); this amounts to 'giving each their due', which requires taking account of all morally relevant differences

(Campbell 1988). What ought to be a relevant consideration is of course contestable. Some of what human beings deserve depends not upon what they have done, but upon the fact of being human. There is a widespread belief that at least some of what children deserve derives from their status as immature human beings. It can plausibly be argued that the younger they are, the less their circumstances are of their own choosing or making, so the less responsible they are for their characters and conduct (Lockyer 1982). Hence all children should have their basic needs met, not as a matter of charity or as a condition of good behaviour, but as a requirement of justice. Given this presumption, differential treatment rather than equality of treatment requires to be justified (Lindlay 1989).

Central to (social) justice is the doctrine of equality of opportunity. When applied to children this entails a general obligation to equalise starting points, to achieve 'a level playing field'. Thus, where possible, provision should be made to compensate for, or mitigate, disadvantages present at birth and equip children for an 'open future' (Archard 2004; Feinberg 1980). The means by which individuals may activate their life plans can be conceived as 'social goods', which include liberties and opportunities, as well as material resources (Rawls 1972). Compulsory education is a very powerful mechanism to compensate for disadvantaged upbringing (Gutmann 1987; Williams 1990). Nonetheless the difficulty of combating disadvantage is highlighted by the persistence of indicators of early childhood disadvantage across the life course (e.g. as regards health, occupational status) (Sealander 2003). Moreover, household poverty and family instability correlate closely with such indicators, including school problems and lack of educational attainment (Hill and Tisdall 1997).

In relation to many social goods, parents and families remain the principal providers (with certain exceptions like formal education and acute specialist medical care). Yet the community and the state have a responsibility to safeguard the welfare of children (*parens patriae*). Hence the state cannot be neutral in relation to family life – even though many would wish it to be (Harding 1996). Many consider a loving home environment to be a necessary condition for children's well-being, their access to other social goods and responsible behaviour. There may be no true substitute that a state can provide (Archard 2003). There is much evidence that state services aiming to give support to failing families or provide satisfactory substitute care tend at best to mitigate disadvantage and in some cases may make things worse (Hill and Tisdall 1997; Ward 1995). If this is the case, the unequal starting point of children will remain relevant in other dealings that the state has with them, as in relation to youth crime, arguably even when they cease to be young.

Communities expect care and protection systems to adjudicate on what degree of parental shortcomings can and cannot be tolerated. When a child's welfare is seriously threatened or a child's behaviour is seen to pose a serious threat to others, then the state may be justified in overriding parental views or even children's own wishes and in seeking to change the child's care environment whether through modifying parental actions or insisting on alternative care. This raises questions about rights, in particular the balance between parents, the state and children themselves in determining what should happen to children and the different kinds of rights accorded to children or claimed by them as a basis for action.

Children and rights

The introduction of the vocabulary of rights, moral or legal, into discourses on children is a relatively modern phenomenon (Franklin 1986; Veerman 1992). Whereas a child's needs (however determined) may invoke a wish to respond, the critical feature of a right is that someone has a *duty* with respect to it. The obligation may be moral or legal. The idea of all human beings possessing rights inherent in their 'natures' is a doctrine that surfaced in seventeenth-century England (Locke 1687). From this time onwards, it has been widely accepted that some human rights are operative from the moment of birth, and that others will be postponed until the onset of rationality or the capacity for informed choice, which some equate with adulthood and some believe comes earlier.

The difference between rights possessed from birth and those acquired later corresponds with a distinction between two kinds of rights involved. One kind of right confers on the right-holder choice and freedoms but the second designates the right-holder as entitled to receive a social good. The first (*rights of action*) require the right-holder to be active and competent, whereas the latter (*rights of recipience*) do not (Raphael 1967). Rights of action cannot be exercised on someone else's behalf, though others may facilitate or hinder them. The right to freedom of expression, assembly or the right to vote are examples. By contrast, rights of recipience can sometimes be at the discretion of the right-holder if they are deemed competent to choose, or at the discretion of others (normally parents or guardians) to consent on the child's behalf, such as the right to medical treatment. (For a range of views on children's rights see Franklin 2002 and Freeman 2004.) Sometimes rights of recipience are considered so important that they are non-optional. The right to compulsory education is the most notable instance of this (Haydon 1977). As a consequence, school has become an influential context for the manifestation of both care and behaviour issues in children. School non-attendance is unlawful and hence a basis for possible legal or administrative actions, occupying an important space between protection and crime.

Justice for those below the age of majority must start with deciding what rights they share with adults, what rights may legitimately be denied them, and what rights they alone deserve in virtue of their particular status (Archard 2003). A minority of theorists subscribe to the so-called 'will or choice theory of rights', which claims all rights to entail the exercise of choice. In their view, a good or benefit cannot be the subject of a right if it is not 'willed' but is compulsory or coerced. Thus children, if they are not entitled to choose, cannot be right-holders, though they can be the beneficiaries of others' duties (Hart 1982; Milne 1973). This theory has been largely discredited by widespread acceptance that rights language is appropriate to describe the entitlements of those below the age of rational choice (Campbell 1983; MacCormick 1976). However, it remains common to think of rights in the first instance as liberties, because in liberal societies we are inclined to favour individuals choosing what benefits them.

On the other hand, where children are concerned, the presumption is reversed. Early international documents concerned specifically with children's rights addressed rights to receive education, protection and welfare (rights of recipience), but not the rights of children to exercise liberty or participate in decision-making (rights of action) (Veerman 1992). The UNCRC was the first to endorse that children have rights to act on their own behalves. The Convention acknowledges both the particular vulnerability of children and their entitlements to share in some of liberties hitherto reserved to adults. The principles embodied in the UN convention are equally applicable whether the recipients of state action are offenders or victims. Arguably participatory rights imply that young people should have a say in the extent to which their care needs and behaviour are handled conjointly or separately.

The rights that the convention endorses are open to wide interpretation and not always compatible with each other (King 1994a). They may not adequately accommodate the legitimate interests of other parties, such as victims who may themselves be children (Hafen and Hafen 1996; Wardle 1996). However, the UNCRC sets a standard for signatory states to recognise the particular responsibility they bear to look to the well-being of those who at present are not yet judged equipped to exercise full adult rights (Freeman 2000).

One of the most intractable difficulties in the generalised discussion of the rights and responsibilities of not-yet-adults, is that the class of human beings referred to is a very diverse one. Different terms, like infants or teenagers, are more specific, but each of these categories is diverse and they intersect or overlap. For some purposes the UN Convention's definition of 'children' may be sufficient: those below the age of majority (which in almost all signatory states is age 18). It must always be borne in mind that, especially with regard to action rights, a child's age and understanding are relevant considerations as acknowledged in the Convention and much national legislation. On the other hand, it may be all too easy for adults to underestimate children's capacities or use their presumed level of understanding as a reason for denying them rights (Franklin 2002; Holt 1975). It will rarely be contrary to a child's welfare for him or her to freely express their views, and such expression will often be pertinent to the determination of where their interests truly lie (Archard 2004).

PROCEDURAL RIGHTS AND JUSTICE

As noted earlier, central to modern western law has been a set of procedures intended to ensure that the accused can answer allegations and have a fair opportunity to influence outcomes, such that individuals are protected from arbitrary treatment. An important distinction must be made between a just procedure and a just outcome. For some institutions, properly following the rules of procedure are the only grounds for judging whether an outcome is fair or just. For example, a just election is one where the appointed candidate receives the most valid votes after an election process that conforms to electoral law. However, in other cases, a fair procedure that observes the rights of parties does not guarantee a just or fair outcome, because the criterion of justness is something other than the procedure itself. A just procedure for hearing and deciding upon the evidence does not guarantee that the guilty are convicted and the innocent are not.

Rights that attach especially to accused persons in a court process have come to be called (following US constitutional language) 'due process' rights (Watkins 1998). These include the right to have notice of the accusation, to challenge it, to cite witnesses and examine others, to have legal representation and rights of appeal. In the USA, the juvenile court's disposition to set aside these rights was criticised most famously in the Gault case, which led to a young person being sent to an institution for many years as a response to a minor legal infringement (O'Brien 2004). According to Omaji (2003) 'Gault signalled a major shift of the focus of delinquency proceedings from a child's best interests to proof of legal guilt in adversarial fashion, and from procedural informality to "due process" requirements' (p.68).

Without doubt procedural rights are important to secure a visibly fair hearing and to protect accused persons against unwarranted loss of liberty. However, it appears that sometimes due process rights have prevented just outcomes. This has occurred in relation to child protection when a proceeding has been abandoned, or court finding set aside, because of a minor 'technically' deficient procedure (e.g. an unsigned warrant to investigate). This suggests that the principle observing the due process rights of accused persons might require on occasion to be balanced by other considerations, such as community safety or victim protection, or even the welfare of the accused themselves (Sealander 2003).

It is highly relevant to ask whether the procedural rights of parties are similar or different, depending on whether the procedure applies to convicting and sentencing, or to care and protection. It is helpful to differentiate the process of proof from disposition. The grounds for intervention with respect to care and protection proceedings may be used in a criminal proceeding against an adult and/or it may result in a civil process alleging harm, risk of harm or absence of care. Different standards of proof often operate in criminal and care proceedings. In some jurisdictions the process in the latter is inquisitorial rather than adversarial, which makes a difference to procedural rights (Koppen 2002). The procedure to determine the facts on the evidence, and the rights of parties, are not essentially different between the types of proceedings, although the range of interested parties may be wider in care proceedings.

Whether the 'due process' applies equally to the disposal decision will be affected by whether the disposal is viewed as a penalty or an outcome aiming to serve the best interests of the child and/or the interests of other legitimate parties. In respect of care and protection proceedings the disposal decisions based on welfare and the assessment of needs tend to be more complex and varied, but this does not make the need for a fair decision procedure any less important. Indeed, when the disposal is not closely prescribed by the finding of fact, the rights of parties to influence dispositions are arguably more to be valued.

The issue of how different should be the application of principles of justice and rights in proceedings associated with young offenders or care and protection depends heavily on whether the state punishment of young people is considered to be legitimate and, if so, whether it is necessarily distinct from compulsory intervention aimed at serving their interests.

PUNISHMENT AND RESPONSIBILITY

The justness of punishing the young is a matter of substantial ideological differences, though also misrepresentation of opponents' views (Acton 1969; Bean 1981). The meaning of punishment has varied connotations (Honderich 1989). For example, if a family member uses extreme violence or neglect as a form of punishment, this constitutes both an illegal act and a basis for child protective intervention. More commonly, use of punishment in family life occurs immediately after an action within a context of long-term, loving relationships and a nexus of shared understandings (Lockyer 1982). Punishments are intended to be educative and constructive. Some states imitate such informality and aims when dealing with crime by younger children.

Usually, however, state punishment for law-breaking is highly formalised. It may be defined for present purposes as deliberate and institutionalised infliction of a penalty or deprivation on an offender for an offence (Quinton 1969). Those punished do not need to experience pain or suffering, but an intended penalty or loss of entitlement. Deprivation of liberty through compulsory alternative care is sometimes justified not as punishment but in terms of the child's interests by providing more effective socialisation, though this may be experienced as punishment by the child or family members.

Punishment by the state ought to be public, impartial and impersonal; it requires a formal procedural framework, involving strict standards of proof, rights of challenge and defence. Conviction is a weighty matter of lasting significance. In these respects public punishment is very different from private punishment in the family (Lockyer 1982). Rather it is to apply to children a similar (though not necessarily identical) mode of court-based justice to that imposed on adults.

A minimal requirement of just punishment is that the offender must be legally responsible, or culpable, for the criminal act. The common law doctrine is that an offender must be proved to have a 'guilty mind' (*mens rea*), one prerequisite of which is that he or she must have the mental capacity to understand the wrong committed (Hart 1968; Williams 1954). It is a concept of ancient origin that below a certain age there can be no criminal capacity (the minor is *doli incapax*) and above that age, but below adulthood, a young person's criminal capacity requires to be proved – quite apart from proof of the facts of the case (Crofts 1998). The problematic nature of the concept of a minimum age of criminal responsibility is illustrated by the fact that in western Europe the ages range from 7 in Ireland and Switzerland to 18 in Belgium (Asquith 1998). Many jurisdictions are also experiencing significant tensions between the growing popular demand to set aside some long-standing protections against treating young people as adult offenders and the acknowledgement of children's rights as defined by the UNCRC, which also specifies that children should be treated separately from adults (Bala *et al.* 2002).

There appear to be two distinct approaches to the association of criminal capacity and age. The first allows that young children may be held legally culpable, open to prosecution in court if their offence is serious enough, but their immaturity is a source of mitigation. The second is to set a higher age threshold for crime and punishment, and treat the equivalent of offending behaviour by those below the age as grounds for other forms of compulsory intervention. Scotland has a peculiar combination of the two in allowing that 'offences' may be committed by children as young as eight (if *doli incapax* is rebutted), but they cannot be prosecuted and punished below 16, unless the offence is especially grave (Kearney 2000).

Ultimately the justification of punishment cannot be grounded upon what Bentham (1789) called its 'efficaciousness'. If social utility was the sole criterion, this could justify punishing the innocent or draconian penalties for minor infringements of the law. To be just, punishment must be deserved and proportionate. This depends upon being able to assign a high degree of responsibility to individual offenders. With children, to whom we attribute less than full moral autonomy, the apportionment of blame for their conduct is not straightforward. The principle of criminal capacity requires that someone has an understanding of right and wrong, but if a child's understanding is greatly at odds with society's morality, this will have something to do with his or her socialisation. Those responsible for a young person's upbringing, and for the culture into which they have been socialised, must at least share some of the responsibility for the child's understanding and conduct (Lockyer 1982). This is not to exonerate the young, nor necessarily blame parents, peers, neighbourhood or educators. It is only to observe that the punitive approach operates with a narrow conception of individual responsibility, which fails to acknowledge much of the social reality that is the moral backdrop to offending and non-socially conforming behaviour.

The issue of punishment also arises when parents or carers unlawfully mistreat children. Intentional harm to children by those with a duty to care is reprehensible and merits punishment of those who abuse their power. Whether or not it merits temporary or permanent loss of parental rights will be matter for careful consideration. However, neglect of children's well-being and interests is not so easy to characterise and condemn, as this may arise from ignorance, incapacity or ill health, and from lack of resources or opportunity (Stevenson 1996).

In some jurisdictions the disposition to prove criminal harm, and punish the perpetrator of it, risks overriding the needs of the young victim (Sealander 2003). The welfare principle (Article 3 of the UNCRC) means that the child's interests in care and protection proceedings should be the primary consideration and may take precedence over meting out just deserts to offenders against children. A state's care and protection system must consider whether any compulsion is justified, on the child or parents, not as an aspect of punishment but as an aspect of welfare. This reinforces the importance of listening to children's views (Article 12), especially on possible parenting, as an essential aspect of any decision procedure concerned with their care and protection, short and long term.

Arguments and evidence for and against separating youth justice and care and protection

Questions of welfare, justice, rights and punishment inform debates about the merits of integrated or separated approaches, but other issues are relevant too, notably ideas about cause and effect. Here we set out five main kinds of argument used, recognising that these may overlap and conflict. We examine each of these in turn, along with associated evidence where pertinent.

Arguments based on welfare and punishment considerations

We have seen that the welfare of a child is pertinent when considering both their needs and behaviour on the basis of social justice. The UN Convention on the Rights of the Child asserts that all actions by courts and other public bodies concerning children should have the child's best interest as a primary consideration (Article 3), while dispositions should be appropriate to their well-being as well as proportionate to both their circumstances and offence (Article 40). Most jurisdictions accept that for younger children this means that children should be 'treated alike on the basis of their needs' (Lockyer 1994, p.118), but to varying degrees many favour differential responses from about ages 14 or 15. Social justice considerations indicate that as long as a young person is at least partially dependent on others for their care, the state has a continuing obligation to seek to offset disadvantage. A whole-child approach to implementation of this principle suggests that, regardless of age, the interlocking nature of a child's needs and deeds requires an integrated, comprehensive appraisal and the same set of options.

As noted earlier, critics of a single system have pointed to evidence that children's welfare has been harmed in practice by decision-makers restricting their liberty for excessive periods of time in the belief that this was in the child's interest. A further suggestion is that young people benefit from seeing a clear separation between responses to their behaviour and to their personal or family needs. As Muncie (2004) expressed it, young people should not be 'sentenced for their backgrounds as well as their offence' (p.156). Also law-abiding children who appear at a hearing on care grounds may resent being associated with those accused of crimes. These points could apply equally well to younger children, but in fact, as we have seen, separation tends to occur only from the mid-teens onwards. One factor in this is that older children who break the law are regarded as more responsible for their actions, so that formal procedures and potentially more restrictive outcomes are seen as desirable. The effects of unequal starting points and socialisation become less prominent considerations, punishment more so.

Arguments based on procedural rights

In North America, England and elsewhere the political and legal impetus to separate out youth justice from welfare considerations was strongly influenced by the belief that welfare-based decision-making overrode rights to due process that had been hard won in criminal matters. Questions of guilt and innocence and the opportunity to have a fair hearing about the facts prompting state intervention were thought to have been sidelined by a well-meaning but overzealous concern to take action 'in the interests' of the child or young person (Crawford and Newburn 2003). Rights to legal representation were often weak or absent. This was not simply a matter of procedural irregularity, since the consequences for some young people involved restrictions of liberty, which could go beyond what many people deemed appropriate. Hence, it is argued, formal procedures are required for young people accused of a crime to protect them from arbitrary decisions, which might be ostensibly in their interests, but in practice serve the interests of society to the detriment of young people.

Conversely, relatively informal processes involving a range of relevant parties, as in Scotland, can help achieve consensus about appropriate actions, in circumstances when strict procedures may divide and polarise (Lockyer 1994). The Scottish Hearings System, which continues to respond to offences on welfare criteria, has been criticised over the years for inadequate legal safeguards. This has in part been based on a mis-perception, since any denial of guilt is dealt with formally by a court and only if proven is the case returned to a hearing for a decision. Also, although decisions are intended to arise from informal dialogue, the Hearings do have a number of procedural requirements, such as ensuring that young people and parents know what the basis for their presence is and understand the potential outcomes (Hallett *et al.* 1998).

Arguments based on causation

It has long been realised that both young people with welfare problems and those who engage in youth crime often have similar background characteristics. Typically these relate to poverty (low-income families, growing up in deprived neighbourhoods) and parenting difficulties (including family separation, mental health problems, violence and conflict). Many studies have shown that youth crime is associated with family 'pathology' and poverty (Farrington 1992). Likewise, these are key factors in child abuse (Corby 2000).

The implication of common causation is that similar measures are needed to address the same underlying causes. The Kilbrandon Report (1964), which led to the setting up of the integrated Scottish Children's Hearings System, stated that the legal distinction between juvenile offenders and other children in need of care was 'very often of little practical significance when the "underlying realities" were examined' (Kilbrandon Committee 1964, p.12). Similarly, neighbourhood-based prevention programmes, whether having a focus on public health, family support or crime reduction, are based on attempts to reduce similar sets of risk factors (France and Utting 2005).

On the other hand, this commonality of causal factors may be seen as only or mainly relevant to long-term prevention, but not to dealing with problems once they have arisen. From this point of view, crime, poor care and abuse are different symptoms or outcomes of similar circumstances with contrasting trajectories and implications, so they require distinctive attention. Linked to this perspective are claims that prevention is difficult to achieve, so it is necessary to concentrate on actions that succeed in reducing 'symptoms' like offending. This relates to a further claim that seeking to modify the welfare-related influences on criminal activity often does not stop reoffending, whereas a structured focus on offence-related patterns of thinking and opportunities is effective, as discussed below (Utting and Vennard 2000).

Arguments based on identity

Even if youth crime and child abuse and neglect may have similar causes, this does not necessarily mean that they occur in the same individuals and families. Evidence suggests that there is no inevitable association between experience of familial care problems and current or later criminal activity (Smith 1995). Peer associations and neighbourhood norms in certain areas may encourage endemic crime almost regardless of family circumstances. Conversely, many young people whose parental or substitute care is problematic, nevertheless have the personal and/or environmental strengths to avoid engagement in crime.

Nevertheless, it is common for children and young people who have serious family care problems to be or become offenders. Many young people who offend were previously ill-treated and/or looked after in public care early in their lives, while disproportionate numbers concurrently face major welfare issues (Huizinga and Jakob-Chien 1998; Taylor 2003; Thornberry, Ireland and Smit 2001). Child maltreatment and early emotional trauma heighten the risk of future delinquency, though this largely concerns those who have experienced prolonged abuse (Greenwald 2002; Thornberry *et al.* 2001). An English study on young adult offenders revealed that at least one-quarter had been in public care (Stewart *et al.* 1994). American studies have shown that early emotional trauma is commonly a precursor of violence and crime in adolescence and that multiple placements in care are associated with 'heightened rates of delinquent outcomes' (Jonson-Reid 2004; McConville 2003). Many young people in detention for offences have been in residential care when younger (Ross, Conger and Armstrong 2002).

This close link means that, where justice and care and protections are separate, the same young people will often at the same time be involved with both welfare and justice agencies and require judicial attention on both welfare and criminal grounds. A national study in the USA showed that a high proportion of young people with serious emotional problems were receiving services from three or more systems (i.e. child welfare, mental health, education, juvenile justice) (Howell *et al.* 2004). Such multi-agency involvement may provide added value in that the input is greater and the different aspects of the individual's problems receive dedicated attention. Equally there are dangers of duplication of time and effort on the part of both professionals and clients, while communication problems and conflicting goals may arise unless there is careful co-ordination. In New York, poor co-operation between child welfare services and youth justice professionals is apparently common and can contribute to high levels of detention (Ross *et al.* 2002). In an integrated system, as in Scotland, it is possible for decision-makers and professionals to address problems in the round and easier to provide a consistent approach, though tensions still arise (Hallett *et al.* 1998; Lockyer and Stone 1998).

Leaving aside organisational considerations, the big overlap in populations strengthens the argument about the interrelatedness of well-being and behaviour, and hence the need for decisions and programmes to take into account and work on that interrelationship. This requires a holistic approach, which is hard to achieve if different aspects of a young person's life and problems are being dealt with in a compartmentalised way.

Arguments based on intervention effects

One of the key reasons why many countries abandoned or modified integrated approaches from the 1970s onwards was the perception that so-called welfare approaches to youth crime had failed. Evidence about reconvictions showed that many young people continued to offend despite the input of supervision or probation in the community or removal from home (Muncie 2004). The record of institutional care was generally poor, although arguably the regimes that operated in the 1960s and 1970s would not now be regarded as welfare orientated. Research indicated that counselling was generally ineffective, though so were punitive regimes (Lipsey 1995).

Equally, research had shown that interventions on care grounds were often ineffective too, especially when children were placed in foster or residential care. Some people who grew up or spent time in public care have done well (Jackson 1998), but many experienced both discontinuities of placement and poor outcomes as regards emotional development, school progress and behaviour (Borland et al. 1998; Ward 1995).

There continues to be empirical and policy support for the notion that when young people offend in a minor way and infrequently (the great majority) the best response is brief and should seek to divert young people from formal intervention (Goldson 2000). Both academics and politicians have increasingly emphasised that it is only serious or persistent offenders who require substantial intervention and should be targeted. The most effective programmes tend to be those that have an explicit focus on the attitudes and circumstances surrounding criminal actions, are well structured and are implemented coherently (McGuire and Priestley 1995; Utting and Vennard 2000). However, it has been found that many young people involved in crime also have serious emotional difficulties and do not usually respond well to short-term targeted interventions. What was needed to achieve positive outcomes was comprehensive integrated services for an extended time (Howell et al. 2004). Moreover, young people appear to respond best to programmes and guidance when they believe that staff are interested in their well-being and are able to build trusting relationships (McNeill and Batchelor

2004). Similarly, in relation to child protection and family support, 'in circumstances of multiple disadvantage, long-term and multi-faceted support programmes produce superior results' (Cameron 2003; Hill 1999). Such multiple approaches are increasingly the norm among practice agencies. Combining attention to offences, relationships and education implies the need for good co-ordination in decision-making as well as service delivery.

Some argue that the shift towards separate systems and a more 'justice' orientation to youth crime in England and Wales during the 1980s and 1990s led to success, at least as regards diminished use of custody (Goldson 2002), while the numbers of children in public care also reduced significantly. However, it is notoriously difficult to draw firm conclusions about policy changes over time from comparative research between countries, because so many other factors impinge.

Conclusions

Evidently the arguments outlined above have to be weighed together. In any case it is open to question whether systems that separate or integrate dealing with young offenders and victims to varying degrees have been constructed on the basis of coherent principles. The arrangements may be the collective product of a series of ad hoc policies that reflect episodic political imperatives, with little overarching design. What is clear is that there is no necessary connection between adopting any specific explanatory theory of youth crime, social deviance or family dysfunction and any one set of institutional responses. All that can be said is that strategies and institutional arrangements comport well or less well with different, explanatory theories, bodies of evidence and normative positions in relation to justice and welfare. This is a subject we will return to when we have learned something of the varieties of arrangements from our contributors in the chapters that follow.

References

Acton, H. (1969) (ed) *The Philosophy of Punishment: A Collection of Papers.* London: MacMillan.

Archard, D. (2003) *Children, Family and the State.* Aldershot: Ashgate.

Archard, D. (2004) *Children's Rights and Childhood* (2nd edn). London: Routledge.

Asquith, S. (1998) 'Children's hearings in an international context.' In A. Lockyer and F.H. Stone (eds) *Juvenile Justice in Scotland: Twenty-Five Years of the Welfare Approach.* Edinburgh: T and T Clark.

Asquith, S. and Hill, M. (1994) *Justice for Children.* Dordrecht: Martinus Nijhoff.

Baker, K. (2004) 'Is *Asset* really an asset? Assessment of young offenders in practice.' In R. Burnett and C. Roberts (eds) *What Works in Probation and Youth Justice: Developing Evidence-based Practice.* Cullompton: Willan Publishing.

Bala, N., Hornick, J.P., Snyder, H.N. and Paetsch, J.J. (2002) *Juvenile Justice Systems.* Toronto: Thompson Education Publishing.

Bean, P. (1981) *Punishment: A Philosophical and Criminological Inquiry.* Oxford: Robertson.

Beck, U. (1992) *Risk Society: Towards a New Modernity.* London: Sage.

Beckett, C. (2003) *Child Protection: An Introduction.* London: Sage.

Bentham, J. (1789) *An Introduction to the Principles of Morals and Legislation* (Hafner edn 1948, edited by L. Lafleur). New York: Hafner Publishing Co.

Booth, T. (1991) *Juvenile Justice in the New Europe.* Sheffield: Joint Unit for Social Services Research.

Borland, M., Pearson, C., Hill, M., Tisdall, K. and Bloomfield, I. (1998) *Education and Care away from Home: A Review of Research, Policy and Practice.* Edinburgh: SCRE.

Bottoms, A. and Dignan, J. (2004) 'Youth Justice in Great Britain.' In A. Doobs (ed) *Youth Crime and Youth Justice: Comparative and Cross-National Perspectives.* London: University of Chicago Press.

Bottoms, A., Shapland, J., Costello, A., Holmes, D. and Muir, G. (2004) 'Towards desistance: Theoretical underpinnings for an empirical study.' *The Howard Journal 43,* 4, 368–389.

Braithwaite, J. (1989) *Crime, Shame and Reintegration.* Cambridge: Cambridge University Press.

Buist, M. and Whyte, B. (2004) *International Research Evidence for Scotland's Children's Hearing Review.* Edinburgh: Scottish Executive.

Burnett, R. and Roberts, C. (2004) *What Works in Probation and Youth Justice: Developing Evidence-based Practice.* Cullompton: Willan Publishing.

Cameron, G. (2003) 'Promoting Positive Child and Family Welfare.' In K. Kufeldt and B. McKenzie (eds) *Child Welfare: Connecting Research, Policy, and Practice.* Waterloo: Wilfrid Laurier University Press.

Campbell, T. (1983) *The Left and Rights.* London: Routledge.

Campbell, T. (1988) *Justice.* Basingstoke: Macmillan.

Cooper, A. (2005) 'Surface and Depth in the Victoria Climbié Inquiry Report'. *Child and Family Social Work, 10,* 1, 1–9.

Corby, B. (2000) *Child Abuse: Towards a Knowledge Base.* Buckingham: Open University Press.

Crawford, A. and Newburn, T. (2003) *Youth Offending and Restorative Justice: Implementing Reform in Youth Justice.* Cullompton: Willan Publishing.

Crofts, T. (1998) 'Rebutting the Presumption of *Doli Incapax.' Journal of Criminal Law 62,* 185–93.

Edwards, I. (2004) 'An Ambiguous Participant: The Crime Victim and Criminal Justice Decision-Making.' *British Journal of Criminology 44,* 967–982.

Farrington, D. (1992) 'Juvenile delinquency.' In J. Coleman (ed) *The School Years.* London: Routledge.

Feinberg, J. (1980) 'The child's right to an open future.' In W. Aiken and H. LaFollette (eds) *Whose Child?* Totowa, NJ: Littlefield Adams and Co.

Fishkin, J. (1983) *Justice, Equal Opportunity, and the Family.* New Haven: Yale University Press.

Flynn, N. (2002) *Public Sector Management.* Harlow: Prentice Hall.

France, A. and Crow, I. (2005) 'Using the "Risk Factor Paradigm" in Prevention: Lessons from the Evaluation of Communities that Care.' *Children and Society 19,* 2, 172–184.

France, A. and Utting, D. (2005) 'The Paradigm of "Risk and Protection-Focused Prevention" and its Impact on Services for Children and Families.' *Children and Society, 19,* 2, 77–90.

Franklin, B. (1986) *Rights of Children.* Oxford: Blackwell.

Franklin, B. (ed) (2002) *The New Handbook of Children's Rights: Comparative Policy and Practice.* London: Routledge.

Freeman, M. (2000) 'The Future of Children's Rights.' *Children and Society 14,* 277–293 also in Freeman (ed) (2004).

Freeman, M. (ed) (2004) *The International Library of Essays on Rights: Children Rights Vols 1 & 2.* Aldershot: Ashgate.

Fuchs, D. (1995) 'Preserving and strengthening families and protecting children: social network intervention, a balanced approach to the prevention of child maltreatment.' In J. Hudson and B. Galway (eds) *Canadian Child Welfare*. Toronto: Thomson.

Fullwood, C. and Powell, H. (2004) 'Towards effective practice in the youth justice system.' In R. Burnett and C. Roberts (eds) *What Works in Probation and Youth Justice: Developing Evidence-based Practice*. Cullompton: Willan Publishing.

Garrett, P.M. (2003) *Remaking Social Work with Children and Families: A Critical Discussion on the 'Modernisation' of Social Care*. London: Routledge.

Gilligan, R. (1999) 'Enhancing the Resilience of Children and Young People in Public Care by Mentoring their Talents and Interests.' *Child and Family Social Work, 4*, 3, 187–196.

Goldson, B. (2000) *The New Youth Justice*. Lyme Regis: Russell House Publishing.

Goldson, B. (2002) 'Children, crime and the state.' In B. Goldson, M. Lavalette and J. McKechnie (eds) *Children, Welfare and the State*. London: Sage.

Goldson, B., Lavalette, M. and McKechnie, J. (2002) *Children, Welfare and the State*. London: Sage.

Greenwald, R. (2002) *Trauma and Juvenile Delinquency*. Binghampton: Haworth Maltreatment and Trauma Press.

Gutmann, A. (1987) *Democratic Education*. Princeton, NJ: Princeton University Press.

Hafen, B. and Hafen, J. (1996) 'Abandoning Children to their Autonomy: The UN Convention.' *Harvard International Law Journal 37*, 2, 449–491.

Haines, K. and Drakeford, M. (1998) *Young People and Youth Justice*. Basingstoke: Macmillan.

Hallett, C., Murray, C., Jamieson, J. and Veitch, B. (1998) *Deciding in Children's Interests*. Edinburgh: The Scottish Office Central Research Unit.

Harding, L.F. (1996) *Family, State and Social Policy*. London: Macmillan.

Hart, H.L.A. (1968) *Punishment and Responsibility*. Oxford: Clarendon Press.

Hart, H.L.A. (1982) 'Legal Rights.' In H.L.A. Hart *Essays of Bentham: Jurisprudence and Political Theory*. Oxford: Clarendon Press.

Haydon, G. (1977) 'The Right to Education and Compulsory Schooling.' *Journal of Educational Philosophy and Theory 9*, 1.

Hetherington, E.M. and Stanley-Hagan, M. (1999) 'The Adjustment of Children with Divorced Parents: A Risk and Resiliency Perspective'. *Journal of Child Psychology and Psychiatry, 40*, 1, 129–140.

Hill, M. (1999) *Effective Ways of Working with Children and their Families*. London: Jessica Kingsley Publishers.

Hill, M. and Tisdall, K. (1997) *Children and Society*. Harlow: Addison Wesley Longman.

Hill, M., Stafford, A. and Green Lister, P. (2003) *'International Perspectives' in the Report of the Child Protection Audit and Review*. Edinburgh: Scottish Executive.

Hill, M., Walker, M., Moodie, K., Wallace, B., Bannister, J., Khan, F., McIvor, G. and Kendrick, A. (2005) *Fast Track Children's Hearings Pilot: Final Report of the Evaluation of the Pilot* (abridged version). Edinburgh: Scottish Executive.

Hirschi, T. and Gottfredson, M. (1991) *Rethinking the Juvenile Justice System*. Sheffield: Joint Unit for Social Services Research.

Holt, J. (1975) *Escape from Childhood*. Harmondsworth: Penguin Books.

Honderich, T. (1989) *Punishment: The Supposed Justifications*. Cambridge: Polity.

Howe, D., Brandon, M., Hinings, D. and Schofield, G. (1999) *Attachment Theory, Child Maltreatment and Family Support*. London: Routledge.

Howell, J.C., Kelly, M.R., Palmer, J. and Mangum, R.L. (2004) 'Integrating Child Welfare, Juvenile Justice and Other Agencies in a Continuum of Services.' *Child Welfare, 83*, 2, 143–156.

Huizinga, D. and Jakob-Chien, C. (1998) 'The contemporaneous co-occurrence of serious and violent juvenile offending and other problem behaviors.' In R. Loeber and D.P. Farrington (eds) *Serious and Violent Juvenile Offenders: Risk Factors and Successful Interventions*. Thousand Oaks: Sage, 47–67.

Jack, G. (2000) 'Ecological Influences on Parenting and Child Development'. *British Journal of Social Work, 30*, 6, 703–720.

Jackson, S. (1998) 'Looking After Children: A New Approach or Just an Exercise in Form Filling? A Response to Knight and Caveney.' *British Journal of Social Work 22*, 1, 45–56.

Jackson, S. and Nixon, P. (1999) 'Family Group Conferences: a challenge to the old order.' In L. Dominelli (ed) *Community Approaches to Child Welfare.* Aldershot: Ashgate.

Jonkman, H.B., Junger-Tas, J. and van Dijk, B. (2005) 'From Behind Dikes and Dunes: Communities that Care in the Netherlands.' *Children and Society 19*, 2, 105–116.

Jonson-Reid, M. (2004) 'Child welfare services and delinquency: The need to know more'. *Child Welfare 83*, 2, 157–173.

Junger-Tas, J. (1998) 'The Netherlands.' In J. Mehlbye and L. Walgrave (eds) *Confronting Youth in Europe – Juvenile Crime and Juvenile Justice.* Copenhagen: AKF Forlaget.

Kearney, B. (2000) *Children's Hearings and the Sheriff Court.* Edinburgh: Butterworths.

Kemshall, H. (2005) 'Risk assessment and young people who offend.' In J. McGhee, M. Mellon and B. Whyte (eds) *Meeting Needs, Addressing Deeds – Working with Young People who Offend.* Edinburgh: NCH Scotland.

Kilbrandon Committee (1964) *Children and Young Persons.* Edinburgh: Scottish Office.

King, M. (1994a) 'Children's Rights as Communication: Reflections on Autopoietic Theory and the United Nations Convention.' *Modern Law Review 57*, 385–401, also in Freeman (ed) (2004).

King, M. (1994b) 'Law's Healing of Children's Hearings: The Paradox Moves North.' *Journal of Social Policy 24*, 3, 315–340.

Koppen, P. van (2002) *Adversarial Versus Inquisitorial Justice.* Dordrecht: Kluwer.

Kufeldt, K. and McKenzie, B. (2003) *Child Welfare: Connecting Research, Policy and Practice.* Waterloo, Ontario: Wilfred Laurier University Press.

Lindlay, R. (1989) 'Teenagers and Other Children.' In G. Scarre (ed) *Children, Parents and Politics.* Cambridge: Cambridge University Press.

Lipsey, M.W. (1995) 'What do we learn from 400 research studies on the effectiveness of treatment with juvenile delinquents.' In J. Maguire (ed) *What Works: Reducing Reoffending.* Chichester: Wiley.

Locke, J. (1687) *Second Treatise on Government.* (ed. P. Laslett, 1967). Cambridge: Cambridge University Press.

Lockyer, A. (1982) 'Justice and welfare.' In F. Martin, S. Fox and K. Murray (eds) *The Scottish Juvenile Justice System.* Edinburgh: Scottish Academic Press.

Lockyer, A. (1994) 'The Scottish Children's Hearings System: internal developments and the UN Convention.' In S. Asquith and M. Hill (eds) *Justice for Children.* Dordrecht: Martinus Nijhoff.

Lockyer, A. and Stone, F.H. (1998) *Juvenile Justice in Scotland: Twenty-Five Years of the Welfare Approach.* Edinburgh: T and T Clark.

Lowe, N., Murch, M., Borkowski, M., Weaver, A., Beckford, V. and Thomas, C. (1999) *Supporting Adoption: Reframing the Approach.* London: BAAF.

Lupton, C. (2000) *Moving Forward on Family Group Conferences in Hampshire: Developments in Research and Practice.* Portsmouth: Social Services Research and Information Unit.

Luthar, S.S. (2003) *Resilience and Vulnerability.* New York: Cambridge University Press.

MacCormick, N. (1976) 'Children's Rights: A Test-Case for Theories of Rights.' *Archiv fur Rechts und Sozialphilosophie 62*, 3, 305–317, also in Freeman (ed) (2004).

Macpherson, C.B. (1977) *The Life and Times of Liberal Democracy.* Oxford: Oxford University Press.

Marsh, P. and Crow, G. (1998) *Family Group Conferences in Child Welfare.* Oxford: Blackwell.

Maxwell, G. and Morris, A. (2002) 'Juvenile crime and justice in New Zealand.' In N.M.C. Bala, J.P. Hornick, H.N. Snyder and J.J. Paetsch (eds) *Juvenile Justice Systems: An International Comparison of Problems and Solutions.* Toronto: Thompson Educational Publishing.

McConville, S. (2003) *The Use of Punishment.* Devon: Willan.

McGuire, J. and Priestley, P. (1995) 'Reviewing what works: past, present and future.' In J. McGuire (ed) *What Works: Reducing Reoffending.* Chichester: Wiley.

McKenzie, N. (2000) 'FGCs and restorative justice.' In C. Lupton (ed) *Moving Forward On Family Group Conferences in Hampshire: Developments in Research and Practice.* Portsmouth: Social Services Research and Information Unit.

McNeill, F. and Batchelor, S. (2004) *Persistent Offending by Young People.* London: NAPO.

Miers, D. (2001) *An International Review of Restorative Justice.* London: Home Office.

Miller, D. (1976) *Social Justice.* Oxford: Clarendon Press.

Milne, A. (1973) 'Philosophy and Political Action: The Case of Civil Rights.' *Political Studies 21,* 4, 453–480.

Muncie, J. (2004) 'Youth justice: globalisation and multi-modal governance.' In T. Newburn and E. Spark (eds) *Criminal Justice and Political Cultures.* Devon: Willan.

Muncie, J., Wetherell, M., Dallos, R. and Cochrane, A. (1995) *Understanding the Family.* London: Sage.

Munro, E. (2002) *Effective Child Protection.* London: Sage.

Newman, T. (2004) *What Works in Building Resilience.* Barkingside: Barnardo's.

O'Brien, T.M. (2004) *Child Welfare in the Legal Setting.* Binghampton: Haworth Press.

Omaji, P.O. (2003) *Responding to Youth Crime: Towards Radical Criminal Justice Partnerships.* Sydney: Hawkins Press.

O'Neill, J. (1994) *The Missing Child in Liberal Theory: Towards a Covenant Theory of Family, Welfare, and The Civil State.* Toronto: Toronto University Press.

Parton, N. (1991) *Governing the Family.* London: Macmillan.

Pinker, R. (1979) *The Idea of Welfare.* London: Heinemann.

Pitts, J. (1988) *The Politics of Juvenile Crime.* London: Sage.

Pitts, J. (2001) *The New Politics of Youth Crime: Discipline or Solidarity?* Lyme Regis: Russell House Publishing.

Pitts, J. and Hope, T. (1998) 'The local politics of inclusion: the state and community safety.' In J. Finer and M. Nellis (eds) *Crime and Social Inclusion.* Oxford: Blackwell.

Polanyi, K. (1968) *The Great Transformation: The Political and Economic Origins of Our Time.* Boston: Beacon Press.

Quinton, A. (1969) 'On Punishment.' In H.B. Acton (ed) *The Philosophy of Punishment: A Collection of Papers.* London: Macmillan.

Raphael, D.D. (1967) *Political Theory and the Rights of Man.* London: Macmillan.

Rawls, J. (1972) *A Theory of Justice.* Oxford: Clarendon Press.

Ross, T., Conger, D. and Armstrong, M. (2002) 'Bridging Child Welfare and Juvenile Justice: Preventing Unnecessary Detention of Foster Children.' *Child Welfare, 81,* 2, 471–494.

Sealander, J. (2003) *The Failed Century of the Child. Governing America's Young in the Twentieth Century.* Cambridge: Cambridge University Press.

Smith, D. (1995) 'Living conditions in the Twentieth Century.' In M. Rutter and D. Smith (eds) *Psychological Disorders in Young People.* Chichester: Wiley.

Smith, R. (2003) *Youth Justice: Ideas, Policy, Practice.* Cullompton: Willan Publishing.

Stevenson, O. (1996) 'Emotional Abuse and Neglect: A Time for Reappraisal.' *Child and Family Social Work, 1,* 13–18.

Stewart, J., Smith, D., Stewart, G. and Fullwood, C. (1994) *Understanding Offending Behaviour.* Harlow: Longman.

Taylor, C. (2003) 'Justice for Looked After Children?' *Probation Journal, 50,* 3, 239–251.

Thornberry, T.P., Ireland, T.O. and Smit, C.A. (2001) 'The Importance of Timing: The Varying Impact of Childhood and Adolescent Maltreatment on Multiple Problem Outcomes.' *Development and Psychopathology, 13,* 957–979.

Tomison, A. (2002) 'Developments in Australia.' *International Perspectives on Child Protection.* Melbourne: Australian Institute of Family Studies.

Trinder, L. (2000) 'The Rights and Wrongs of Post-Adoption Intermediary Services for Birth Relatives.' *Adoption and Fostering, 24,* 3, 19–25.

Utting, D. and Vennard, J. (2000) *What Works with Young Offenders in the Community?* Ilford: Barnardo's.

van der Laan, P. (and Committee of Experts) (2003) *European Committee on Crime Problems: Final Activity Report.* Strasbourg: Council of Europe.

Veerman, P. (1992) *The Rights of the Child and the Changing Image of Childhood.* Dordrecht: Martinus Nijhoff.

Waldfogel, J. (2001) *The Future of Child Protection.* Cambridge, Mass.: Harvard University Press.

Walgrave, L. (1996) 'Restorative juvenile justice: a way to restore justice in western European systems?' In S. Asquith (ed) *Children and Young People in Conflict with the Law.* London: Jessica Kingsley Publishers.

Walgrave, L. and Mehlbye, J. (1998) 'An overview: comparative comments on juvenile offending and its treatment in Europe.' In J. Mehlbye and L. Walgrave (eds) *Confronting Youth in Europe – Juvenile Crime and Juvenile Justice.* Copenhagen: AKF Forlaget.

Ward, H. (1995) *Looking After Children: Research into Practice.* London: HMSO.

Wardle, L. (1996) 'The Use and Abuse of Rights Rhetoric: The Constitutional Rights of Children.' *Loyola University of Chicago Law Journal 27,* 321–348, also in Freeman (ed) (2004).

Waterhouse, L. (1993) *Child Abuse and Child Abusers.* London: Jessica Kingsley Publishers.

Waterhouse, L. and McGhee, J. (2004) 'International themes in juvenile justice policy.' In J. McGhee, M. Mellon and B. Whyte (eds) *Meeting Needs, Addressing Deeds – Working with Young People who Offend.* Glasgow: NCH Scotland.

Watkins, J. (1998) *The Juvenile Justice Century.* Durham, NC: Carolina Academic Press.

Weitekamp, E.G.M., Kerner, H.-J. and Herberger, S.M. (1998) 'Germany.' In J. Mehlbye and L. Walgrave (eds) *Confronting Youth in Europe – Juvenile Crime and Juvenile Justice.* Copenhagen: AKF Forlaget.

Williams, G. (1954) 'The Criminal Responsibility of Children.' *Criminal Law Review 498,* 493–499.

Williams, K. (1990) 'In Defence of Compulsory Education.' *Journal of Philosophy of Education 254,* 2, 285–294.

Zermatten, J. (2004) *The Swiss Federal Stature on Juvenile Criminal Law.* Sion: Juvenile Court of Valais.

1

Different Approaches to the Youth Justice–Child Care and Protection Interface

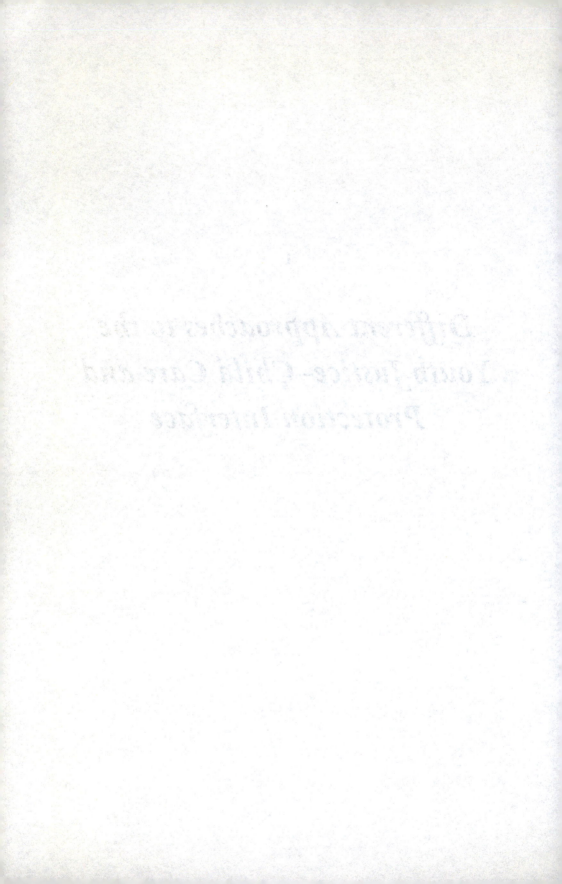

Approaching Youth Crime through Welfare and Punishment: The Finnish Perspective

Johanna Korpinen and Tarja Pösö

Introduction

In a recent legal article, Kimmo Nuotio (2004) noted that only a couple of years ago it would have seemed strange to use such a concept as youth criminal justice in Finland. Even now the concept is used inconsistently and no wide agreement exists yet as to what it means. Despite this fact – or perhaps because of it – youth criminal justice is at present a focus of attention within academic literature.

The recent use of this concept demonstrates that we are living through an era of change. Youth crime policy and its associated systems and practices go back as far as the end of the nineteenth century – if not even earlier (Harrikari 2004a) – with the fundamental legislation having been established in the early part of the twentieth century. Since then Finland has generally approached youth crime by keeping separate the justice and child protection measures and systems. Of the two, the tasks and duties of child protection are much wider. However, recent policy proposals suggest that the role of child protection and the justice system should be rethought and that new approaches should be developed. When the Ministry of Justice launched a commission to reassess the Finnish juvenile justice system in 2001, the aim was to establish a more rehabilitative perspective (Marttunen 2004).

These challenges for change are set against a social, economic and cultural situation where deep concerns about the state of well-being of children and young people have been debated to a great extent both in the mass media as well as academically (Bardy, Salmi and Heino 2001; Järventie and Sauli 2001). There have been reports about the deterioration of welfare and educational services for children, young people and families, who have traditionally been the key target for the Nordic welfare states through social services and income transfers. The core of concern has been directed towards the social stratification of families and childhood. Poverty among families with children increased sharply during the 1990s (Sauli, Bardy and Salmi 2002). It is estimated that 17 per cent of children and young people under the age of 18 experience or witness violence in their homes (Oranen 2001). Furthermore, unemployment is high among young people: in fact, there are regions where every third young person under the age of 24 is unemployed (Suutari 2002). Children and young people have become increasingly polarised into those who have many psychosocial problems of various kinds and those who live a safe childhood with many educational, cultural and social opportunities.

The issues of youth crime and child protection are thereby located at a juncture of debates, changes and crises of different types concerning the role of formal society and the social position of youth. This chapter aims to describe these ongoing discussions as well as to present the systems and practices for dealing with youth crime. The opening section will look at, first, child protection and, second, youth crime from the point of view of the relevant legislation and systems, together with the issues those institutions deal with. The second section will discuss some of the current tendencies and contradictions in policies for children and young people.

Child care and protection

Legislation

The Finnish system for child care has a long history in family and population policy. At present, child care consists of a variety of services and benefits targeted at children and families with children (Millar and Warman 1996). Most of the services and benefits, universalist by their nature, are meant for all children and families. Child protection is directed especially to children and families in trouble and in need but, even so, the approach is broad.

The legislation that governs Finnish child protection is both national and international. The UN Convention on the Rights of the Child 1989 and the European Convention on Human Rights, as well as the Finnish Constitution provide the basic principles that also direct the practices of child protection work. The leading principle in the so-called 'child laws' in Finland, the Child Welfare Act 1983 and the Child Custody and the Rights of Access Act 1983, is the best interest of the child. For their part, the general laws of social welfare (e.g. the Social Welfare Act 1982 and the Act on Client's Position and Rights in Social Welfare 2000) play a major role in defining the rights of clients and the obligations for local authorities to act.

The starting point of Finnish child protection is that it covers all children in society and that it should extend to schools, the health services, housing policy, the family and culture. All children under 18 years of age are covered and in some cases even persons under 21. Despite the wide nature of the concept, the Child Welfare Act 1983 set out specific criteria specifying when the local authorities have to intervene. According to the Act, family-orientated and individual child welfare comprises assistance in 'open care', taking into care, substitute care and aftercare (Section 8).

Open care

In Finland, support for children and families who are considered to be in need of child protection services is provided through so-called 'open care', which is roughly equivalent to family support in the UK. Open care covers a wide range of services, from assistance at home to temporary placement in foster or residential care. The need for open care measures are met if the health or development of a child or young person is endangered or not safeguarded by the environment in which she or he grows up, or if a child or young person endangers this environment through his or her behaviour (Section 12). This means that when social workers are informed (for example, via school, neighbours or a child health clinic) of a child who may be in need of some kind of support they will contact the family. If there is a need for help or support, open care measures can then be considered. This may take the form of, for example, financial support, lay helpers, support families, therapy, assistance in education and training, job and house finding, leisure activities or temporary placement outside the home (for a maximum of six months).

Social workers are also obliged to make a care plan that should be revised regularly together with the child and the parents.

Open care is voluntary and there are no time limits for its duration. It may last only a short time or continue for several years. Open care is a mixture of support and control and therefore its intensity varies depending on the situation. If open care measures prove to be inadequate, there is the option that the child is taken into care by the local authorities, even against the child's or the parents' will. However, Hurtig (2003) argues that open care measures may last several years even if the requirements for taking into care have been met earlier. The strong emphasis on supporting whole families may in some cases neglect children's individual needs. Despite these problems, open care creates the basis for Finnish child protection social work with the ultimate aim of solving and preventing problems before they become too serious.

Taking into care and substitute care

Taking into care means that the local authorities become responsible for the child's care and upbringing away from the child's own home. It can occur only if all three of the following preconditions are fulfilled: the child's health or development has been seriously endangered; the open care measures taken have proved to be inappropriate or inadequate; substitute care is deemed to be in the best interest of the child (Section 16). Substitute care may take the form of foster care, residential care or some other appropriate form of care. Compared with Sweden and Norway, a relatively large number of children are placed in residential care in Finland. In 2002, 57 per cent of the children in substitute care were in institutions and 45 per cent in foster care (Rousu and Holma 2003). Substitute care terminates when the child reaches 18 years of age, or earlier if it is considered there is no longer such a need.

Aftercare

The local authorities are also required to provide aftercare for children or young persons who have been in substitute care. The idea is to support both the child and the parents in everyday life when the child returns to his or her home or moves to his or her own apartment. The help and support is provided through 'open care'. Financial support and different types of sheltered homes are important forms of assistance for young people. The obligation ends when the young person turns 21.

The system of child protection

Historically, the social welfare boards have been important actors in carrying out child protection work. Their role was defined in the first child protection law in 1936, since when they have been central decision-makers concerning child protection issues. Prior to 1936, children's well-being was based mostly on the patriarchal and autonomous family. On the whole, only orphans and children abandoned by their parents were taken into public care as part of poor relief. Children who had committed criminal offences were looked after by the justice system (Hearn *et al.* 2004).

The law of 1936 gave the local authorities the right to remove a child from his or her parents into the care of local authorities (Forsberg 1998). It emphasised the need to protect children from their parents, and contact with the biological parents was not seen as being important. The guardianship of the child was transferred to the social welfare board, which meant both the custody of the child and the administration of his or her property. The new Child Welfare Act 1983 abandoned the old problem-based perspective and broadened the idea of child protection. In particular, it emphasised preventive work, which is the cornerstone of the current system.

Social welfare boards are part of the local administration. The seats on the board are occupied by politically elected lay people. The number of seats for each political party is based on the percentage won in the civic elections. The board is responsible for overseeing the operations and finances of its specific sector. The board can, however, delegate its decision-making power to municipal office-holders, that is to say social workers, except when the measures are compulsory. Therefore, social workers have a lot of discretionary power to decide when and how to intervene. The board itself will handle child protection issues if a child is taken into care against the parents' will or if a child over 12 years of age opposes the taking into care or has not been heard. The board can hear different parties in their meetings, but it is not obligatory. The board has to submit its decision to the Provincial Administrative Court within 30 days, which may also arrange oral hearings. However, in most cases, the Court's decisions are based on documents.

The functions of the welfare board have been criticised for contravening Article 6 of the European Convention on Human Rights, on fair trial. There have also been doubts regarding whether lay people are sufficiently qualified to make decisions concerning difficult family situations, especially in small communities. It has been said that lay people do not possess the kind of expertise that decision-makers need; however, this critique is not based on any research and there are no studies of how the boards actually work. There are also contradictory views of what kind of expertise counts and what qualifications decision-makers need. Proposals have been made to transfer all the decisions concerning the taking into care of children from the municipal boards to the administrative courts except in cases of emergency care orders (Oikeusturva-asiain 2001). However, opposing views suggest this would have negative effects on child protection work carried out at a local level. From a social work perspective it might increase 'legalism' (for example, the use of solicitors would increase) and reduce the discretionary powers of social workers. On the other hand, it could clarify the decision-making process, clearly identify social workers as the children's advocates and lessen the differences between municipalities.

Although municipalities are responsible for official child protection work, different voluntary organisations, the Church and private service providers are also important actors in the field of child protection. They provide information and training, carry out research and sell services to municipalities.

Children, families and social work methods in child protection

The clients of child protection services could be described as a last resort when universal services have failed (Forssen 1998). The recession at the beginning of the 1990s resulted in many cuts in social service provision while also heightening the number of child protection problems (Bardy *et al.* 2001). Therefore the need for services increased but there were fewer resources with which to respond. The cuts have not been compensated for, even though the number of children in open care has more than doubled in ten years. There were 23,456 children in open care in 1992 and by 2002 it was 54,458 children (4.9% of all children under the age of 18) (Sosiaali- ja terveydenhuollon 2003). The clientele in open care has also become long term, which suggests that the problems are more severe (Bardy *et al.* 2001).

There are two specific age groups that seem to arouse concern and need for action: the very young and adolescents (Bardy *et al.* 2001). For example, in 2002, 42 per cent of placements outside the home concerned young people aged 12–17 (Sosiaali- ja terveudenhuollon 2003). Family conflicts, alcoholism and problems in daily care are the major problems experienced by this group (Bardy *et al.* 2001). In the case of small children, the typical reason for intervention is a lack of basic care and welfare, while for adolescents, antisocial behaviour, substance abuse and difficulties at school are typical (Laakso and Saikku 1998).

Although a child could be taken into care after committing an illegal act, this has rarely been used as the primary reason. Crimes represented only 1 per cent of all the care decisions that have been made in Helsinki in recent years (Nuorisorikostoimikunnan mietintö 2003). A recent study (Pösö 2004) analysing a small number of formal documents articulating the reasons for young people's placements in reform schools suggests that crimes were referred to as reasons much more rarely in 2001–2002 than in 1989–1990. The explanation may be found simply in the discursive practices of social work. Although 'criminality' was not used as a reference for intervention, there were notions about 'uncontrollable and aggressive behaviour', among others. The young people might still have committed crimes (Kitinoja 2004) but these are not categorised in formal documents as the main reasons for placements. As Finnish child protection practice nowadays uses more holistic and interpretive descriptions of problems, the role of crimes has become less visible.

While there is ongoing discussion about the limited resources in child protection work, there are also several projects that aim at improving child welfare practices. One of the leading themes has been to develop a child-orientated way of working, by which is meant spending more time seeing and listening to children, as well as making parents aware of the children's needs and feelings. As a result, several books about direct work with children have been published recently (e.g. Möller 2004; Muukkonen and Tulensalo 2004). Family Group Conferences have also been developed to meet the needs of children and to get together people who are in position to support the child or young person in his or her life at home (Heino 2000). The experiences of the conferences have proved to be successful. Furthermore, different practice models have been developed to visualise and standardise child protection (Rousu and Holma 2004). The training of social workers has been expanded in such a way that professional social workers with master's degrees may specialise in child and youth social work by doing a four-year training programme at university, leading to a Licentiate Degree.

Most importantly, the government of Finland has committed itself to giving priority to child protection within social welfare for the five-year period starting 2004 (Valtioneuvoston periaatepäätös 2003). This major programme aims to improve key areas of the child protection services.

Youth crime and the juvenile justice system

Legislation

There are three different age categories in the Finnish juvenile justice system: children under the age of 15 (the age of criminal responsibility), young persons between 15 and 17, and young offenders between 15 and 20. As can be seen, the category of young offenders is the most important as it covers all the young people who are seen as responsible for their crimes. The category of young persons is needed because, before reaching the age of adulthood at the age of 18, the young people are entitled to child protection measures and the criminal procedure is slightly different from that used with young people between the ages of 18 and 20.

The main (non-parental) responsibility for the care and supervision of minors committing crimes belongs to the social welfare authorities and not to the criminal law authorities. Young persons can be subject to either criminal law sentences or a variety of care and protection measures, whereas children under 15 are subject only to care and protection measures. Young offenders between the ages of 18 and 20 are subject to some special features of the criminal procedure and may be sent to juvenile prison (Marttunen 2004).

The notion of juveniles as a special category of offenders can be traced back as far as the eighteenth century (Harrikari 2004a). Towards the end of the nineteenth century the differentiation of children and adults became stronger (Harrikari 2004b). The Penal Code of 1889 set the age of 15 as the point at which criminal responsibility could be established. Similarly, a growing number of statements argued that children required special consideration as offenders. Meanwhile, in the context of the care of poor people, 'poor houses' were starting to be divided into adult and children units, while special institutions such as reform schools for offending and delinquent children were also being established.

In international terms, the end of the nineteenth century was the era when the systems and practices for dealing with 'delinquent' children were established, with Chicago and Norway as the leading examples (Dahl 1985; Morris and McIsaac 1978; Platt 1967). Finland, by contrast, introduced its own laws much later. The first child protection law was established in Finland in 1936, stating that children committing crimes form a special category for child protection interventions. The distinction was clear: the criminal system was to look after the legal responses to youth crime while the child protection system would look after the well-being of children and young people in those cases where the crimes might be a threat of some kind to the young person him/herself or his/her environment (Nuotio 2004). The second and latest child protection law is 20 years old now, with a less specific approach to youth criminality than before. At present, legislation concerning young offenders is undergoing fundamental change with the variety of sentences widening. Similarly, there are pressures to introduce major changes to child protection legislation as well.

The youth justice system

In keeping with the legal distinctions outlined above, youth criminality is dealt with by two different systems: the child protection system, as part of municipal social welfare, and the justice system. Child protection services not only have the main role for minors below the age of 15 but play an important role for other young offenders too (Laitinen and Nyholm 1995). This reflects the Finnish view that youth crime is different in nature from adult crime (Nuorisorikostoimikunnan mietintö 2003).

Marttunen (2004) describes three elements of the justice system for young people. The first comprises the duties of the police department who investigate alleged offences. There is no special youth police department in Finland, although there can be arrangements at a local level for specialising in youth crime. In a criminal investigation, the police may question the young person, and apprehend, arrest and remand him or her in custody. When the person to be questioned is under the age of 18, the custodial parent and Social Welfare Board must be given the opportunity to be present. The Board should be informed about any crimes committed by minors. According to Tommo (2004), social workers react to the crimes differently depending on their seriousness and frequency. When the crime is interpreted to be part of the normal behaviour of young people very minimal or no action will be taken. However, if the social workers receive several reports from the police and the crimes are considered to be serious, different kinds of open care measures are used. The final outcome may be to take a child into the care of the local authorities but only if substitute care is seen to be serving the best interest of the child. The process then follows the same route as other child protection cases.

The second part of the justice system for young people consists of prosecution. The prosecutor may prosecute young people for offences, but may waive charges, or caution the offender in some cases. For each young person who is charged with an offence, including young adults, a specific personal investigation report must be prepared. The reports on young people under the age of 18 are prepared by the social welfare authorities, while the Probation Association prepares reports on young adults (18–20 years). The report describes the young person's social situation as well as the circumstances of the offence. The position of these reports has been the focus of criticism by the Commission on Youth Crime because, among many other things, their contents are seen to vary considerably between the different agencies. Also such crime-focused reports are seen to threaten those young people who might experience them as a part of a labelling process (Nuorisorikostoimikunnan mietintö 2003). One of the proposals made by the Commission on Youth Crime has been to reshape the report in such a way that there would in fact be two reports: one prepared by the social welfare authorities concerning the social situation of the young person, and the other prepared by probation officers focusing on the issues concerning the crime and the recommended sentences. The Commission also challenges social welfare authorities to ensure that the offender gets all the services he or she might need.

The third part of the justice system for juveniles described by Marttunen (2004) is the local court, which hears cases that are prosecuted. Appeals are heard by the courts of appeal and the highest level is the Supreme Court. The normal composition of the local court in juvenile cases is one legally trained judge and three lay judges. The composition may change according to the seriousness of the case, but a legally trained judge should always preside (Marttunen 2004). If the minor is held to be responsible for the offence, the only option is to pass a criminal sentence. The sentences applicable are a fine, conditional and unconditional imprisonment, community service and juvenile punishment, which outlines community service and supervision. Finnish criminal policy has strongly emphasised the importance of not using unconditional imprisonment for offenders under the age of 18 (Nuorisorikostoimikunnan mietintö 2003).

Mediation is, at the moment, an alternative to court proceedings for young people who offend (Marttunen 2004; Mielityinen 1999). The mediation programmes are managed by the municipal social welfare offices. The initiative for submitting cases to mediation comes from the police or from the prosecutor. The consent of all parties is required before going to reconciliation.

When analysing the present system of young offenders, the Commission for Youth Crime has suggested that the range of sentences for young offenders should be expanded in Finland. Juvenile punishment, including several social and rehabilitative goals, is proposed to cover all offenders under the age of 21 (Nuorisorikostoimikunnan mietintö 2003). The experiences resulting from a pilot period between 1997 and 2004 were sufficiently positive to suggest that juvenile punishment (community service and supervision) should be introduced across the country as an option in 2005. The evaluation research of that period informs us that during a 12-month follow-up period, at least 57 per cent of those sentenced to juvenile punishment committed a new offence for which they received at least a conditional prison sentence. Marttunen and Takala (2002) argue that the rate of recidivism does not mean that juvenile punishment has failed but that the sanction has been used for the most difficult group of offenders.

A principle is being expressed here: juvenile punishment can be seen as a compromise between the neoclassicist and the social and rehabilitative perspective. Juvenile punishment incorporates punishment in the sense that the sanction involves a censure for the offence. Having the offenders realise the impact of their offences, getting them to understand why that act is wrong and what impact it has on other people – for example, the victim – are significant objectives of juvenile punishment (Marttunen and Takala 2002). In the future, the Commission for Youth Crime suggests that juvenile punishment should also include the option of having treatment for substance abuse or psychiatric problems, which has not been possible so far. Therein lies one of the main messages of the present proposal: the justice system for juveniles should include more social and treatment approaches than it has done so far.

The changing nature of youth crime

The series of surveys of Finnish ninth grade (15–16-year-old) pupils and their self-reported crimes during the years 1995, 1996 and 1998 suggest that juvenile delinquency has become more polarised over recent years in Finland. The number of youths who refrain completely from law-breaking activities seems to be increasing, and the attitude of adolescents towards delinquent behaviour has become less tolerant. The number of those young people who did not report any offence during the year of inquiry increased from 25 per cent to nearly 30 per cent of all respondents (in 1995 and in 1998) (Kivivuori 1999). These results regarding the division of crime activity support the thesis that a stratification process in childhood and youth is producing a polarisation in well-being of those who are worst and best off (Kivivuori 2002).

The numbers of juveniles suspected of crimes against the Penal Code have been relatively stable in the last two decades, according to the National Research Institute for Legal Policy (Rikollisuustilanne 2002, 2003). Although most crimes are committed by adults, the years of youth are nevertheless marked by intense criminal activity (Marttunen and Kivivuori 2003, p.144). Of all persons suspected of crimes, the proportion of young persons has slowly decreased, being 9.5 per cent in 2002. The most typical juvenile offences are status offences related to alcohol possession and identity documents, as well as car thefts, damage to property, robberies, thefts and assaults. There is, however, a slight growth in violent crimes committed by young people. Nevertheless, the figures for violent crimes are still so low that, for example, the World Health Organization (WHO) does not count the figures at all in its statistics (Krug *et al.* 2002).

In May 2004, there were 96 young people under the age of 21 serving their sentence in Finnish prisons. This was 3 per cent of the total prison population (3107) (Muiluvuori 2004). The number of young people under the age of 18 serving a sentence in prison was three in 2003; these young persons were placed in prison units meant for young offenders, with separate provision for male and female offenders.

In terms of international comparisons, these figures are low. According to Muncie (2004), in 1996 3.6 per cent of the prison population was under the age of 21 in Finland. The same figure was 18.8 per cent for Scotland and 17.8 per cent for England.

Between the justice system and child protection: dimensions, experiences and implications for the future

Challenging professionalism and lay expertise

In child protection, social workers have traditionally been the key professional group planning, implementing and making decisions about child protection measures. Social workers have functioned within the limits of local administration and politics as well as civil society (Lehtinen 2001). They often collaborate with other professions working with families and children, such as family workers, teachers, psychologists and psychiatrists, and not forgetting the police. The ultimate legitimisation and framework for child protection has always been presented by legislation; in order to exist, child protection has to follow the principles of the Child Welfare Act and other pieces of legislation related to it. However, some recent tendencies suggest that a legalisation process of a new sort is taking place. This means that, on the one hand, the accuracy and documentation of the formal process of decision-making are being given more attention and, on the other, legal actors and institutions have started to play an important role during the different stages of child protection clienthood, using argumentative power to influence specific actions by professionals and families instead of only setting the general framework (Sinko 2004).

This development could be seen in the context of attempts to safeguard human rights in the complicated and conflict-sensitive situations of child protection (Sinko 2004). However, the impact of the new kind of legalism can also be found in the attempts to make the professional and bureaucratic elements of child protection stronger in order to meet the criteria set by the juridical parties. That tendency is in tension with the role of civil society and its lay and political representatives in the municipal social welfare boards, which traditionally have been there to guide, regulate and control (local) child protection and the position of social workers. Most interestingly, the tendency towards legalisation is strong at a time when professional methods such as the use of Family Group Conferences have become highly valued, with an emphasis on diversion from formal decision-making. In such approaches, the authority of professional expertise is challenged by the expertise of those who, as members of the family and local community, would like to become involved in solving a problem a child/family has met.

Meanwhile, the justice system dealing with juvenile crimes has introduced mediation, relying strongly on the willingness of civil society to become involved in negotiating and solving the conflict (crime) between the young offender and the victim. Juvenile punishment also requires other parties, such as employers, to offer young offenders a place to work in order to complete their community service; lay people may also be the supervisors for conditional imprisonment or juvenile punishment. In other words, both the involvement and co-operation of civil society are necessary in order to carry out the tasks of sentencing for young people.

The tendencies are, as it turns out, rather contradictory: although there is, on the one hand, a strong emphasis on lay expertise and the involvement of civil society, on the other, the professional and bureaucratic elements are particularly emphasised in formal child protection decision-making and especially in the frame of legal system and expertise. The different discourses of expertise are common in any area of human services, and indeed are often seen as characteristic of the postmodern era, where uncertainty and ambiguity as elements of expertise exist side by side with demands for authoritative expertise (Parton and O'Byrne 2000). In the context of children and young people in trouble, this self-evidently means extra expectations for the children, young people and their families to work out and constantly negotiate how to act in different contexts with different expertise discourses.

Dialogue and psychosocial programmes vs institutional placements

In the early days of specialised interventions in the lives of children and young people in trouble, institutional care was one of the major instruments. In Finland, the first reformatory schools were established at the end of the nineteenth century, providing care and upbringing in isolated conditions for 'delinquent' children and young people (Harrikari 2004b, p.21). They still exist, but their number and the numbers of young residents they work with has decreased enormously: at the moment, there are only six institutions of this kind and they take about 200 young persons a year compared with the considerably higher figures of the 1980s and 1990s.

The weakening role of the reformatory schools indicates a major shift in understanding public care and in the expectations placed upon it: residential care has largely been replaced by other forms of support provision, upbringing and control. A very strong example of such ideology is the most recent report on youth justice (Nuorisorikotoiimikunnan mietintö 2003): youth sentencing should take place as much as possible in the everyday environment of the offender and imprisonment should be used only when absolutely necessary. Institutional care, if used, should be integrated into society as much as possible. Child protection practices tend to emphasise the importance of 'open care measures' while the justice system stresses different forms of community sentencing. The principles of social belonging and dialogue have replaced the idea of sending young persons to the isolation of institutional space, except for a small minority.

There are different reasons for such policy changes and they are not separate from what has taken place in social welfare and health care generally. In criminal justice, the importance of dialogue has increased especially as a part of mediation. The mediation movement has criticised the criminal justice system for its 'facelessness' and inadequacy in dealing with emotions (Takala 1998, p.136). Therefore the face-to-face contact between the offender and the victim is important to facilitate the resolution of the human reactions of different types, including moral sense and emotions. In social work, interaction between people, including the social worker and his/her client, has traditionally been seen as one of the core elements of practice, as that is the arena for expressing and (re)formulating needs and directions for change.

It seems that the power of dialogue is given a special status in juvenile justice. The report of the Commission of Juvenile Crime (Nuorisorikostoimi-kunnan mietintö 2003) suggests that young people, when arrested, should be taken to a special reprimand session to make sure that the wrongness of committing crimes is known to the offender. The expectations are thus that this dialogue would change the offender's understanding of his/her behaviour. With regard to the impact of mediation, the dialogue in the institu-tional context of mediation seems to influence the offenders. In Eskelinen's study (2005, p.161) of mediation for persons under 15 years of age, the coming face to face of the victim and the offender was found to be a very important part of the mediation process. The experience had had positive effects on how they could attend their problems through interaction. How-ever, the research done in this field does not allow us to make any statements about the influence of dialogue in other professional or lay settings.

Promoting change

In Finland, the idea of punishment is not uppermost in the case of young offending. One of the key principles of the Finnish system is the strong belief that change can be promoted even in cases when children or young people harm themselves or their environment by their behaviour. Such individuals are seen to be in need of support, control, education and resocialisation.

In many policy documents concerning both social welfare (Heikkilä, Kaakinen and Korpelainen 2003) and youth justice (Nuorisorikostoimikunnan mietintö 2003) early intervention is prioritised as being the essential tool for dealing with childhood and youth problems. The very idea of early intervention is not new. Preventative issues have long belonged to the agenda of child welfare and work with young offenders (Laitinen and Nyholm 1995). However, recent policy documents make prevention central. Crime prevention has been rooted in the practices of criminal policy, while early childhood education and care, including day care, is partly legitimated as a practice preventing the deterioration of the psychosocial problems of children and their families. In its most fundamental meaning, early intervention is meant for everyone – every child should be entitled to a happy and safe childhood. Therefore, the general functioning of universalist family policy, through financial benefits and other support, is important. However, a growing number of arguments emphasise the importance of practices that focus only on high-risk childhoods in order to avoid the possible marginalisation process.

Early intervention policies have increased co-operation between different agencies and professionals. Networking and co-operation are highly valued and practised in social welfare in general. The police, day care professionals, teachers, youth workers, child and youth psychiatrists, and not forgetting social workers in different organisations, constitute the key group. A great challenge is to expand the approach in such a way that other actors, notably children and young people, could be included as equal partners, as well to define what kind of changes are needed. As part of child policy, children and young people have been involved as active subjects in their living or school environments, but not so commonly when planning crime prevention or child protection.

In the area of youth offending, the systems of child protection and justice have existed side by side. The future might mean a stronger interdependency between these two systems due to the suggested increase of social and rehabilitative elements of youth sentencing. We may see some risks in this development. First, is the possible growth of professional power previously mentioned. Second, the key tasks of each system might become blurred: for example, the justice system will include care and support functions as part of youth sentencing and at the same time child protection will function in order to prevent crimes. Third, and most importantly, although the expanding networks of professionals, organisations, approaches and programmes may offer an opportunity for the children and young people to find solutions to their problems, on the other hand the variety of networks might introduce a new type of managerialism, regulated more by the interests of the system than by the individual children and young people.

Conclusions

The welfare of children and young people has been high on the Finnish social policy agenda for more than a decade. The position of children and young people in trouble should therefore be looked upon from the point of view of the functioning of the welfare state which, in a very contradictory way, may exclude the most vulnerable children and young people with their special needs (Hearn *et al.* 2004; Pösö 2001). In that respect, the early 2000s form a distinctive period of social debate as so many social concerns as well as policy documents have been targeted at those vulnerable children and young people.

The present statements, analysis and proposals for change are rich in their ambition to promote the welfare of children and young people. Although child protection issues are to some extent separate from justice issues, there are several interconnections, especially in terms of young people committing crimes. Even though a proposal for thorough changes in juvenile justice has been made, youth criminality is not currently prominent among the concerns articulated in Finnish society. This could be explained by the fact that in Finland serious youth crime is not quantitatively an important issue, compared to, for example, the UK, and also by the strong holistic and psychosocial discourses among professionals who work with children and young people.

However, at this very moment, the strong stratification process among children and young people may fundamentally challenge the traditional approaches to social problems in Finnish society. Even more, professional practice with children and young people in trouble is expected to go through major changes. There are some contradictory tendencies – for instance, the emphasis on both the importance of the role of formal institutions and the need to involve members of civil society in decision-making and the different programmes for looking after young people and their troubles. At worst, the practices are asked to solve problems that cannot be resolved by individually based programmes. There is, nevertheless, the opportunity to move towards such a practice, which is sensitive enough to the needs of children and young people in trouble as well as to the special social and cultural conditions in which those troubles are created and dealt with.

References

Bardy, M., Salmi, M. and Heino, T. (2001) *Mikä lapsiamme uhkaa? Suuntaviivoja 2000-luvun lapsipoliittiseen keskusteluun* [What Threatens our Children?] (Perspectives for 2000's child policy debate). Raportteja 263. Helsinki: Stakes.

Child Welfare Act (683/1983) Unofficial translation at www.finlex.fi/fi/laki/kaannokset/1983/en19830683.pdf/.

Dahl, T. (1985) *Child Welfare and Social Defence.* Oslo: Norwegian University Press.

Eskelinen, O. (2005) *'Hermot vapautu ja tuli puhdas olo.' Alle 15-vuotiaiden rikosten sovittelun käytännöt ja vaikutukset.* Lapset rikoksen sovittelussa – tutkimusprojektin raportti ['I stopped being nervy and felt clean.' Practices and Impact of Crime Arbitration among Children under 15 Years of Age]. Report 3. Helsinki: Sosiaali- ja terveysministeriö.

Forsberg, H. (1998) *Perheen ja lapsen tähden. Etnografia kahdesta lastensuojelun asiantuntijakulttuurista.* [For the Sake of the Family and the Child]. Helsinki: Lastensuojelun keskusliitto.

Forssen, K. (1998) *Children, Families and the Welfare State. Studies on the Outcomes of the Finnish Family Policy.* Report 92. Helsinki: Stakes.

Harrikari, T. (2004a) *Alaikäisyys ja rikollisuuden muuttuvat tulkinnat suomalaisessa lainsäätämiskäytännössä* [The Status of Minors and Changing Interpretations of Crime in Finnish Legislation]. Report 48. Helsinki: Nuorisotutkimusverkosto.

Harrikari, T. (2004b) *Tahdon vahvistamisesta tarpeen tyydytykseen. Suomalaisen koulukodin lainsäädäntöhistoriaa 1860–1980* [From Enforcment of the Will to Fullfiling of the Needs. The History of the Legislation on the Finnish Reform Schools in 1860–1980]. In M. Jahnukainen, T. Kekoni and T. Pösö (eds) *Nuoruus ja koulukoti* [Youth and the Reform Schools]. Raportteja 43. Helsinki: Nuorisotutkimusverkosto, 21–60.

Hearn, J., Pösö, T., Smith C., White, S. and Korpinen J. (2004) 'What is child protection? Historical and Methodological Issues in Comparative Research on Lastensuojelu/Child Protection.' *International Journal of Social Welfare 13*, 1, 28–41.

Heikkilä, M., Kaakinen, J. and Korpelainen, N. (2003) *Kansallinen sosiaalinen kehittämisprojekti* [National Project for Developing Social Welfare]. Työryhmämuistioita 11. Helsinki: Sosiaali-ja terveysministeriö.

Heino, T. (ed) (2000) *Läheisneuvonpito – Uusi sosiaalityön menetelmä* [Family Group Conferences – A New Social Work Method]. Oppaita 40. Stakes: Helsinki.

Hurtig, J. (2003) *Lasta suojelemassa – etnografia lasten paikan rakentumisesta lastensuojelun perhetyön käytännöissä* [Protecting the Child: An Ethnographic Study of the Place of the Child as Contructed in Family Work Practices]. Acta Universitatis Lappiniensis 60. Rovaniemi: University of Lapland.

Järventie, I. and Sauli, H. (eds) (2001) *Eriarvoinen lapsuus* [Unequal Childhood]. Porvoo: WSOY.

Kitinoja, M. (2004) *Kujan päässä koulukoti* [The Reform School as the End Stop]. Unpublished manuscript of a doctoral dissertation. Helsinki: University of Helsinki.

Kivivuori, J. (1999) *Nuorten rikoskäyttäytyminen 1995–1998* [Criminal behaviour of young people in 1995–1998] Julkaisuja 161. Helsinki: Oikeuspoliittinen tutkimuslaitos.

Kivivuori, J. (2002) *Nuoret rikosten tekijöinä, uhreina ja kontrollin kohteina 1995–2001* [Young People as Actors, Victims and Social Control Targets in Crime 1995–2001]. In J. Kivivuori (ed) *Nuoret rikosten tekijöinä ja uhreina* [Young People as Actors and Victims of Crime]. Julkaisuja 188. Helsinki: Oikeuspoliittinen tutkimuslaitos, 14–63.

Krug, E., Dahlberg, L.L., Mercy, J.A., Zwi, A.B. and Lozano, R. (2002) *World Report on Violence and Health*. Geneva: World Health Organization.

Laakso R. and Saikku, P. (1998) *Hyvä huostaanotto?* [Good Practice of Taking into Care?] Aiheita 28. Helsinki: Stakes.

Laitinen, A. and Nyholm, M.-L. (1995) *Luvaton nuoruus* [Illegal Youth]. Helsinki: Painatuskeskus.

Lehtinen, T. (2001) *Pienen kunnan sosiaalityöntekijä valtasuhteiden verkostossa: omakohtaisen kokemuksen analyysi* [Social Worker in the Middle of Power Webs in a Small Municipality: Analysing One's Own Experience]. Unpublished manuscript for a Licentiate Degree in Social Sciences. Tampere: University of Tampere.

Marttunen, M. (2004) *Finnish Juvenile Criminal Justice*. Scientific Report on European Youth Involved in Public Care and Youth Justice Systems at www.ensayouth.cjsw.ac.uk.

Marttunen, M. and Kivivuori, J. (2003) *Nuorisorikollisuus* [Juvenile Delinquency]. In *Rikollisuustilanne 2002. Rikollisuus tilastojen valossa* [Crime Trends in Finland]. Helsinki: National Research Institute for Legal Policy, 143–157.

Marttunen, M. and Takala, J.-P. (2002) *Nuorisorangaistus 1997–2001. Uuden rangaistuslajin arviointi* [Juvenile Punishment 1997–2001. Evaluation of a New Punishment]. Report 192. Helsinki: National Research Institute of Legal Policy.

Mielityinen, I. (1999) *Rikos ja sovittely* [Crime and Mediation]. Julkaisu no 167. Helsinki: National Research Institute of Legal Policy.

Millar, J. and Warman, A. (1996) *Family Obligations in Europe*. London: Policy Studies Centre.

Möller, S. (2004) *Sattumista suunnitelmallisuuteen. Lapsen elämäntilanteen kartoitus lastensuojelussa* [From Coincidence to Systematic Practice. Discovering the Child's Conditions of Life in Child Protection]. Opas- ja käsikirjat 1. Jyväskylä: Pesäpuu ry.

Morris, A. and McIsaac, M. (1978) *Juvenile Justice? The Practice of Social Welfare*. London: Heinemann.

Muiluvuori, M.-L. (2004) *Vangit vankiloittain ja vankeinhoitoalueittain, 1.5.2004* [Prisoners in Jails and in Prison Administration Districts, 1 May 2004]. Rikosseuraamusviraston monisteita 6. Helsinki: Rikosseuraamusvirasto.

Muncie, J. (2004) *Youth & Crime*. (2nd edn). London: Thousand Oaks New Delhi: Sage.

Muukkonen, H. and Tulensalo, H. (2004) *Kohtaavaa lastensuojelua. Lapsikeskeisen lastensuojelun sosiaalityön tilannearvion käsikirja* [Handbook for the Assessment of Situations in Child-Centered Social Work]. Selvityksiä 1. Helsingin kaupungin sosiaalivirasto.

Nuotio, K. (2004) Nuorisorikosoikeus? [Youth Criminal Justice?] *Lakimies 3*, 466–478.

Nuorisorikostoimikunnan mietintö (2003) [Report by the Commission on Juvenile Crime]. Helsinki: Oikeusministeriö.

Oikeusturva-asian neuvottelukunnan kertomus toiminnastaan 2000–2001. [Report of the Consultative Board for Legal Security], online at www.oikeusturva-asiainneuvottelukunta.fi.

Oranen, M.(2001) *Perheväkivallan varjossa: raportti lapsikeskeisen työn kehittämisestä* [In the Shadow of Family Violence]. Report 30. Helsinki: Ensi- ja turvakotien liitto.

Parton, N. and O'Byrne, P. (2000) *Constructive Social Work. Towards a New Practice*. Basingstoke and London: Macmillan.

Platt, A. (1967) *The Child Savers: The Invention of Delinquency*. Chicago: University of Chicago Press.

Pösö, T. (2001) 'Child protection without children – or Finnish children without problems?' In J. Best (ed) *How Claims Spread. Cross-national Diffusion of Social Problems.* New York: Aldine de Gruyter, 283–304.

Pösö, T. (2004) *Vakavat silmät ja muita kokemuksia koulukodista* [Serious Eyes and other Experiences of Reform Schools]. Tutkimuksia 133. Helsinki: Stakes.

Rikollisuustilanne (2003) Rikollisuus tilastojen valossa 2002 [Crime Trends in Finland]. Helsinki: The National Research Institute for Legal Policy, at www.om.fi/optula/20195.htm.

Rousu, S. and Holma, T. (2003) *Lastensuojelupalvelujen hankinta ja tuottaminen* [Buying and Producing Child Protection Services]. Helsinki: Suomen kuntaliitto.

Rousu, S. and Holma, T. (2004) *Lastensuojelupalvelujen laadunhallinta* [Quality Management in Child Protection Services]. Helsinki: Suomen Kuntaliitto.

Sauli, H., Bardy, M. and Salmi, M. (2002) 'Elinojen koventuminen pikkulapsiperheissä.' [The detoriating living condition in families with small children]. In M. Heikkilä and M. Kautto (eds) *Suomalaisten hyvinvointi 2002* [The Well-being of the Finns 2002]. Helsinki: Stakes, 32–61.

Sinko, P. (2004) *Laki ja lastensuojelu* [Law and Child Protection]. Helsinki: Palmenia –kustannus.

Sosiaalialan kehittämishanke. Toimeenpanosuunnitelma (2003) [Developing the Social Sector. Enforcement Plan]. Monisteita 20. Helsinki: Sosiaali- ja terveysministeriö.

Sosiaali- ja terveydenhuollon tilastollinen vuosikirja 2003 (2003) *Suomen virallinen tilasto* [Statistical Yearbook for Social and Health Welfare 2003]. Sosiaaliturva 4. Helsinki: Stakes.

Sosiaalityön kehittämisryhmän linjaus- ja toimenpide-ehdotukset 2002 (2003). Helsinki, at www.hel.fi/sosv/julkaisu/suse/2003/sokeri.pdf.

Suutari, M. (2002) *Nuorten sosiaaliset verkostot palkkatyön marginaalissa.* [The Social Networks of Young People in the Margins of Paid Labour]. Report 26. Helsinki: Nuorisotutkimusverkosto.

Takala, J.-P. (1998) *Moraalitunteet rikosten sovittelussa* [Moral Emotions in Victim–Offender Mediation]. Report 151. Helsinki: The National Research Institute for Legal Policy.

Tommo, E. (2004) *Lapsirikollisuus lastensuojelussa* [Youth Crime in Child Protection]. Unpublished master's thesis. Department of Social Policy and Social Work. Tampere: University of Tampere.

Valtioneuvoston periaatepäätös sosiaalialan tulevaisuuden turvaamiseksi (2003) [The Council of State's Decision to Ensure the Future of the Social Sector). Esitteitä 5. Helsinki: Sosiaali- ja terveysministeriö.

2

The Interface between Youth Justice and Child Protection In Ireland

Helen Buckley and Eoin O'Sullivan

Introduction

There is a widespread acceptance that factors such as poverty, abuse and neglect, poor educational outcomes and behavioural problems are characteristic of the majority of children and young people who find themselves embroiled in either the child protection system or in the juvenile justice sector. In the light of this, recent developments in Ireland indicate an ideological acceptance that the most effective provision of services to children and young people is through proactive community-based interventions that draw on local resources and incorporate familial involvement. One of the provisions of the new and not yet fully implemented Children Act, 2001 raised the age of criminal responsibility from 7 to 12 years of age. This modification, accompanied by the implementation of diversionary programmes for young offenders, signifies a refocusing on local participatory methods to address the underlying causes of children and young people's problems. This chapter will look at the Irish systems for child care and protection and for youth justice, with a focus on some of the challenges to the provision of a comprehensive, holistic and non-stigmatised approach to troubled children and young people.

Sociological analyses demonstrate that the development of social systems rarely occurs in a logical or systematic manner, but is rather the result of what are described as 'radical ruptures', global, local and political events, as well as ideological movements that have waxed and waned at different times (Skehill

2004). To that extent, the system in each society has been shaped by the combination of a number of specific and unique events, rather than a rational progression informed by international knowledge and research. For example, in Ireland, two forces combined to produce a system that was initially very reactive, taking large numbers of children into state care: namely the power and dominance of the Catholic Church, and the readiness of different governments to adopt a model of child care and protection orientated to use of residential institutions, particularly during the early and mid-twentieth century (Raftery and O'Sullivan 1999).

This approach further evolved under the legislative framework of the Children Act 1908, a relict of British rule in Ireland that regulated the provision of welfare services to children until the enactment and implementation of the Child Care Act 1991. A series of tribunals and child abuse inquiries is still dealing with the legacy of that approach, an inheritance that, unfortunately, transcended international borders following the travels of Irish religious orders to Canada, Australia and other parts of the world. As O'Sullivan (1997) has argued, the 1908 Act was largely concerned with protecting children from 'moral danger' and dealing with the very small number of crimes committed by children, and paid little attention to the maltreatment of children or interventions to protect them. Despite a common perception that the Irish state could do little to intervene in Irish family life due to the exalted status of the family in the Irish Constitution (1937) (e.g. the Kilkenny Incest Inquiry, 1993), the historical evidence shows that the state intervened in multiple ways and removed thousands of children from their families for reasons such as non-attendance at school (Fahey 1992).

Thus, for many years, Ireland followed a 'social risk' model of child care. It was only from the late 1960s that this was displaced by a more developmental model (O'Sullivan 1979). This was brought about by the discovery of the 'deprived child' in Ireland. Prior to this period child care intervention was viewed as 'a means of social control rather than of individual fulfilment'. The primary facets of the emerging developmental model were a disenchantment with institutionalisation and the espousal of a wider interpretation of the basis for child care policy. Rather than focusing almost exclusively on the physical needs or moral behaviour of the child, increasingly attention was paid to emotional and psychological dimensions in promoting the welfare of children.

Thus, the discourse of the (morally) 'depraved' child, which had long shaped intervention by the state and those to whom it delegated child care responsibilities, shifted to a discourse that placed a premium on the notion of deprivation. In this spirit, the Child Care Act 1991, fully implemented in 1996, placed a statutory duty on Health Boards to promote the welfare of children who are not receiving adequate care and protection up to the age of 18; it enhanced the powers of the Health Boards to provide child care and family support services; enabled the courts to place children who have been assaulted, ill-treated, neglected or sexually abused or who are at risk, in the care of or under the supervision of regional Health Boards; and it established new procedures for the registration and inspection of residential centres for children. In 1987 the Status of Children Act was passed, which abolished the concept of illegitimacy. In 1996, a Children Bill was published, which aimed to repeal the provisions of the Children Act 1908 in respect of juvenile justice and introduce an amendment to the Child Care Act 1991, allowing Health Boards to detain children in their own interest. The Children Bill 1996 was, for various reasons, abandoned and replaced three years later with the Children Bill 1999, which was signed into law in 2001 as the Children Act 2001.

The triggers for policy change in the 1990s have undoubtedly been the child abuse inquiries and high-profile scandals that have challenged two of Ireland's strongest institutions: the family and the Catholic Church. The media have played an enormous role in both raising and reflecting public concern, and much of the impetus for change emerged from publicity given to the criminal trials of perpetrators as well as some hard-hitting television documentaries about abuse in residential care. The system is now characterised by a vastly expanded network of services, more elaborate structures and increased accountability. These have, together, contributed to the new paradigm of child care and protection that has developed alongside a growing realisation of the value of family support, prevention, co-operation and inclusiveness. However, despite the aspirations underpinning the Child Care Act 1991, research, policy and inquiry reports continued to highlight the absence of preventive services and the piecemeal nature of interventions in the overall continuum of child welfare provision (Buckley 2002, 2003; Buckley, Skehill and O'Sullivan 1997; Department of Health 1993; Ferguson and O'Reilly 2001).

A parallel development, at the border between child protection and youth justice, demonstrated a 'new' concern of the late 1990s and early 2000s, which evoked considerable political and media reaction. This was the emergence of the alleged 'out of control' or 'hard to manage' child, who was not necessarily offending but was seen to require a special type of intensive intervention. There has also been a concern to destigmatise very troubled children who may otherwise have entered the justice system, and maintain them within the child care and protection system. As a result, a small but significant number of children whose behaviour puts their health and safety, and that of others, at risk come to the attention of the statutory services each year, requiring a particular type of response. In the absence of legislation to place children needing special care in appropriate settings, individual case law in the form of high court orders has been the main determinant of practice, resulting in an uneven and fragmented delivery of services in this sector and attracting considerable criticism (Kenny 2000). It has meant that disproportionate amounts of public money are being spent on cases that have attracted significant attention in the courts, to the detriment of preventive services (O'Sullivan 1996).

In the broader field of child care and protection, research has also indicated that a greater proportion of resources are invested and expended in responding to suspicions of child abuse rather than in the sort of support services that may prevent abuse from occurring (Buckley 2002; Department of Health 2001; Eastern Health Board/Impact 1997). There is evidence too, that even though child neglect, associated with poverty and disadvantage, continues to be the most widely identified and reported category of maltreatment, child sexual abuse still tends to be the most dominant and symbolically powerful form of child abuse in terms of its propensity to attract an assertive multidisciplinary response (Buckley 2002, 2003; Buckley *et al.* 1997). Despite the fact that research continues to demonstrate the link between child neglect and diminished life chances, the child care and protection system has, to date, been unable to provide the sort of integrated response or early intervention necessary to tackle the issue in a holistic way.

Integration of services

Meeting the challenge of integrating justice, health, education and social welfare services for children and young people will require strategic planning.

This is particularly pertinent given the involvement of police, probation officers, teaching and Health Board staff in the operation of the legislation, and the fact that funding of services is divided between different government departments. The first and most basic hurdle will be to deal with the structural aspects of integrated service delivery. As Lupton *et al.* (2001) argue, provider networks are rarely context-free but are rooted in substructural influences. Government departments that deal with a range of issues will inevitably have competing priorities, and will be subject to pressure from different sectors. An example would be the announcement by the government in 2002, following an incident where two police officers were killed in a car chase involving two young people, of plans to open a juvenile prison for 14- to 16-year-olds, staffed by prison officers. This was a move that flew directly in the face of the aspirations underpinning the proposed legislation, which sought to use incarceration only as a last resort when all other alternatives had been tried. These plans were later shelved, but illustrate how political forces can create a rift between organisations allegedly pursuing the same goal.

There are few existing formal links between, or even within, protective, mental health and juvenile justice services, either at community or residential levels (Barnardo's 2000; Children's Legal Centre 1996). As the foregoing section has pointed out, certain recent policy initiatives have been put in place to address these difficulties, but in the meantime research demonstrates that child care and protection systems are operated differently both between and within different regions (Buckley 2002; Horwarth and Bishop 2001) and there is little evidence to demonstrate that youth justice services operate any differently. When a service is itself disjointed, it is very difficult to see how it can promote partnership and participation among those whom it is intended to serve and with whom it is intended to collaborate. An alternative model exists in New Zealand, where a single government ministry of Child, Youth and Family (CYF) deals directly with provision of child welfare, protection and youth justice services. If a similar model were applied in Ireland it would eliminate the chasm between policy-making and service delivery by creating strong connections between the front line and central government, ensure greater accountability from voluntary services, eliminate the influence of local politics and facilitate the flow of information.

Early intervention

The dual aspirations of the current children's legal framework in Ireland are to enhance the welfare of children and protect them from adverse outcomes including early school leaving and involvement in crime. This is heavily dependent on a commitment to provide universalist services embedded in a broad welfare system. While this is the case in certain parts of Europe, the tendency in Ireland and the UK, and indeed most of the English-speaking world, is towards residual and selective provision where services are offered to children when harm or abuse has already occurred. The latter model tends to produce the often-identified tension between a narrow form of child protection and broad-based child welfare (Parton 1996). International research has demonstrated that in the UK, Ireland, Australia and New Zealand child welfare services for families who need help receive less attention and fewer resources than child protection services focused on child abuse, despite evidence that most children coming to the attention of services are 'in need' rather than abused (Department of Health (UK) 1995; Ferguson and O'Reilly 2001; Thorpe 1994). In Ireland priority is given to cases identified as 'at risk' partly because this is seen as a statutory duty, even though the Child Care Act 1991 obliges Health Boards to promote the welfare of children in need. The dearth of early intervention and family support services means that more children end up requiring much stronger interventions with less positive outcomes. The absence of a preventive framework, within a context of relatively defensive practice means that front-line practitioners have become accustomed to working in a very proceduralised, reactive fashion that functions well when dealing with some of the more severe manifestations of child abuse but does not lend itself to less easily defined concerns about children, such as neglect and vulnerability (Buckley 2005; Graham 1998). It is suggested that the reasons why the systems in England, North America, Canada, Australia and New Zealand are so focused on harm rather than need are the shortage of resources, combined with defensiveness and a lack of confidence prevailing in agencies, which are afraid of being open to criticism if issues like child safety or juvenile crime are seen to have been inadequately addressed (Parton 1996; Spratt 2001). The raising of the age of criminal responsibility from 7 to 12 by the Children Act 2001 means that child care and protection staff will inherit from the police an area of work for which they have little expertise or capacity at present. Hence it is over-optimistic to expect that supportive interventions to divert vulnerable youngsters from crime will be readily provided by these services.

Participation and partnership

One of the more positive developments in both the child protection and youth justice areas has been the development in Ireland of the Family Welfare Conference model. Legislation now requires that conferences involving families will be held to deal with situations where secure care is being considered, and in certain instances where offences have been committed by children. The main principle underpinning the family conference is the prioritising of a family- and community-based solution to the presenting difficulty, and the limiting of the state's role in direct intervention.

The Children Act 2001

The remainder of the chapter aims to highlight some of the implications for children at the interface of the child protection and youth justice system through interrogating some of the tensions evident in the Children Act 2001. This Act is the culmination of over three decades of agitation, research and debate on how to reform children's services in Ireland (Burke, Carney and Cook 1981; CARE 1978; Dail Eireann 1992; Department of Health 1980; Reformatory and Industrial Schools Systems 1970).

Both the Children Act 2001 and its predecessor the Child Care Act 1991, were claimed by their respective authors to be radical departures from past practices in the manner in which Irish society regulated those parents and young people who were deemed to have transgressed both societal and legal norms. Nevertheless, they represent a striking continuity of ideology regarding the treatment of errant children and their families. This new legislative framework results in 'a new emphasis on the personal responsibilities of individuals, their families and their communities for their own future well-being, and upon their own obligation to take active steps to secure this' (Rose 1996, pp. 327–328).

It is of note that in the various debates leading up to the Children Act 2001, more attention was given to the additions to the Child Care Act 1991 than the sections dealing with juvenile justice. Two issues dominated the debates: first, when was the legislation going to be implemented and, second, the structures for gaining a special care order. Many of the other amendments and changes were relatively minor. For example, existing places of detention for 16- and 17-year-olds were renamed 'Children Detention Schools' and remand institutions became 'Remand Centres'. In relation to the operation of the Children Detention Schools, a minimum period of three months' detention is now specified, regular inspections are now defined as at least every six months, and the Inspector of Children Detention Schools has been given the power to investigate the grievances of individual children.

Implementation of the Act

In light of the considerable delays in implementing the Child Care Act 1991 and the long gestation of the Children Act 2001, members of the Irish parliament (Oireachtas) were particularly concerned at what stage the legislation would be implemented. Although the government's stated intention was to implement the legislation as soon as possible, in practice, by the end of 2004, the only sections enacted were Part 2, which deals with family welfare conferences, and Part 3, the special amendment to the Child Care Act 1991 (see below). Thus, none of the sections dealing with youth justice is currently operational.

Special care orders

The second substantive issue was in relation to Part 3, Section 16, which amends the Child Care Act 1991 in relation to special care units (secure accommodation for non-offending children) and private foster care. The changes made included a requirement that the Special Residential Board be consulted before an application to court for a special care order can be made. Also, the minimum time that a child can be detained in special care is three months, on the understanding that a special care unit should be used only as a last resort and for as short a time as possible.

Custodial vs non-custodial sanctions

The 2001 Act declared a preference for utilising non-custodial sanctions, which has been welcomed in most quarters. Two principal provisions raised the age of criminal responsibility to 12 (from 7) and stipulated that the detention of children will be utilised only as a last resort. However, the actual commitment to developing such services must be questioned in light of the Minister for Justice's statement that the Children Act 2001, will create a requirement for a separate, secure detention centre, for up to 20 juvenile female and 90 juvenile male offenders. Funding additional detention places appears to indicate a readiness on the part of government to incarcerate more young people rather than divert them from custody. Furthermore, if non-custodial sanctions are developed we need to be wary of how they are utilised. It has been argued (Cohen 1985; Muncie 1999) that, unless carefully monitored, such measures can result in the tendency for non-custodial sanctions to become additions, rather than alternatives, to custodial sanctions.

Given the preoccupation of recent governments with incarceration (Kilcommins *et al.* 2004; O'Donnell and O'Sullivan 2001), and a media that sensationalises and distorts the reality of crime in Ireland (O'Connell 1999), it is difficult to see any substantial change in the ideology of the juvenile justice system in the new Act. More significantly, the recommendations of the 1998 *Report of the Expert Group on the Probation and Welfare Service*, which argued for a decisive shift from custodial to non-custodial sanctions, have not been implemented and the urgency evident in recruiting prison officers and Gardai (police) has not been replicated with regard to probation and welfare officers.

Children Detention Schools vs Special Care Units

Effectively, the Children Act 2001 proposes three sites for the 'incarceration of children'. Existing Reformatory and Industrial Schools will be known as Children Detention Schools. These are aimed at those young people between 12 and 16 convicted of a criminal act, and are managed by the Department of Education. Detention Centres are for those aged between 16 and 18 convicted of a criminal act, and Special Care Units are aimed at children under 18 who have not committed an offence but are deemed to be a risk to themselves and others.

In practice, we could argue that there would be very little difference in the personal characteristics of the children committed to these places (Harris and Timms 1993) – that is, they are likely to be poor and underachieving educationally. The role of the experts charged with regulating unruly children will change to one of evaluating the child's capacity for self-management. Failures to govern oneself appropriately will trigger different professionals depending on the degree or form of lack of self-government and the age of the child (i.e. out of control or engaged in delinquent activity). In some cases, the young person will be subject to the 'gaze' of all the experts as they travel through the panoply of expert interventions (Geiran *et al.* 1999). Most importantly, it signals that any attempt to locate offending by children within a welfarist framework is now effectively terminated.

The role of the expert is not to engage in seeking out the 'cause' of the offending behaviour or most certainly not to locate it in any socio-economic context, but to evaluate the site of appropriate intervention by means of audit that can best induce a successful 'output' (Feeley and Simon 1994). Thus, while we may welcome the fact that children under 12 will no longer be subject to the formal criminal justice system, this does not mean that children under the age of criminal responsibility will not be 'incarcerated', rather they may be subjected to the 'special care' of the Health Boards. In practice, the regime in a Special Care Unit will not be very different from that of a Children Detention School, except for one ironic difference: those children committed to Detention Schools and Places of Detention will have stronger procedural rights than those placed in Special Care Units because they will have determinate sentences, regular inspections and access to a visiting panel. Children placed in Special Care Units have, under the Children Act 2001 weaker safeguards (Child Care Regulations 2004). This leads us to the third key issue in the Act.

Parental responsibility vs state responsibility

As indicated above, over the past decade or so, the central role of parents in both regulating and protecting their children has been reinvented as the panacea to the perceived deficits in state management of these issues (Bessant and Hil 1998). Family welfare conferences, parental sanctions, community sanctions, restrictions on movement, group work programmes that challenge offending behaviour, and other family-based crime prevention projects have been developed and are incorporated in the Children Act 2001. These measures co-opt families into the child regulation and protection systems. Parents are urged to exercise more effective care and control of their children in order to prevent or curtail juvenile offending. Under the Children Act 2001 parents and guardians may be subjected to a range of 'normalising' activities and required to engage in practices that ensure compliance with judicial inter-pretations of appropriate behaviour. For example, under Section 111 (6), parents may be ordered by the courts to: undergo treatment for alcohol or other substance abuse, where facilities for such treatment are reasonably available; participate in any course that is reasonably available for the improvement of parenting skills; comply with any other instructions of the court that would in its opinion assist in preventing the child from committing further offences. This to be done by judges who, if appointed prior to 1995, do not have to undergo any training to assist them in making these decisions (Section 72).

Although this could be regarded as a recent instance of neo-liberal governance, historically the state has more or less continuously attempted to apportion responsibility for protecting and regulating children to their parents (Allen 1991; Brank and Weiss 2004). For example, When Herbert Samuel was introducing the Children Act 1908, he outlined three principles informing the section on juvenile justice, the second of which was:

> that the parent of the child offender must be made to feel more responsible for the wrong-doing of his child. He cannot be allowed to neglect the upbringing of his children, and having committed the grave offence of throwing on society a child criminal, wash his hands of the consequences and escape scot free.

The basic philosophy underpinning the concept is that parents must be made responsible for the offences committed by their offspring. At the heart of this concept is the notion that the aetiology of much juvenile crime is the result of inadequate supervision and care of children, and defective socialisation into the norms of society. This interpretation of juvenile crime has been reinforced in public discourses by nostalgic yearnings for tradition, and appeals to idealistic notions of family values, community norms and consensus. For example, Mr Paddy Culligan, the former Garda Commissioner (chief of police) identified some of the causes of crime in Ireland as 'dismantling the authority of the family; dismantling teachers' authority; the abandonment of the religious ethic and the social pressures for both parents to go into the labour force' (Culligan 1994).

In contrast, the assumption that the state might have some responsibilities to its vulnerable citizens has dissipated. Indeed, the Children Act 2001 appears to exempt the state, acting *in loco parentis*, from the sanctions that can be imposed upon parents. It becomes clear that there are discrepancies between the laws imposed on individual parents and guardians in society and those accepted by the state in its capacity as the responsible parent/guardian. In light of recent revelations regarding the experiences of children in the care of the state in Ireland, this instance of differential justice hinders the development of meaningful relationships between state agencies and the families of children ensnared in child care and protection/youth justice systems.

Conclusions

The legislative framework for both the protection and punishment of children has changed considerably over the past decade or so. Indeed the pace of change compared to the relative inertia of the previous 60–70 years is remarkable, which explains in part the hesitant, fragmentary and fragile nature of many services as they attempt to adapt to changing realities. The Children Act 2001 represents a combination of traditionalism and new regulatory practices to ensure compliance with this traditionalism. It also signals that responsibility for juvenile crime is located both at the level of the individual and that the individual child and parent must be empowered to exercise responsibility and become a good citizen. That social conditions and the state might have a degree of responsibility for the creation of the conditions that could have contributed to such actions in the first instance is minimised. Instead an infrastructure has been developed to ensure that children, through teaching, coaxing, cajolement, threats and ultimately banishment, conduct themselves responsibly.

The challenge of inter-agency co-operation, greater scrutiny and account-ability of service delivery, active rather than passive clients and fear of litigation are but some of the elements that are reshaping the manner in which services to children are evolving. The interface between the services and agencies that manage and deliver both child welfare and youth justice services are, as a consequence of these developments, particularly fluid and unsettled. Ideolog-ically, the dominant professional view appears to be that those children who are involved with child welfare services and those who appear before criminal justice agencies share many of the same difficulties and many of the same characteristics. Thus, the interface between the differing agencies requires greater coherence and tangible relationships, but administrative and legal boundaries remain powerful impediments to the development of such practices.

References

Allen, R. (1991) 'Parental responsibility for juvenile offenders.' In T. Booth (ed) *Juvenile Justice in the New Europe*. Sheffield: Joint Unit for Social Services Research.

Barnardo's (2000) *Responding to the Needs of Troubled Children: A Critique of High Support and Secure Care Provision in Ireland*. Dublin: Barnardo's.

Bessant, J. and Hil, R. (1998) 'Parenting on Trial: State Wards' and Governments' Accountability in Australia'. *Journal of Criminal Justice 26*, 2, 145–157.

Brank, E.M. and Weiss, V. (2004) 'Paying for the Crimes of their Children: Public Support of Parental Responsibility.' *Journal of Criminal Justice 32*, 5, 389–499.

Buckley, H. (2002) *Child Protection and Welfare: Innovations and Interventions*. Dublin: Institute of Public Administration.

Buckley, H. (2003) *Child Protection Work: Beyond the Rhetoric*. London: Jessica Kingsley Publishers.

Buckley, H. (2005) 'Neglect: no monopoly on expertise'. In J. Taylor and B. Daniel (eds) *Child Neglect: Practice Issues for Health and Social Care*. London: Jessica Kingsley Publishers.

Buckley, H., Skehill, C. and O'Sullivan, O. (1997) *Child Protection Practices in Ireland: A Case Study*. Dublin: Oak Tree Press.

Burke, H., Carney, C. and Cook, G. (eds) (1981) *Youth and Justice: Young Offenders in Ireland*. Dublin: Turoe Press.

CARE (1978) *Who Wants a Children's Prison in Ireland*. Dublin.

Child Care (Special Care) Regulations (2004) *Statutory Instrument No. 550 of 2004*. Dublin: Stationery Office.

Children's Legal Centre (1996) *Secure Accommodation in Child Care*. Dublin: CLC.

Cohen, S. (1985) *Visions of Social Control*. Cambridge: Polity.

Culligan, P. (1994) 'Crime in Ireland.' *Irish Times*, September.

Dail Eireann (1992) *First Report of the Select Committee on Crime. Juvenile Justice – Its Causes and its Remedies*.

Department of Health (1980) *Task Force on Child Care Services. Final Report*. Dublin: Stationery Office.

Department of Health (1993) *Report of the Kilkenny Incest Investigation*. Dublin: Stationery Office.

Department of Health (UK) (1995) *Messages from Research*. London: HMSO.

Eastern Health Board/Impact (1997) *Report of the Eastern Health Board/Impact Review Group on Child Care and Family Support Services*. Dublin: Eastern Health Board.

Fahey, T. (1992) 'State, Family and Compulsory Schooling in Ireland.' *Economic and Social Review 23*, 4, 369–395.

Feeley, M. and Simon, J. (1994) 'Actuarial justice: the emerging new criminal law.' In D. Nelkin (ed) *The Futures of Criminology*. London: Sage.

Ferguson, H. and O'Reilly, M. (2001) *Keeping Children Safe: Child Abuse, Child Protection and the Promotion of Welfare*. Dublin: A & A Farmar.

Geiran, V., McCarthy, M., Morahan, M. and O'Connell, V. (1999) *Young Offenders in Penal Custody: Contact with the Probation and Welfare Service and Experience of Community Sanctions Prior to Custodial Sentence*. Dublin: Probation and Welfare Service.

Graham, B. (1998) *Overwhelmed or Under-whelmed? The Response of an Area Social Work Team to Neglect*. Unpublished dissertation: Trinity College, Dublin.

Harris, R. and Timms, N. (1993) *Secure Accommodation in Child Care*. London: Routledge.

Howarth, J. and Bishop, B. (2001) *Child Neglect: Is My View Your View?* North Eastern Health Service Executive and the University of Sheffield.

Kenny, B. (2000) *Responding to the Needs of Troubled Children: A Critique of High Support and Secure Special Care Provision in Ireland*. Policy Briefing 3. Dublin: Barnardo's.

Kilcommins, S., O'Donnell, I., O'Sullivan, E. and Vaughan, B. (2004) *Crime, Punishment and the Search for Order in Ireland*. Dublin: Institute of Public Administration.

Lupton, C., North, N. and Khan, P. (2001) *Working Together or Pulling Apart? The National Health Service and Child Protection Networks.* Bristol: The Policy Press.

Muncie, J. (1999) *Youth and Crime: A Critical Introduction.* London: Sage.

O'Connell, M. (1999) 'Is Irish Public Opinion towards Crime Distorted by Media Bias?' *European Journal of Communication 14,* 2, 191–212.

O'Donnell, I. and O'Sullivan, E. (2001) *Crime Control in Ireland: The Politics of Intolerance.* Cork: Cork University Press, 102.

O'Sullivan, D. (1979) 'Social Definition in Child Care in the Irish Republic: Models of Child and Child Care Intervention.' *Economic and Social Review 10,* 3, 209–229.

O'Sullivan, E. (1996) 'Juvenile Justice in the Republic of Ireland – Future Priorities.' *Irish Social Worker 14,* 2/4, 4–7.

O'Sullivan, E. (1997) 'Restored to Virtue, to Society and to God" Juvenile Justice and the Regulation of the Poor.' *Irish Criminal Law Journal 7,* 2, 171–194.

Parton, N. (1996) 'Child protection, family support, and social work.' *Child and Family Social Work 1,* 3–11.

Raftery, M. and O'Sullivan, E. (1999) *Suffer the Little Children: The Inside Story of Ireland's Industrial Schools.* Dublin: New Island Books.

Reformatory and Industrial Schools Systems (1970) *Report.* Dublin: Stationery Office.

Rose, N. (1996) 'The Death of the Social? Re-figuring the Territory of Government.' *Economy and Society 25,* 3, 327–356.

Skehill, C. (2004) *History of the Present: Child Protection and Welfare Social Work in Ireland.* New York: Edwin Mellen Press.

Spratt, T. (2001) 'The influence of child protection practice orientation on child welfare practice.' *British Journal of Social Work 31,* 933–954.

Thorpe, D. (1994) *Evaluating Child Protection.* Milton Keynes: Open University Press.

3

Child Welfare and Juvenile Justice in the USA: A Practice Perspective

Mark Creekmore

Introduction: practice and policy in child welfare and juvenile justice

This chapter focuses on issues that arise in separating child welfare from juvenile justice functions in the USA. I will examine policy and practice developments and the interface between the two. Policy and practice are related though distinct systems of codifying organisational activities. Usually formal policies do not translate directly into practice, but form one among several sets of influences involved in 'doing the work'. Practice is routine, purposeful activity involving typologies about cases, which may concern individuals, families or members of communities. Cases having a consistent set of characteristics are the essential units of practice. For example, practices that work with children who have mental health problems are different from practices that work with children who are drug abusing. Practices involve ideals (norms), some of which are embodied in laws. General norms such as confidentiality and client participation in decisions apply to all cases. More local community and organisational norms also affect how certain cases should be handled. For example, community norms about how developmentally disabled youth should be dealt with are different from those concerning delinquency. Finally, practices also rely on bodies of knowledge and methods of knowing (epistemologies), and the sources and types of this knowledge also vary by the types of cases. Here, traditional 'practice wisdom' still has an important place alongside current emphasis on 'evidence-based practices'.

The relationships between practice and policy are complex. Practice knowledge is usually more emergent, amorphous and flexible than policies, which are usually codified in writing. Policies are derived from various sources, including laws, government reports and agency procedures. In the USA, both laws and public agency rules are stratified further by levels of federal, state and local government. Policies affect worker activities through varied routes (e.g. procedures, training, staff recruitment). Their application depends on how individuals interpret them in the light of organisational and community norms.

Policies may fail or fall into disuse if they conflict with important, established practices. Barton and Creekmore (1994) documented the failed policy that applied risk assessment tools to dispositional decisions in New Hampshire. Case practices are more flexible than policies. Based on professional norms and bodies of knowledge, practices develop strategies that apply policies to complex cases. For example, practitioners make choices about which policy to apply; they may ignore or work around the policy by partial compliance; and they may attempt to resolve problems that sometimes follow from competing or inflexible policies and procedures.

The next part of this chapter examines the history concerning the separation of child welfare and juvenile justice. At some times policies have followed or merely codified practice; at others, they have led practice. After that, consideration is given to the present organisational and social contexts that coincide with the separation of child welfare and juvenile justice. Finally examples are given of practices that 'work around' policies dividing child welfare and juvenile justice, and of experiments that unify child welfare and juvenile justice practices.

The historical context of service practice for youth and families

This brief history will show that most of the fundamental strains among current practices and policies were present from the start and have stubbornly avoided systematic solution. They include differing definitions of childhood, the identification of perpetrators and victims, and the appropriate roles for individual, family and community responsibility.

Table 3.1 summarises in parallel columns the trends in child welfare (based on the works of Gordon (2002) and Schene (1998)) and the trends in juvenile justice (Krisberg and Austin 1993).

Table 3.1: Historical summary of child welfare and juvenile justice

Child welfare	Juvenile justice
1875–1890: Child Savers. Children's Aid Society, settlement houses, public schools. Practice focused on child abuse.	1850–1890: Child Savers. New York Juvenile Asylum. Practice focused on institutionalisation.
1880–1920: Progressive Era. Regulation of institutions, child labour laws, (state) mothers' pension laws, compulsory school attendance. Practice focused on neglect. Juvenile Court: youth segregated by age.	1880–1920: Progressive Era. Juvenile court: youth segregated by age. 1907–1940s: Child Guidance Clinic Movement. Practice focused on psychological evaluation and counselling.
1930–1940: Depression Era Practice focused on economic stress.	1930s–1950s: Chicago Area Project. Psychological counselling, Youth Authority model. Practice focused on community (dis)organisation.
Second World War and 1950s: Practice focused on neurotic complexes and individual adaptation.	1950s and 1960s: Mobilisation for Youth, Youth Service Bureaus. Practice focused on prevention and community intervention.
1960s and 1970s: Practice focused on child abuse, mandatory reporting, family preservation, specialised foster care (Indian Child Welfare Act).	1970s: Institutional change and Gault decision. Practice focused on centralised state services through youth authorities and creation of community-based corrections.
1980s–1990s: Numerous and shifting policies. Practice focused on 'reasonable efforts' (Adoption Assistance and Child Welfare Act); on termination of parental rights and adoption (and against cross-racial placements and adoptions (Adoption and Safe Families Act); on prevention and early intervention (Wraparound and Family Group Decision Making).	1980s–1990s: Practice focused on violent crime and gang activity through transfer and direct file to adult courts; on balanced and restorative justice; on community development; on speciality dockets (e.g. drug courts, truancy courts).

Child welfare and juvenile justice practices had common beginnings in the immigration and urban poverty prior to the US Civil War (Bernard 1992, p.58). During the era of the Child Savers (dated between 1850 and 1890) juvenile justice reformers criticised the work of established social institutions like churches. Juvenile justice focused on social control using institutional 'asylums' that separated children from adults, removed them from urban environments and attempted to inculcate values and habits, especially about work. Child welfare, however, focused on family strategies such as home placement. This meant the removal of some children from urban poverty to rural homes, but settlement houses provided less disruptive and more integrative educational and community strategies.

From 1880 to 1920, the so-called Progressive Era, formal policies increasingly differentiated child welfare and juvenile justice. The juvenile court began in 1899 in Illinois and, by 1925, all but two states had legislation to create juvenile courts. The primary focus of juvenile courts was delinquency, but at first they also dealt with some children who were neglected. Whenever possible these were kept with their own families or referred to probation officers. Later legislation for juvenile courts formally separated the delinquent from the dependent and neglect cases by limiting the definition of criminal intent by age. Separate institutions were established to rehabilitate young offenders, and children under 12 years were no longer admitted to reform schools.

One far-reaching effect of the juvenile court was to deal with social problems on a 'case-by-case basis, rather than through broad-based efforts to redistribute wealth and power throughout the society' (Krisberg and Austin 1993, p.31). This reinforced a shift in practice towards a focus on individual change, contrasting with the community development strategies of the settlement house movement. This realignment was supported by class-based, community norms about individual responsibility, which are still very strong in the practice of juvenile justice. In juvenile justice the emphasis was placed on 'treating' individual problems leading to delinquency via the child guidance clinic movement.

Child welfare policies during the Progressive Era focused on child neglect, pension laws and ways to keep children out of exploitative labour markets. Services became more formalised and practice more professionalised, drawing on new systematic research about children. Regulatory laws introduced inspections of welfare agencies (O'Connor 2001, p.297).

During the Depression, the Second World War and the 1950s, juvenile justice and child welfare practices and procedures continued to develop 'out of phase'. By the late 1960s, however, the disaffection with existing institutional practices of both child welfare and juvenile justice became more focused and intense. The concern expressed in the Gault decision (see Chapter 12) was widespread: that children (and others) were being harmed by service systems that were large, non-reflective and unchallenged. Such concerns led to greater specialisation of both decision-making and services. Child welfare became dominated by responses to child abuse. In 1974 the federal government provided model legislation for states to develop mandatory reporting laws and create child protective services. Referrals for child protection escalated (Waldfogel 1998). The use of out-of-home care grew, but stays in foster care were criticised for being long and sometimes destructive. In reaction, in 1980 new legislation encouraged 'reasonable efforts' via family services to keep children with their parents or return them home quickly. In juvenile justice during that same period alternatives to institutional treatment were being developed, and diversion of non-serious and status offences was encouraged (Krisberg and Austin 1993, p.48). Starting in the mid-1970s more juvenile cases were transferred to adult courts, and juvenile sentences (called dispositions) emphasised punishment ('accountability') instead of treatment. For some cases the juvenile court became more similar to the adult criminal court. The role of the prosecuting attorney expanded to the point that prosecutors reviewed intake decisions, as in adult courts. Judicial autonomy was also reduced through sentencing guidelines. The number of youths in adult correctional facilities grew. These changes were influenced by three trends: the reduction (in age) of the 'threshold of adolescence'; increased due process as a result of Supreme Court decisions like Gault; and public anxiety about the increase in serious and violent juvenile crime (Fagan 1995, pp.241–243).

The divergence of child welfare and juvenile justice has been accompanied by variation in policies that is structured by American federalism. Responsibility for child welfare and juvenile justice policies is divided among counties, states and the federal government. Furthermore, county juvenile courts and public social service agencies within each state can pursue different policies and priorities. Laws governing child and family services in the USA are still the responsibility of states, although some uniformity has occurred through imitation. Largely in the wake of the civil rights movement, the federal government has been more active as a policy leader using both legislation and financial incentives to encourage states to follow its objectives (Mechanic and Rochefort 1990, p.304).

Current conditions for child welfare and juvenile justice practice

The history of family services shows that child welfare and juvenile justice diverged early and followed separate paths. Current social and organisational conditions, especially among line workers, also affect the separation and conduct of child welfare and juvenile justice.

Child welfare workers are usually young women with college (bachelor) degrees, frequently in a first job, the pay being markedly below salaries for nurses, teachers, police and firefighters. Some work under the auspices of private, not-for-profit agencies, but most are located in large state agencies equivalent to departments of social service. Some child welfare functions are shared between state and county agencies (American Public Human Services Association 2005).

The primary functions of child welfare agencies are to investigate allegations and process complaints about child abuse (Child Protection Services), offer family support (home protection) and provide fostering and adoption services (Littell and Schuerman 1994). Following their investigations, CPS workers may refer cases to the criminal court for the prosecution of parents for neglect or abuse, and to the juvenile court for a decision on whether to remove a child. Juvenile courts also review placements to ensure that a permanency plan is developed and followed. Once a child is removed, other child welfare workers may place the child in foster care and supervise the placement, the adoption or the return home (Schene 1998).

Most child welfare workers handle complex, demanding caseloads within a high-pressure organisational setting (Tittle 2002). Workers perceive a daunting set of problems in carrying out their roles: imbalance of job demands relative to remuneration; starting salaries relative to other positions; other, better job alternatives; budget constraints (not related to hiring); hiring freezes (restrictions); negative media reports (American Public Human Services Association 2005, pp.5–6; also Gunderson and Osborne 2001).

'Child protective staff fear errors, especially the failure to take endangered children into care, and the subsequent public response to deaths or severe abuse and neglect' (Kamerman and Kahn 1990). Furthermore, when a judge's order is not carried out, the judge may order the child welfare agency to a formal hearing to 'show cause' why they should not be held in contempt of court, threatening workers and supervisors with jail for non-compliance. Not surprisingly, then, the yearly turnover of front-line workers is high (Hochman, Hochman and Miller 2003).

Conditions for caseload practices for juvenile justice in the USA

The profiles of juvenile justice workers and their practices differ from those of child welfare workers in several respects. Juvenile probation officers are usually college-educated white males, 30–49 years old, with five to ten years' experience in the field. Typically they earn much more than their counterparts in child welfare (Torbet 1996). Unlike child welfare workers, many are employees of juvenile courts. Probation was 'the single most important component of the juvenile court program' and even now is rarely performed by private agencies (Rothman 1980, p.218). As Duquette has suggested (Chapter 12), many think that probation services should not be located under court auspices.

The primary functions of probation officers are to screen cases, divert minor cases, conduct predisposition or pre-sentence investigations, and supervise cases in probation (Torbet 1996). Most probation officers' interactions with young people are limited to office contacts and are normally short term. Some courts have developed field offices away from the court, and intensive probation programmes with smaller caseloads to increase the amount of contact with youth at home and in schools. Officers rarely keep in touch when youth are admitted to detention or residential care (Bercovitz, Bemus and Hendricks 1993). Child welfare workers, in contrast, typically oversee their most risky cases in foster and adoptive placements.

Whereas child welfare work is plagued with high turnover, poor salaries and public pressure over case errors, probation faces other issues. One of the biggest for juvenile probation is on-the-job safety. Probation also faces large caseload sizes, limited resources for programmes and intense accountability. Like child welfare, probation is also a 'catch basin' that cannot control rates of referral, though some decision-making systems have been developed to allocate cases according to levels of difficulty and risk (Torbet 1996).

Table 3.2 summarises some of the fundamental differences between the practice of child welfare and juvenile probation in the USA.

Table 3.2: Differences in the practice of child welfare and juvenile justice

Functional area	Child welfare workers	Juvenile probation officers
Workforce composition	Female, young, little experience	Male, middle-aged, 5–10 years' experience
Typical annual salary	~$36,000	~$46,000
Functions	CPS investigation	Intake
	In-home services	Diversion
	Recommendations for termination of parental rights	Predisposition investigation
		Supervision of youth through office contacts
	Foster care and adoption supervision through field contacts	
Auspices	State/county social services department	State/county courts
Does worker directly supervise most risky cases?	Yes. High-risk cases retained in birth homes, or placed in foster or adoptive homes	No. High-risk cases transferred to adult court or placed in residential care
Caseload control	Limited by the adequacy of assessments and service options	

The table highlights that, commonly, child welfare workers have less experience, lower pay, a higher community profile, more exposure to public criticism and more direct responsibility for risky cases than their counterparts in juvenile justice. The capacity of both child welfare and juvenile justice to manage adequately their caseload depends on the adequacy of assessments and service options. In several respects, the differences between child welfare and juvenile justice seem gendered. Most child welfare workers are women and their contributions seem less valued than those of juvenile justice workers.

Child welfare practices address vulnerable children and families; juvenile justice predominantly concerns the delinquency of boys.

The future of child welfare and juvenile justice practices

Despite the long-standing policy and organisational divergence of child welfare and juvenile justice a movement exists to support the merger of the two. Three recent critiques are driving practice and policy changes. Two trends have emerged to address these critiques.

First there are the managerial critiques about the general state of human service agencies. The public, elected officials and professionals fault these service systems as being isolated from other service systems, overly procedural, inflexible and non-reflective (Hutchison and Charlesworth 2000; King 1997). Correctional, mental health, welfare and educational systems have difficulty working together on cases. It has been suggested that proceduralism can be moderated and the system made more responsive to individual needs if practice is more strongly influenced by research, training or norms (Green 2003), and accountability through collaborative models of service (King 1997).

Second are the structural critiques, which argue that the resources, the kind and amount of services, and the logic systems that link them, are inadequate to achieve the needed outcomes, especially for multi-problem families (McCroskey and Meezan 1998, pp.56–60). These claims gain credibility with the projection that funding for services will continue to contract as almost all US states face deficits (Rivlin 2002). One structural critique has asserted that more services need to focus on prevention and even the alleviation of poverty. Another suggests the need to develop local community-based support to supplement public funds that are shrinking.

Third are the normative critiques. Services have been criticised for their undemocratic quality, being controlled by experts. Practices that have resulted in the disproportionate control over minorities have also been criticised. Traditional services are isolated from key stakeholders in the community, especially their 'clients' (Kretzman and McKnight 1996; Roussos and Fawcett 2000). Service activities should be balanced and include active participation by both immediate stakeholders and the larger community (Waldfogel 1998). The appeal to democratic values has been one of the strongest arguments for Balanced and Restorative Justice (BARJ) and its counterpart in child welfare,

Family Group Decision Making (FGDM). These approaches hold not only that children and families should be accountable to the community, but also that the community should be accountable to children and families. BARJ and FGDM have reintroduced skills training and motivation into social welfare and juvenile justice systems that had become largely retributive and narrowly focused on compliance and short-term outcomes.

Another normative critique is that services should not be funded unless research has supported their effectiveness. The funding of services that have not been evaluated may not only waste resources it also may do harm. Jonson-Reid (2004) concludes that while child welfare intervention may prevent delinquency, '[it] is also possible to envision an inverse association between services and delinquent outcomes due to inept or insufficient services...' (Jonson-Reid 2004, p.163).

Currently, US federal and state governments are promulgating two initiatives that have the potential to transform child welfare and juvenile justice practices: community-based problem-solving approaches and evidence-based practice (EBP). The two initiatives are complementary, and they hold out the potential for integrating child welfare and juvenile justice for some cases.

For example, problem-solving courts have become very common and include community courts, drug treatment courts, mental health courts, family courts, domestic violence courts and re-entry courts. Other community approaches include community prosecution, Family Group Decision Making and Balanced and Restorative Justice. These initiatives go beyond individual treatment to community-based and multifactor/multisector interventions, with scope for combining aspects of child welfare and juvenile justice practices.

The second initiative from federal and state governments, evidence-based practice (EBP), has been made possible by the expanded use of experimental research designs and the meta-analysis of results over the last 20 years. The federal government and private foundations have for some time made research and programme evaluation a routine component of service grants, as is now the case for the Office of Juvenile Justice and Delinquency Prevention. Networks and institutions have been established to assist in the application of research evidence to practice. On the other hand, two concerns have been expressed about EBP. The first is methodological and concerns the amount of research that is available, the degree to which application depends on local contexts (services), the role of 'practice wisdom' and professional values, personal experience, and participation from 'clients' (Gilgun 2005, p.58). The second is structural and concerns the degree to which service agencies will be able to incorporate research and evaluation into their ongoing operations.

Conclusions

These relatively new federal initiatives of community-based problem-solving and evidence-based practice address all three critiques of present service systems (managerial, structural and normative). They also provide a basis for bridging service systems such as child welfare and juvenile justice, among others. The sustainability of these initiatives should not be taken for granted, however. The separation of child welfare and juvenile justice has deep historical roots. The differences have been solidified by the development of separate work systems, including the composition of the workforce, compensation, functions, auspices and the exposure to risk.

The managerial critique suggested that proceduralism is an outgrowth of closed systems. Community-based problem-solving and evidence-based practice provide the venues and the means to cross system boundaries and make closed systems more open, especially in terms of their ability to provide assistance to families and communities rather than merely to individuals.

The structural critique suggested the need to address the adequacy of and accessibility to resources. These reforms suggest increased access to new resources. They can provide not only access to new resources in the community, but also can suggest more effective use of existing resources. Support for these system changes comes from a broad range of political and cultural viewpoints that have recently divided American political practice, as illustrated by the support for BARJ from people with very different viewpoints. An important set of resources are those of the children and families themselves, whose participation has been discounted in traditional service systems. Resources may be more effective if service recipients are more motivated to change and take advantage of them. Traditional services, on the other hand, disempower children and families and often commit the system to using the most expensive services, like jail, to compel participation. These initiatives also address normative critiques through increased democratic participation by service recipients and by community members.

The costs of collaborative projects may diminish the effects of these reforms. Collaborations are difficult to start and expensive to sustain. These reforms depend to a great extent on the commitment of government or private sponsors. At the local level, collaborations are process intensive and draw on community resources; they require education and staff structures to support both leadership by a few and participation by the community. Many project-based collaborations are vulnerable because they are not embedded permanently into an organisational   structure. Yet some falter when they are expanded, requiring more resources to maintain (Roussos and Fawcett 2000; Sandfort 2004; Waldfogel 1998).

For the most part, recent innovations with a community- and evidence-based focus in the child welfare and juvenile justice fields have been adjuncts to existing court administrations and services, leaving the existing systems relatively unaffected. For changes to be substantial and sustainable, it remains for the staff and communities to embed the principles and practices into mainstream structures and activities.

References

American Public Human Services Association (2005) *Report from the 2004 Child Welfare Workforce Study: State Agency Findings.* Washington, DC.

Barton, W.H. and Creekmore, M. (1994) *Use of Dispositional Guidelines in New Hampshire.* Ann Arbor, MI: New Hampshire Department of Children and Families.

Bercovitz, J., Bemus, B. and Hendricks, W.S. (1993) *Probation Case Classification and Workload Measures System for Indiana.* Indianapolis, IN: Indiana Judicial Center.

Bernard, T.J. (1992) *The Cycle of Juvenile Justice.* Oxford: Oxford University Press.

Braithwaite, J. and Mugford, S. (1994) 'Conditions of Successful Reintegration Ceremonies: Dealing with Juvenile Offenders.' *British Journal of Criminology 34,* 2, 139–171.

Fagan, J. (1995) 'Separating the men from the boys: the comparative advantage of juvenile versus criminal court sanctions on recidivism among adolescent felony offenders.' In J.C. Howell, B. Krisberg, J.D. Hawkins and J.J. Wilson (eds) *A Sourcebook: Serious, Violent, and Chronic Juvenile Offenders.* Thousand Oaks, CA: Sage Publications.

Gilgun, J.F. (2005) 'The Four Cornerstones of Evidence-based Practice in Social Work.' *Research on Social Work Practice 15,* 1, 52–61.

Gordon, L. (2002) *Heroes of their Own Lives: The Politics and History of Family Violence: Boston, 1880–1960.* Urbana: University of Illinois Press.

Green, M.Y. (2003) 'Balancing the Scales: Targeting Disproportionality in Child Welfare and Juvenile Justice.' *Children's Voice,* January/February.

Gunderson, D. and Osborne, S. (2001) 'Addressing the Crisis in Child Welfare Social Worker Turnover.' *North Carolina Journal for Families and Children,* Winter, 2–6.

Hochman, G., Hochman, A. and Miller, J. (2003) *Foster Care: Voices from the Inside.* Washington, DC: Pew Commission on Children in Foster Care and Georgetown University Public Policy Institute.

Hutchison, E.D. and Charlesworth, L.W. (2000) 'Securing the Welfare of Children: Policies Past, Present, and Future.' *Families in Society 81,* 6, 576–585.

Jonson-Reid, M. (2004) 'Child Welfare Services and Delinquency: The Need to Know More.' *Child Welfare 83*, 2, 157–173.

Kamerman, S. and Kahn, A. (1990) 'Social Services for Children, Youth and Families in the United States.' *Children and Youth Services Review Special Issue, 12*, 1–184.

King, M. (1997) *A Better World for Children? Explorations in Morality and Authority.* New York: Routledge.

Kretzmann, J. and McKnight, J.P. (1996) 'Assets-based Community Development.' *National Civic Review 23*, 9.

Krisberg, B. and Austin, J.F. (1993) *Reinventing Juvenile Justice.* Newbury Park, CA: Sage Publications, Inc.

Littell, J. and Schuerman, J.R. (1994) *Putting Families First: An Experiment in Family Preservation.* New York, NY: Aldine de Gruyter.

McCroskey, J. and Meezan, W. (1998) 'Family-centered services: approaches and effectiveness.' In M.B. Larner (ed) *Protecting Children from Abuse and Neglect.* Los Altos, CA: David and Lucille Packard Foundation.

Mechanic, D. and Rochefort, D.A. (1990) 'Deinstitutionalization: An Appraisal of Reform.' *Annual Review of Sociology 16*, 301–327.

O'Connor, S. (2001) *Orphan Trains: The Story of Charles Loring Brace and the Children he Saved and Failed.* Boston: Houghton Mifflin Co.

Rivlin, A.M. (2002) *Another State Fiscal Crisis: Is there a Better Way?* The Brookings Institution.

Rothman, D.J. (1980) *Conscience and Convenience: The Asylum and its Alternatives in Progressive America.* Boston: Little, Brown & Company.

Roussos, S.T. and Fawcett, S.B. (2000) 'A Review of Collaborative Partnerships as a Strategy for Improving Community Health.' *Annual Review of Public Health 21*, 369–402.

Sandfort, J. (2004) 'Why is Human Services Integration so Difficult to Achieve?' *Focus 23*, 2, 35–39.

Schene, P.A. (1998) 'Past, present, and future roles of child protective services.' In M.B. Larner (ed) *Protecting Children from Abuse and Neglect.* Los Altos, CA: David and Lucille Packard Foundation.

Tittle, G. (2002) *Caseload Size in Best Practice: A Literature Review.* Urbana-Champaign, IL: University of Illinois, Children and Family Research Center.

Torbet, P.M. (1996) *Juvenile Probation: The Workhorse of the Juvenile Justice System.* Washington, DC: US Department of Justice, Office of Justice Programs, Office of Juvenile Justice and Delinquency Prevention.

Waldfogel, J. (1998) 'Rethinking the paradigm for child protection.' In M. B. Larner (ed) *Protecting Children from Abuse and Neglect.* Los Altos, CA: David and Lucille Packard Foundation.

Further reading

Allen, N.E. (2005) 'A Multi-level Analysis of Community Coordinating Councils.' *American Journal of Community Psychology 35*, 1/2, 49–63.

Angelotti, S. (2003) *Background Information on Mental Health Issues.* Lansing, MI: State of Michigan, Senate Fiscal Agency.

Association for Retarded Citizens (1980) *The Plymouth Case and Decree.* Lansing, MI.

Belsky, J. (1993) 'Etiology of Child Maltreatment: A Developmental-ecological Analysis.' *Psychological Bulletin 114*, 3, 413–434.

Braithwaite, J. (2000) 'Democracy, community and problem solving.' In G. Burford and J. Hudson (eds) *Family Group Conferencing: New Directions in Community-centered Child and Family Practice.* New York: Aldine de Gruyther.

Braithwaite, J. (2001) 'Restorative Justice and a New Criminal Law of Substance Abuse.' *Youth & Society 33*, 2, 227–248.

Bruyere, S.M. (2000) 'Civil Rights and Employment Issues of Disability Policy.' *Journal of Disability Policy Studies 11*, 1, 18–28.

Catchpole, R.E.H. and Gretton, H.M. (2003) 'The Predictive Validity of Risk Assessment with Violent Young Offenders.' *Criminal Justice and Behavior 30*, 6, 688–708.

Drake, B. and Jonson-Reid, M. (2000) 'Substantiation and Early Decision Points in Public Child Welfare: A Conceptual Reconsideration.' *Child Maltreatment 5*, 3, 227–235.

English, D.J. (1998) 'The extent and consequences of child maltreatment.' In M.B. Larner (ed) *Protecting Children from Abuse and Neglect.* Los Altos, CA: David and Lucille Packard Foundation.

Fantuzzo, J.W. and Mohr, W.K. (1999) 'Prevalence and effects of child exposure to domestic violence.' In L.S. Carter and C.S. Stevenson (eds) *Domestic Violence and Children.* Los Altos, CA: David and Lucille Packard Foundation.

Farabee, D., Hser, Y.-I., Anglin, M.D. and Huang, D. (2004) 'Recidivism among an Early Cohort of California's Proposition 36 Offenders.' *Criminology and Public Policy 3*, 4, 563–584.

Farole, D.J., Puffett, N.K., Rempel, M. and Byrne, F. (2005) 'Applying Problem-solving Principles in Mainstream Courts: Lessons for State Courts.' *Justice System Journal 26*, 1, 57–75.

Feld, B.C. (2004) 'Juvenile Transfer: Editorial Introduction.' *Criminology and Public Policy 3*, 4, 599–604.

Findlater, J.E. and Kelley, S. (1999) 'Child protective services and domestic violence.' In L.S. Carter and C.S. Stevenson (eds) *Domestic Violence and Children.* Los Altos, CA: David and Lucille Packard Foundation.

Gambrill, E.D. (2003) 'Evidence-based Practice: Sea Change or the Emperor's New Clothes?' *Journal of Social Work Education 39*, 1, 3–23.

Geen, R. (2002) *Shoring up the Child Welfare-TANF Link.* Washington, DC: The Urban Insistute.

Gibbs, L. and Gambrill, E. (2002) 'Evidence-based Practice: Counterarguments to Objections.' *Research on Social Work Practice 12*, 3, 452–476.

Gran, J. (1996) 'Community Services Litigation: Experiences and Outcomes.' *TASH Newsletter 22*, 2/3, 11–13.

Green, M.Y. (2002) 'Minorities as Majority: Disproportionality in Child Welfare and Juvenile Justice.' *Children's Voice,* November/December.

Hayward, R. (1992) 'Users' Guides to Evidence-based Medicine.' *Journal of the American Medical Association 268*, 17, 2420–2425.

Holsinger, A.M., Lurigio, A.J. and Latessa, E.J. (2001) 'Up to Speed: A Review of Research for Practitioners.' *Federal Probation 65*, 1, 46–50.

International Child and Youth Care Network (2003) 'New Jersey Department of Youth and Family Services Pleads for Help.'.International Child Protection and Youth Network, 17 January.

Jonson-Reid, M. (2002) 'Exploring the Relationship Between Child Welfare Intervention and Juvenile Corrections Involvement.' *American Journal of Orthopsychiatry 72*, 4, 559–576.

Karp, D.R. and Drakulich, K.M. (2004) 'Minor Crime in a Quaint Setting: Practices, Outcomes, and Limits of Vermont Reparative Probation Boards.' *Criminology and Public Policy 3*, 4, 665–686.

Kelley, B.T., Thornberry, T.P. and Smith, C.A. (1997) 'In the Wake of Childhood Maltreatment.' *Juvenile Justice Bulletin.* NCJ 165257

Lane, J., Turner, S., Fain, T. and Sehgal, A. (2005) 'Evaluating an Experimental Intensive Juvenile Probation Program: Supervision and Official Outcomes.' *Crime and Delinquency 51*, 1, 26–52.

Latessa, E.J., Cullen, F.T. and Gendreau, P. (2002) 'Beyond Correctional Quackery – Professionalism and the Possibility of Effective Treatment.' *Federal Probation 66*, 2, 43–49.

McCullough, C. (2003) *Better Results for Kids: Financing and Contracting Options and Considerations.* Washington, DC: Public Strategies Group.

McKnight, J.L. (1992) 'Redefining Community.' *Social Policy 23*, Fall/Winter, 56–62.

Mentaberry, M. (1997) 'Permanency Planning for Abused and Neglected Children.' *OJJDP Fact Sheet 65.*

Morton, M.J. (2000) 'Institutionalizing Inequalities: Black Children and Child Welfare in Cleveland, 1859–1998.' *Journal of Social History 34*, 1, 141–162.

Oriega, S. and Simpson, J. (2004) 'Promoting systemic change through collaboration.' *The Community Psychologist 37*, 4, 37–40.

Osofsky, J.D. (1999) 'The impact of violence on children.' In L.S. Carter and C.S. Stevenson (eds) *Domestic Violence and Children.* David and Lucille Packard Foundation.

Platt, A.M. (1977) *The Child Savers: The Invention of Delinquency.* Chicago, IL: University of Chicago Press.

Prochaska, J.O., DiClemente, C.C. and Norcross, J.C. (1992) 'In Search of How People Change: Applications to Addictive Behaviors.' *American Psychologist 47*, 9, 1102–1114.

Task Force on Employment and Training for Court-involved Youth (2000) *Employment and Training for Court-involved Youth.* Washington, DC: US Department of Justice, Office of Justice Programs, Office of Juvenile Justice and Delinquency Prevention.

Tilbury, C. (2004) 'The Influence of Performance Measurement on Child Welfare Policy and Practice.' *British Journal of Social Work 34*, 2, 225–241.

Trickett, E.J. and Espino, S.L.R. (2004) 'Collaboration and Social Inquiry: Multiple Meanings of a Construct and its Role in Creating Useful and Valid Knowledge.' *American Journal of Community Psychology 34*, 1–2, 1–69.

US Department of Justice (2005) *Community-based Problem-solving Criminal Justice Initiative: FY2005 Competitive Grant Announcement.* Washington, DC: Office of Justice Programs, Bureau of Justice Assistance.

Vaughn, M.S. and Smith, L.G. (1999) 'Practicing Penal Harm Medicine in the United States: Prisoners' Voices from Jail.' *Justice Quarterly 16*, 1, 175ff.

Webb, S.A. (2001) 'Some Considerations on the Validity of Evidence-based Practice in Social Work.' *British Journal of Social Work 31*, 57–79.

Widom, C.S. (1991) 'Childhood victimization: risk factor for delinquency.' In M.E. Colten and S. Gore (eds) *Adolescent Stress: Causes and Consequences.* New York: Aldine de Gruyter.

Wolfe, D.A. and Jaffe, P.G. (1999) 'Emerging strategies in the prevention of domestic violence.' In L.S. Carter and C.S. Stevenson (eds) *Domestic Violence and Children.* Los Altos, CA: David and Lucille Packard Foundation.

4

Juvenile Crime and the Justice System in Sweden

Anna Hollander and Michael Tärnfalk

Introduction

Youth crime is very much a topic of discussion in public, political and legal debates both in Sweden and internationally. Youth criminality is problematic for many reasons. The literature on juvenile justice is largely concerned with offenders, but young people come to the attention of the justice system also as victims. For example, many of the runaways and other status offenders apprehended by the police are victims of abuse or neglect, which may be why they ran away (Chesney-Lind and Pasko 2004). This is rarely the main cause of the justice system's involvement with youth, however (Finkelhore, Pascall and Hashima 2001). In Sweden as in other counties in Europe, throughout the last decade, children have been focused on as 'offenders' first and 'children', or children in need, second. It seems as if both the ideology, policy and practice is less interested in supporting children than accusing them, although this view is fundamentally against the principles on children in welfare and child protection legislation, and in the UN Convention on the Rights of the Child (Goldson 2000; Levin 1996; Muncie 1999; Proposition 1997/98:96). By contrast the UN Convention (Article 3) and the principle of the best interest of the child are of major importance for the social welfare system in Sweden in that this Article was implemented into the Social Services Act in 1998 and in the Compulsory Care of Young Persons Act in 2003 (Proposition 1996/97:124; Proposition 2002/03:53).

The extent of youth crime is difficult to measure. As no country is perfect in terms of its use of statistics, it is difficult to compare nations in terms of official statistics (Barberet 2001; Estrada 1999, 2001; Hofer 1998). The definition of what constitutes a crime varies between countries, as do the lower and upper age limits for juvenile status, police practices and differences in the administration of justice. There are also legal, linguistic and other cultural differences (Barberet 2001). Because of these differences in how the statistics are compiled, it is easier to compare trends than levels (Hofer 1998).

Youth crime trends are difficult to describe for the same reason. Whether juvenile crime is increasing or decreasing is a constant topic of debate in Sweden (Ahlberg 1992; Estrada 1999, 2001; SOU 2004:122). Some Swedish criminological studies show that youth crime has both increased and become more violent since the 1970s, whereas others suggest little change since the Second World War (Ahlberg 1992; Knutsson 1993; Tham 1995). In Sweden, studies on self-reported crime show no increase in juvenile crime since the 1970s (SOU 2004:122).

When we speak about youth crimes we mostly mean crimes committed by boys. Girls are as good as invisible in this context, a circumstance that has worked to the detriment of girls and young women; this situation creates difficulties in developing resources to address the problems girls experience (Chesney-Lind 2001).

For girls the most common crimes are shoplifting and theft. However, girls' crimes are described as becoming more violent and more frequent (Chesney-Lind and Pasko 2004). The most common types of crime committed by boys in Sweden are pilfering, criminal damage, car theft, burglary, physical assault and minor thefts such as shoplifting. Although there have been only a few changes in the number and types of reported youth crimes, there have been important changes in the last 10–15 years in terms of the way the criminal justice system has responded to youth offenders (BRÅ 2000a).

In this chapter we give an overview of the youth justice system in Sweden, where different sets of legal rules are applied for persons under 15 years of age, between 15 and 17 years of age, and between 18 and 21 years of age. Our main focus is the 15–17 age group, which has received most attention in recent national strategies and legislation. In Sweden, co-operation between the social services and the criminal juvenile justice system is crucial throughout the whole legal process, from the preliminary investigation to the final decision in court. As King and Piper (1995) describe it, the welfare and justice perspectives have significance for everyone involved in the decision-making that concerns children. They also point out that both welfare and justice are dualistic concepts (King and Piper 1995). From a Swedish perspective, social services interventions can mean both voluntary (consensual) and coercive interventions/sanctions, and justice can mean both social and legal justice. Generally, when referring to the social services in this connection, it is mostly in terms of voluntary and care-orientated interventions, but recent changes in the criminal justice system have imposed new duties on social welfare authorities to provide 'appropriate sanctions' to handle youth offenders in a credible way (Proposition 1997/98:96; SOU 2004:122).

Welfare and justice

A long-standing theme in the debates on youth crime is the extent to which the sanction system should be the same for youths and adults. Diverting offenders from the criminal courts – for example, by issuing cautions – has traditionally been used for young boys and girls rather than for adults because the legal process itself is thought to harm children. It first became legally possible in 1902 to replace punishment for a crime by treatment provided by the social services authorities (Kumlien 1997). Since then there has been a recurrent conflict between proponents of welfare-orientated and formal justice-orientated approaches to reducing youth crime (Bramstång 1964; Levin 1996; SOU 1993:35). There is a long-standing principle, though, in the Swedish model whereby the courts are generally expected to surrender offenders between 15 and 17 years of age to the social services system. This is one of the fundamental pillars of the Swedish youth justice model and it has remained intact despite recent legislative reforms (Proposition 1962:10; Proposition 1979/80:1; Proposition 1997/98:96). The goal in both the Social Services Act 1998 and in the Compulsory Care Act 2003 is to provide protection, help and support for abused or neglected children as well as children with criminal behaviour and other social problems (Proposition 2000/01:80; Proposition 2002/03:53). The legal prerequisites of children in need, though, are almost the same today as they were in the first Child Act in 1902 (Bramstång 1985; Hollander 1985; Mattson 2002). It is the local social services board – a municipal, political, organ – that decides about care for children and families according to the Social Services Act. If consent to care is not given by the child's guardians, or by the young person if the person is 15 years of age, the Compulsory Care Act can be applied. In such situations the local social services board applies to the County Administrative Court to decide whether the conditions set out in the Compulsory Care Act have been fulfilled (Hollander 1985; Mattson 2002; Proposition 1989/90:28).

Young persons who commit crimes can also be dealt with under the Criminal Code (CC), which includes more coercive measures for youth crime, such as custodial youth care, introduced in 1989. However the local social services boards will still have the main responsibility for young offenders (Proposition 1997/98:96; SOU 2004:122). Actual and proposed reforms during the last decade have aggravated the conflict between dealing with young people who commit crimes as 'children in need' or as 'young offenders'.

As in many other western welfare states, the trend has been away from the welfare approach and towards more control, more punishment and the notion of 'just deserts' (Garland 1991, 2001; Goldson 2000; Littlechild 1997). The offence is given priority at the expense of the young person's circumstances and needs. Strong demands have been made for the social services authorities to follow new punitive strategies and standards concerning young offenders (Proposition 1997/98:96; Proposition 2002/03:53). At the same time, the Criminal Code concepts of proportionality and consequences have been strengthened when deciding about interventions in relation to the crime rathert hen in relation to the child's needs (Proposition 1997/98:96; SOU 2004:122).

The social services have long been criticised for being both too weak and too vague in their plans and interventions for young offenders (Proposition 1997/98:96; SOU 1993:35). Care and treatment used by the social services authorities have not been accepted as suitable in relation to criminal justice. On the other hand, it is stressed by the government that young persons who commit crimes shall be kept outside the criminal justice system for as long as possible (Proposition 1997/98:96; SOU 2004:122).

The swings of the pendulum between different values and strategies used by the social services authorities and the justice systems – care, rehabilitation or sanctions – make an interesting study, but the consequences for young offenders are not easy to discern. The changes are mainly driven by ideology and make little difference to the behaviour of young offenders. However, the changes can distance juveniles in trouble from ordinary child and family policy and social work, and separate them from the welfare domain. This consolidates the label of the 'dangerous criminal child' (Goldson 2000; Levin 1996).

Responses to youth crime

In Sweden, children under 15 years of age are not subject to legal sanctions (CC 1:6). The age of criminal responsibility is relatively high in Sweden compared with other countries in Europe where the age of responsibility varies between 7 and 18 years (Jareborg and Zila 2000). There are many contradictions in the reasoning behind the setting of different age limits and the determination of children's competence and maturity (e.g. if young children actually have the capacity to understand that they have committed a crime, and the consequences of it) (White 2001).

Children, unlike adults, are perceived as lacking legal competence, and therefore particularly vulnerable and in need of special protection. This view of children as being innocent and in need of protection is, however, of recent origin, which indicates that our understanding of children is historically and culturally relative (Hollander 1998). Children's competence is also very much a question of their lack of power in society (John 2003). Variable competence is an idea towards which the varied legal treatment of children might aspire (Minow 1986).

It seems more reasonable to interpret children's competence according to their life conditions in that, for children as for adults, competence is a mutual question of how well one manages life. The great majority of criminal or violent children come from problematic social environments (Chesney-Lind and Pasko 2004; Garbarino 2000). In ascertaining a child's legal competence, it is a delicate task to find a balance that takes into account the child's life situation, the crime committed and his or her need of protection and care.

Proportionality and legality

In the criminal justice system the principle of proportionality and the concept of culpability have taken on added importance as a result of reforms introduced in 1989 to criminal policy. These were based on the principle that the sentence must reflect the severity of the crime: the more reprehensible the crime, the harsher the punishment or sanction (Proposition 1987/88:120).

Since 1999 this principle has been applied to a greater extent in the youth justice system as well, with the aim of bringing sanctions towards young people who offend more in line with the justice system for adults (Proposition 1997/98:96; SOU 2004:122). The principle of legality is also of great importance (CC 1:1). All reactions to a crime must be grounded in law and it is the prosecutor's task to substantiate the criminal charge before a court of law (Wennberg 2000).

This has always been the case but renewed emphasis on legality has highlighted the ambiguity of the role of the local social services. They are expected to prepare a report about the young offender to the prosecutor before the decision is made in court about both facts and, if proven, consequences (Proposition 1997/98:96). This means that the social worker has to suggest a plan for the young person based on an assessment of her/his situation and needs before it is decided if he or she is guilty of the crime. It is not unusual that the young person denies any involvement in the crime he or she is accused of.

Youth justice sanctions

Sweden does not have special youth courts. All cases of crime by young people aged 15 years and over are prosecuted in the same criminal courts used for adults, in a similar legal process. There are five sanctions that can be imposed for young offenders who have been proved guilty:

1. fine (CC 25)

2. conditional sentence (CC 27)

3. probationary sentence (CC 28)

4. imprisonment (CC 26) and

5. youth custody (CC 31:1a).

These represent a hierarchy, with fines expected to cover the least serious offences, while probation and conditional sentences are seen as alternatives to custody.

Youth custody was introduced in 1999 for young people between 15 and 17 years of age. It represents a combination of punishment and care. Usage depends on the severity of the crime, yet it is carried out with treatment aims under the social services, which retain the main responsibility for the young person and run the closed institutions according to the Enforcement of Custodial Youth Care Act 1998 (603). The minimum time juveniles may serve in closed care is 14 days, and the maximum four years.

The government intended this sanction to be used as sparingly as a sentence of imprisonment would be. In the 1999 reform, youth custody was made equivalent to imprisonment and is thus considered an equally strong punishment (Proposition 1997/98:96). Evaluation of youth custody has shown that it has been used more frequently than expected, instead of both imprisonment and a probationary sentence. This has been explained as partly due to changes in the types of crime committed by young people but also as a result of a policy shift towards greater use of institutions (SOU 2004:122). A major dilemma is that this form of closed institutional care is also a form of treatment/sanction within the social services system (Compulsory Care Act, Section 12). The Compulsory Care Act can be applied because of a young person's criminal behaviour but also because of drug abuse and other situations that place the child's health and development at serious risk. Consequently, young people may be placed in youth custody not only by a criminal court but also by the social services board or an administrative court.

Hence, young people in closed institutional care have come there via both criminal and welfare procedures. This results in confusion for the children as well as social services as to the balance of care functions and punishment embodied in the institutional practices (Tärnfalk 2001).

Ironically, youth custody was introduced partly due to Sweden's ratification of the Child Convention with the aim of avoiding the imprisonment of children alongside adults. At the same time, it was intended to create a more credible criminal sanction for the courts compared with the social services' interventions in cases of more severe crime. Young people under 18 years of age can be sentenced to prison only under very special circumstances and their age alone warrants a less severe sentence than for adults (CC 29:7; CC 30:5). In Sweden the maximum punishment for crimes is life imprisonment, but for convicted offenders under the age of 21, the maximum sentence is ten years' imprisonment (CC29:7; CC30:5).

Special care measures

A court considering any crime committed by a young person aged 15 and over can impose measures of special care instead of a criminal sentence (e.g. fine, probation, custody). This means that the court can decide to give the social services authorities the responsibility to provide care or treatment for the convicted young offender. This decision can be made only if the social authorities have submitted a written report to the prosecutor or the court describing what interventions will be carried out if the young person is placed in their care. The Criminal Code requires the court to determine the nature and length of the social intervention according to the concept of culpability, the severity of the crime and the convicted person's prior criminal record, if any (CC 31:1). The suggested intervention can be compulsory or voluntary institutional care or supervision. If the court regards the intervention as insufficiently severe, it can combine this measure with a fine or with youth service. Youth service is a form of programme with a restorative or rehabilitative purpose (CC31:1).

From the government's perspective, this sentence of surrender to special care challenges the social services authorities on the one hand, and the prosecutors and courts on the other, to collaborate in ways that meet the young person's welfare needs while also addressing the offence with an element of punishment or reparation (SOU 2004:122).

Stages in handling youth crime

From the moment a crime is reported until the final decision has been taken, there is a long chain of events. Increasingly, policy-makers stress the importance of a prompt response so that young people can more easily see the link between the law-breaking incident and the associated decision.

No action

The police officer, as the crime investigator, has the option of not reporting the crime to a prosecutor if it is considered 'less serious' and if the sanction would probably be a fine. The most common crime where this option is used is shoplifting. However, most cases remain unsolved because of a lack of investigative resources. In consequence, the number of unsolved shoplifting cases has increased in the last ten years (Lindström 1998).

Preliminary criminal investigation

The preliminary investigation is an important element in both care and protection and the youth justice system (Proposition 1997/98:96; Clevesköld and Thunved 2001). The prosecutor has a duty to complete the criminal investigation within six weeks, and sooner if possible. If the investigation is complicated because of the severe nature of the crime, or if there are many suspects or different crimes are involved, the time limit can be extended at the discretion of the chief prosecutor (Provision Act, Section 4). There are special demands on the investigator in youth cases to take account of the child and family circumstances (Section 2, 1st LUL (Act on Certain Provisions Concerning Youthful Offenders); Proposition 1994/95:12). In practice, though, few prosecutors have received education or training about children or children's issues.

Both the child's parents as custodians and a social worker are to be informed about the investigation and they are expected to be present at the child's hearing (Provision Act, Section 5–7). From a welfare perspective it is important that both the parents and a social worker are informed at an early stage so that they can participate actively in the investigation and gain better knowledge of the process. The aim of the regulations is to ensure that they assume responsibility for the child and lend their full support (Provision Act, Sections 5–7).

The child should be asked about his or her attitude towards the parents being present at the child's hearing, although there must be a very strong reason not to allow them to be present. There are situations, however, when parental participation can be prohibited by the investigator – for example, where there is a severe conflict between parent and child, or if the parents attempt to impede the investigation (Clevesköld and Thunved 2001). The child cannot stop a social worker being present at the investigation, as he/she is obliged, by law, to be there (Provision Act, Section 5). There are very strong restrictions on taking a child between 15 and 17 years of age into custody during a criminal investigation (Provision Act, Section 23). In such situations the social welfare officer has the opportunity to intervene on the child's behalf (Compulsory Care Act, Section 6). If the case goes to trial, the child has the right to a lawyer.

The social welfare officer's report

The social services are, as mentioned above, obliged to submit a report concerning the young person to the prosecutor before a decision is taken as to whether or not to prosecute. The report must provide concrete information about the plans for the young person (Proposition 1997/98:96; Provision Act, Section 11). This has a dual function. From a criminal justice perspective, it is important that, by means of the statement, the court is able to foresee the type of intervention being planned and the relation it bears to the crime. From a social welfare perspective, it is important that the child's needs have been properly assessed; it is the young person's current situation and prognosis for development that must be taken into account, not the crime itself.

Actions by the prosecutor

When the investigation has been concluded the prosecutor must choose between three types of decision:

1. no legal action

2. summary penalty, and

3. prosecution.

The first type of decision may occur if the crime is considered less serious and the juvenile has confessed. A decision not to press charges may also be accompanied by the imposition of a fine and registration of the child for the offence. Prosecution applies when the crime is more severe or the juvenile denies responsibility for it (Provision Act, Sections 15–17).

During the last decade, there has been a substantial change in the types of decisions made by prosecutors with respect to young people. Children are brought before criminal court twice as often today, but the option of 'no prosecution' has decreased by nearly 50 per cent. During the same period the use of surrender to special care by the court has increased from 35 to 54 per cent of all court decisions, and is now the most common sentence for young offenders between 15 and 17 years of age (BRÅ 2000b, Sweden's official crime statistics). One reason for this increase is that the social services are more focused on the crime and therefore suggest interventions seen as more acceptable to the prosecutors and the courts. Research also shows an appreciable rise during the 1990s in the number of children taken into custody by the local services boards and the administrative courts (Lundström and Vinnerljung 2001; SOU 2004:122).

Protection of the child – protection of society

One of the aims of the Swedish social welfare reform of 1982 was to ensure that interventions for young offenders would be motivated solely by the child's need for care. The intentions of the legislation introduced then were to change the earlier emphasis on repression and the protection of society that had earlier dominated child welfare legislation concerning young offenders (Proposition 1979/80:1). Actions taken for the sake of the child's care and protection may be an indirect way of protecting society because a child who has committed a crime can still be taken into custody compulsorily. Nevertheless, while protecting society may be an effect, it is not itself the aim of child welfare legislation (Bramstång 1985; Proposition 1979/80:1; Clevesköld and Thunved 2001).

By contrast, the 1990s reforms were passed to bring the sanction system for young offenders aged 15 and over more in line with that for adults, while the existing law remains applicable in the case of younger offenders. One tension is that the criminal legislation focuses on events that occurred in the past, whereas child welfare legislation focuses on the child's current situation and prognosis for development in the future. This situation creates a difficult role for social workers, prosecutors and the courts when dealing with young offenders. The government's official aim is to encourage more consultations, co-operation and co-ordination between the social services and the juvenile justice system in order to bring about a common strategy that ensures their public responsibility for young offenders has been fulfilled. However, the youth justice system plays the dominant part in this situation and the UN Convention, ratified by Sweden in 1990, has not changed the situation for young offenders in that respect (Proposition 1997/98:96; Proposition 1999/00:137; 2002/03:53; SOU 2004:122).

Conclusions

The youth justice system encompasses a broad range of perspectives on both welfare and justice, and these vary from jurisdiction to jurisdiction. In Sweden, where the social welfare system is deeply integrated in the criminal justice system, it is difficult to separate these considerations. The debate among lawyers, criminologists and social workers in Sweden has for a long time been concerned with divergent approaches of the social welfare and justice systems. Today the conflict between them is more evident and more complex than ever before. There is an inherent conflict between the different systems in terms of how to deal with young offenders. This became evident from a recent study on how prosecutors and judges perceive the option of surrendering young offenders to special care by the social services. The majority of both prosecutors and judges assumed that, in the statements submitted by social workers to the prosecutor, due regard had been paid to the principles of proportionality and culpability in the planning of interventions for young people prosecuted for criminal offences. The implication is that the social workers' interventions should be in proportion to the culpability of the crime (BRÅ 2002). This implies that the social welfare system should correspond with the criminal justice system both in judging the severity of the crime and in imposing the sentence. This highlights the difficulties involved in correctly apprehending what are the responsibilities of the social services system when dealing with young offenders. Social work plans therefore have to combine responses to welfare need with judgements about appropriate sanctions for the crime. The difficulty of reconciling these considerations is exacerbated by the timing of reports, as the report made by the social welfare officer is submitted to the prosecutor before the suspect's guilt has been proved. If guilt has not clearly been proven, how can the report reflect the severity of the crime?

By intertwining the social welfare with the criminal justice system it becomes more difficult for all involved to decide on what grounds interventions should be made. There is an apparent risk that interventions are generated from the crime rather than from the needs of the child. There are truly challenges facing welfare and justice research to develop theories and methods that could be credible options in the cases of children who commit crimes.

References

Ahlberg, J. (1992) 'Myten om en minskande ungdomsbrottslighet.' [The Myth about Decreasing Juvenile Criminality]. *Apropå nr 1*.

Barberet, R. (2001) Youth crime in western Europe. In S. White (ed) *Handbook of Youth and Justice*. New York: Kluwer Academic/Plenum Publishers.

Bramstång, G. (1964) *Förutsättningar för barnavårdsnämnds ingripande mot asocial ungdom.* [Conditions for the Child Welfare Board to Intervene in the Case of Delinquent Youth]. Glerup Lund. Sweden.

Bramstång, G. (1985) *Sociallagstiftningen. En Kommentar.* [Commentary on The Social Welfare Legislation]. Stockholm: Norstedts.

BRÅ (2000a) *Påföljdssystemet för unga lagöverträdare* [Crime Prevention Council, The Juvenile Justice System]. Rapport 2000:7. Stockholm: Fritzes.

BRÅ (2000b) *Sveriges officiella brottsstatistik.* [Crime Prevention Council, Official Crime Statistics of Sweden].

BRÅ, Socialstyrelsen och Statens institutionsstyrelse (2002) *Sluten ungdomsvård – en uppföljning.* (Compulsory Institutional Care – A Follow-up Study]. The Crime Prevention Council, National Board of Health and Welfare, and the National Board of Institutional Care.

Chesney-Lind, M. (2001) Girls, violence and delinquency. Popular myths and persistent problems. In S. White (ed) *Handbook of Youth and Justice.* New York: Kluwer Academic/Plenum Publishers.

Chesney-Lind, M. and Pasko, L. (2004) *The Female Offender. Girls, Women and Crime.* (2nd edn). Sage Publications.

Clevesköld, L. and Thunved, A. (2001) *Samhället och de unga lagöverträdarna* [Society and Juvenile Delinquents]. Stockholm: Norstedts.

Estrada, F. (1999) Juvenile Crime Trends in Post-war Europe. *European Journal on Criminal Policy and Research 7.*Kluwer Academic Publishers, 23–42.

Estrada, F. (2001) Juvenile Violence as a Social Problem. Trends, Media Attention and Societal Response. *British Journal of Criminology 41,* © Centre for Crime and Justice Studies (ISTD), 639–655.

Finkelhore, D., Pascall, M.J. and Hashima, P.Y. (2001) Juvenile crime victims in the justice system. In S. White (ed) *Handbook of Youth and Justice.* New York: Kluwer Academic/Plenum Publishers.

Garbarino, J. (2000) *Pojkar som gått vilse. Varför våra söner blir våldsamma och hur vi kan rädda dem.* [Lost Boys. Why our Sons Turn Violent and how We Can Save Them. Stockholm: Norstedts tryckeri AB.

Garland, D. (1991) *Punishment and Modern Society. A Study in Social Theory.* Oxford: Oxford University Press.

Garland, D. (2001) *The Culture of Control. Crime and Social Order in Contemporary Society.* Oxford: Oxford University Press.

Goldson, B. (2000) '"Children in need" or "young offenders"? Hardening Ideology, Organizational Change and New Challenges for Social Work with Children in Trouble.' *Child and Family Social Work 5,* 255–265.

Hofer, von H. (1998) *Svårt att jämföra internationell statistik.* [Difficulties in comparing international statistics]. Stockholm: BRÅ-Apropå 5–6.

Hollander, A. (1985) *Omhändertagande av barn.* [Taking Children into Custody]. Stockholm: Aktuell Juridik Förlag.

Hollander, A. (1998) 'Barns rätt att komma till tals – ökat inflytande för barn eller vuxna?' [Children's Right to be Heard – Greater Influence for Children or for Adults?] *Nordiskt Sosialt Arbeid 4,* 194–201.

Jareborg, N. and Zila, J. (2000) *Straffrättens påföljdslära.* [The Sentencing Doctrine in Criminal Justice]. Stockholm: Norstedts.

John, M. (2003) *Children's Rights and Power, Charging up for a New Century. Children in Charge 9.* London: Jessica Kingsley Publishers.

King, M. and Piper, C. (1995) *How the Law Thinks about Children.* Aldershot: Arena.

Knutsson, J. (1993) 'Missvisande beskrivningar av brottsutveckling.' [Misleading Descriptions of the Criminal Development]. Stockholm: Apropå 1.

Kumlien, M. (1997) *Uppfostran och Straff. Studier kring 1902 års uppfostringslagar.* [Upbringing and Punishment. Studies on 1902 Laws Considering Troubled Youth]. Stockholm: Nerenius & Santérus förlag.

Levin, C. (1996) Barnen mellan straff och behandling [Children between correction and care]. In B-Å. Armelius, S. Begtzon, P-A. Rydelius, J. Sarnecki and K. Söderholm Carpelan (eds) *Vård av ungdomar med sociala problem (Treatment and Care of Youth with Social Problems)*. Statens Institutionsstyrelse: Liber Stockholm.

Lindström, P. (1998) 'Fler åtalade unga lagöverträdare' [More Prosecuted Juvenile Delinquents]. *Nordisk Tidskrift for Kriminalvidenskap 2*.

Littlechild, B. (1997) 'Young Offenders, Punitive Policies and the Rights of Children.' *Critical Social Policy. A Journal of Theory and Practice in Social Welfare 17*, 4, 73–92.

Lundström, T. and Vinnerljung, B. (2001) 'Omhändertagande av barn under 1990-talet.' [Children taken into custody during the 1990s]. In Välfärdstjänster i omvandling. Antologi/Kommittén Välfärdsbokslut, SOU 2001:52 (Official Report). Stockholm: Graphium/Norstedts AB.

Mattson, T. (2002) *Barnet och rättsprocessen*. [The Child and the Legal Process]. Lund: Diss. Juristförlaget.

Minow, M. (1986) 'Rights for the Next Generation: A Feminist Approach to Children's Rights.' *Harvard Women's Law Journal 9*, 1, 1–23.

Muncie, J. (1999) *Youth and Crime: A Critical Introduction*. London: Sage.

Proposition 1962:10 Om brottsbalkens införande [Government Bill: The New Criminal Code in Sweden].

Proposition 1979/80:1 Socialtjänstlagen [Government Bill: The Social Services Act].

Proposition 1987/88:120 Om ändring i brottsbalken, straffmätning och påföljdsval m.m. [Government Bill: Reforms in the Criminal Code, Sentencing and Sanctions].

Proposition 1989/90:28 Vård i vissa fall av barn och ungdom [Government Bill: Care of Children and Youth in Certain Situations].

Proposition 1996/97:124 Barnkonventionens införande i Socialtjänstlagen [Government Bill: Introducing the UN Convention on the Rights of the Child into the Social Services Act].

Proposition 1997/98:96 Vissa reformer av påföljdssystemet [Government Bill: Some Reforms in the Juvenile Justice System].

Proposition 1999/00:137 Barn – här och nu. Redogörelse för barnpolitiken i Sverige med utgångspunkt i FN:s konvention om barnets rättigheter [Government Bill: Children – Here and Now. Swedish Child Policy from the Perspective of the UN Convention of Children's Rights].

Proposition 2000/01:80 Ny socialtjänstlag [Governement Bill: A New Social Services Act].

Proposition 2002/03:53 Stärkt skydd för barn i utsatta situationer m.m. [Government Bill: Strengthening the Protection for Exposed Children].

SOU 1993:35 Reaktion mot ungdomsbrott. Betänkande av Ungdomsbrottskommittén [The Swedish Government Official Report: Reaction to Juvenile Crime. Statement from the Committee of Juvenile Crimes].

SOU 2004:122 Ingripande mot unga lagöverträdare [The Swedish Governments Official Report: Actions against Juvenile Offenders]. Betänkande av Ungdomsbrottsutredningen.

Tärnfalk, M. (2001) Sluten ungdomsvård år 2000: Redovisning av intervjuundersökning [Compulsory Institutional Care. An Interview Study]. Allmän SiS-rapport nr 6 Stockholm: Statens Institutionsstyrelse (SiS).

Tham, H. (1995) 'Från behandling till straffvärde – kriminalpolitik i en förändrad välfärdsstat' [From treatment to just desert – criminal policy in a changing welfare state]. In D. Victor (ed) *Varning för straff. Om vådan av den nyttiga straffrätten* [Beware of Punishment. About the Risks of Useful Criminal Justice]. Stockholm: Norstedts.

Wennberg, S. (2000) *Introduktion till straffrätten, Sjätte upplagan*. [Introduction to Criminal Law, 6th edn). Stockholm: Norstedts Juridik AB.

White, S. (2001) *Handbook of Youth Justice*. New York: Kluwer Academic/Plenum Publishers.

5

Child Protection and the 'Juvenile Secure Estate' in England and Wales: Controversies, Complexities and Concerns

Barry Goldson

Introduction

This chapter engages with the difficult and contested question of child protection within locked institutions. The primary objective is to illuminate some of the key intersecting controversies, complexities and concerns that relate to the practices of locking up children and protecting them once their liberty has been withdrawn. For present purposes, 'child protection' is taken to have three core dimensions: the protection of children's human rights as provided by domestic statute and international standards, treaties, rules and conventions; the protection of their emotional, developmental and psychological well-being; and the protection of their physical (including sexual) integrity. In England and Wales, the 'juvenile secure estate' comprises three different types of institution:

1. local authority secure children's homes

2. secure training centres

3. young offender institutions.

Secure children's homes contain children whose liberty is restricted by either the civil courts (Family Proceedings Courts and County Courts) or the criminal courts (Youth Courts and Crown Courts), whereas secure training centres and young offender institutions are exclusively reserved for children whose liberty is restricted in criminal proceedings.

Controversies

Locking up children is, and should be, a controversial practice per se. This is compounded by the paradoxical fact that the law provides for the institutional restriction of children's liberty in both *civil* and *criminal* proceedings, on both welfare and offending grounds. In child care proceedings, children are detained in secure children's homes under the provisions of civil law because their vulnerabilities in the community are considered so great that institutional confinement is sanctioned by the courts in order to keep them safe. In this context the restriction of the child's liberty is conceived as a protective measure, a benign intervention in order to safeguard and promote their welfare. On the other hand, the rationale for detaining children in secure children's homes, secure training centres and young offender institutions under criminal law (in youth justice proceedings) is quite different. Here, it is the risk that children are thought to pose to the community, rather than the vulnerabilities that they might experience within it, that is imperative. The restriction of liberty is legitimised by reference to control, correction and even punishment. For the former group of children, child safety and child protection is the stated priority; the locked institution is seen as a place of safety. For the latter, community safety and public protection takes precedence; the locked institution is seen as a site of control, correction and, ultimately, punishment.

The means by which children are 'socially constructed' (James and Prout 1997) and formally conceptualised, lies at the root of such a paradox. A victim–threat dualism operates, whereby children can be perceived either as troubled and in need of protection (the child as *victim*), or as troublesome and in need of control, correction and punishment (the child as *threat*) (Goldson 2004). Despite such tidy conceptual differentiation, however, in practice children can rarely, if ever, be crudely dichotomised in this way. There is significant overlap between such categories, and the backgrounds, social circumstances, welfare needs and child protection requirements of such children are often very similar (Goldson 2002). The initial source of controversy, therefore, is that the restriction of liberty is incongruously legitimised by its appeal to care and welfare on the one hand, and with reference to control and punishment on the other. This is not only theoretically problematic but it also provides the potential for the inconsistent and excessive application of institutionally imposed restrictions of children's liberty. This, in turn, gives rise to further controversy.

The United Nations Convention on the Rights of the Child provides that:

> No child shall be deprived of his or her liberty unlawfully or arbitrarily. The [restriction of liberty]…shall be used only as *a measure of last resort* and for the *shortest appropriate period of time* (United Nations General Assembly 1989, Article 37b, emphases added)

It follows that closely and consistently observed legal safeguards are necessary in order to protect children's human rights. Yet the evidence outlined below suggests that in England and Wales children's liberty in institutions is restricted inconsistently and excessively, contrary to the principles of 'last resort' and 'shortest appropriate period of time'. This implies insufficient protection of children's human rights.

Restriction of liberty as 'care'

Placing children in secure children's homes in civil proceedings raises many controversial issues with regard to ethics, human rights and professional licence. Hodgkin, for example, has questioned:

> …why exactly is it necessary to lock up young people who are only a risk to themselves? What if their behaviour is untreatable within the locked placement? …How can one determine which to lock up of the many thousands of young people whose behaviours make them eligible for security… ? What filters, judicial or otherwise, ensure that *only* the necessary minimum are locked up? (Hodgkin 1995, p.7, original emphasis)

Indeed, research that has focused upon the characteristics, behaviours, vulnerabilities and protection needs of children placed in secure children's homes within the child care context adds weight to Hodgkin's queries. Thus, O'Neill (1999, p.290) observed that: 'it seems that many young people in secure accommodation are not significantly different from those accommodated in non-secure provision', and Aymer and her colleagues noted that:

...it is not necessarily the hard core of dangerous and self-damaging children and young people, those for whom secure accommodation was designed, who go into security... This was our finding and it...begs questions about who is being locked up and why? (Aymer *et al.* 1991, p.93)

Similar findings are echoed by O'Neill (2001a) and Vernon (1995). Although the legal criteria that must be satisfied before a child's liberty can be restricted in child care proceedings are ostensibly strict, in practice the processes that determine the 'placement' of children in secure children's homes comprise something of a lottery. Furthermore, the inconsistencies and excesses of such a 'lottery' have both gendered and geographically centred dimensions. In other words, girls are more likely than boys to be detained in secure children's homes for reasons of 'care' and 'protection', and some local authorities are significantly more likely than others to resort to institutional restrictions of children's liberty (for a fuller discussion see Goldson 2002).

Restriction of liberty as 'control' and 'correction'

Rates of detention in locked institutions (of young people who offend) have increased rapidly in recent years in England and Wales. The total number of custodial sentences imposed upon children rose from approximately 4000 per annum in 1992 to 7600 in 2001, a 90 per cent increase (Nacro 2003, 2005). During the same period the child remand population grew by 142 per cent (Goldson 2002). In March 2004, there were 3251 children (aged 10–17 inclusive) in penal custody in England and Wales, 80 per cent of whom were held in prison service young offender institutions (Youth Justice Board 2005, p.78).

Such patterns of child imprisonment in England and Wales are excessive when compared to most other industrialised democratic countries in the world (Youth Justice Board 2004, para. 9; for a fuller discussion see Muncie and Goldson 2006). They also bear no direct relation to the general incidence or severity of youth crime itself. Although it is always necessary to exercise care and caution in reading, analysing and interpreting 'official' youth crime data (Muncie 2004, pp.15–19), incidence of youth crime in England and Wales has been stable, if not diminishing, in striking contrast to the law and policy allowing for substantial penal expansion. More specifically, the number of child prisoners aged 12–14 increased by 800 per cent in the ten-year period

1992–2001 (Home Office 2002), the use of penal custody for girls increased by 400 per cent over a similar period (Nacro 2003), and black children are consistently over-represented within the population of child prisoners (Feilzer and Hood 2004). None of this bears any direct relation to the age, gender or ethnic distribution of crime, rather it represents a crude politics of toughness with child-focused, gendered and racialised inflections.

In sum, the protection of children's human rights in accordance with the 'measure of last resort' principle is fundamentally compromised. While controversy surrounds the excessive number of cases in which decisions are made to restrict children's liberty in locked institutions, complexity characterises the context, policies, procedures and practices relating to child protection once children are detained.

Complexities

Applying child protection principles to the practice of locking up children is, in many respects, intrinsically paradoxical. It follows that child protection policies, procedures and practices within the 'juvenile secure estate' are pitted with myriad complexities. There is not space for a comprehensive analysis of such complexities here. Instead two illustrations, the first relating to secure children's homes and the second to young offender institutions, are considered.

Protecting the mix? Children's differences and similarities

As noted, secure children's homes draw their statutory authority from both civil and criminal statute and, as such, they fulfil specific but different functions within both child welfare and youth justice systems. Consequently, children are 'placed' in secure children's homes under highly varied circumstances, and for very different purposes:

- *sanctuary* because they are thought to be especially vulnerable and in need of concentrated forms of care and protection ('looked after' children)

- *containment* in order to protect others, to deter them from offending and/or to guarantee that they attend court for trial or sentence (remanded children)

- *correction and punishment* because they have been convicted of offences (sentenced children).

The diverse and potentially conflicting purposes, associated with widely differing needs of the children concerned, pose major challenges for the operational rationale of secure children's homes; and their routines, regimes and practices:

> the considerable differences in terms of the age, gender, ethnic origin…antici-pated length of stay and distance from home area typify the profiles of children in secure facilities nationally. The implications that such differences raise in terms of managing and meeting the respective needs of such a 'mix' of children in closed facilities are profound…an intricate matrix of needs, rights and responsibilities calls for quite staggering versatility. (Goldson 1995, p.5)

Some commentators have problematised such a diverse mix by emphasising issues of incompatibility particularly along the axis (frequently gendered) of 'non-offender' (child welfare)–'offender' (youth justice). Thus research by O'Neill (2001b, p.6) revealed that 'non-offenders' were concerned about living alongside those convicted of violent and sexual offences. This applied particularly to those who were known to have been sexually abused and/or to have been engaged in child prostitution prior to admission. Similarly, Hodgkin (1995, p.42), referring to girls with long histories of appalling sexual abuse and violation, questioned how they 'could benefit from being locked up with convicted rapists and violent offenders'.

Indeed, children detained in secure children's homes on the basis of their 'welfare' and 'protection' needs, and the staff who work with them, typically illuminate such tensions and complexities (Goldson 2002, pp.119–21):

> Not all of us are in here for our own safety. It's not right that we are mixed – we should be kept separate. Sentenced and welfare are here for very different reasons and yet we are just all put together. We should not be in mixed units. (Girl aged 16 yrs)

> All Secure Units should be closed down. It is not going to help anybody. They are like prisons. Prisons are for bad people. I am not a bad person. There are more criminals in here than welfare people. I am here for welfare, I have not done anything to anyone to get myself in here. (Girl aged 15 yrs)

> 90% of them don't think they should be here because they can't see what they are doing wrong... There are welfare kids who could spend a year in here and who have they mixed with? They've mixed with muggers, rapists, robbers and car thieves. They are here because they are at risk. It makes no sense. (Secure Unit Residential Social Worker)

> Generally they think that they are here to be punished. How can you explain to a girl who has been abused for years and comes in here for self-harming and overdosing that she is not being punished when the abuser is walking about freely on the outside... More to the point how do you explain to her that it is not punishment when she comes in here and is mixing with children serving sentences? (Secure Unit Team Leader)

The mix of children within secure children's homes raises some extraordinarily complex issues, therefore. On the one hand, the practice is tantamount to the criminalisation of children with compelling welfare needs. Moreover, locking up such children alongside convicted 'offenders' might expose them to heightened risks of emotional, developmental, psychological, physical and/or sexual abuse. On the other hand, as noted, the victim–threat dichotomy is oversimplified, which means that many of those admitted for offences are very vulnerable too. Although the 'welfare' and 'justice' constituencies of children enter secure children's homes along quite different legal pathways, their background circumstances and consequent needs are often very similar (Goldson 2002, p.122):

> The other way of looking at this is that the justice kids have welfare needs, and we have to be careful not to lose welfare issues for justice kids. (Secure Unit Shift Manager)

> When you read the files there is not as much difference in their backgrounds at all. (Secure Unit Team Leader)

Indeed, while children's differences within secure children's homes are sources of tension, similarities in their collective circumstances and needs are also evident. Most of the children in secure children's homes, irrespective of their legal status at the point of admission, have experienced unsettling and unstable family and domestic circumstances; chequered education; emotional, psychological, physical and/or sexual abuse; and invariably have poor self-images that are the net result of multiple disappointments and histories of failed and neglectful relationships (Boswell 1996; Goldson 1995, 2002). Such differences and similarities give rise to particular complexities, and impose formidable demands on staff with child care and child protection responsibilities in secure children's homes.

'Safer custody'? Punishment and protection

Young offender institutions are prisons to which children in England and Wales are sent as punishment. It is increasingly recognised, however, that child prisoners typically endure serious welfare neglect and 'import' multiple vulnerabilities into prisons. Moreover, penal regimes tend to accentuate such vulnerabilities and in so doing they expose children to significant risks and harms. The requirements of child protection, within a conceptual and institutional context of punishment, raise a range of theoretical and practical complexities, therefore. With regard to the latter, the Youth Justice Board for England and Wales (YJB) advised the Home Secretary in 1998 that: 'there is clear evidence that the current arrangements for juvenile secure facilities are highly unsatisfactory' (Youth Justice Board 1998, p.12). This echoed serious concerns about the conditions and treatment of child prisoners expressed in previously published reports (Her Majesty's Chief Inspector of Prisons 1997; Utting 1997). As a result, the YJB has since endeavoured to apply a 'safer custody' agenda to the 'juvenile secure estate'. The processes of 'placement' and 'assessment' have been substantially reformed, with a focus on developing child protection policies, practices and procedures (Goldson 2002; Goldson and Coles 2005).

This effort was galvanised following an action for judicial review brought by the Howard League for Penal Reform in November 2002. Prior to the Howard League's action, the statutory protections provided in England and Wales, by the Children Act 1989, had been interpreted as *not* applying to children in penal custody. As Valier (2004, p.15) has observed, however: 'the League successfully challenged the legality of the Home Secretary's policy on statutory child protection duties towards children held in young offender institutions'. Since the judgment (Munby 2002), a range of child protection initiatives have been implemented.

The Association of Directors of Social Services, the Local Government Association and the Youth Justice Board (2003) have made a series of recommendations in respect of the applicability of the Children Act 1989 to child prisoners, and the associated duties of statutory agencies to ensure that robust child protection processes are in place. Prison Service Order 4950, 'Regimes for Under 18 Year Olds', has been revised to include a detailed sequence of 'annexes' and 'appendices' setting out child protection law, guidance, policy, procedure, process and practice, together with a range of pro-forma documents for the purposes of executing and recording child protection interventions in young offender institutions (Her Majesty's Prison Service 2003). Her Majesty's Prison Service 'Juvenile Group' and the Youth Justice Board (2003) have undertaken a 'Child Protection and Safeguards Review'. The Department for Education and Skills (2004) has issued a Local Authority Circular entitled 'Safeguarding and promoting the welfare of children and young people in custody'. The Circular advises Local Authorities in areas where there is a young offender institution or a secure training centre to: 'ensure that they have agreed local protocols with custodial establishments…in line with legislation, guidance and local procedures, including the local Area Child Protection Committee (ACPC) child protection procedures' (Department for Education and Skills 2004, p.2). Finally, the YJB has published a three-year 'Strategy for the Secure Estate for Juveniles' in which it states its determination to 'ensure that young offenders are cared for in custodial establishments where they are kept safe and healthy in decent conditions' (Youth Justice Board 2004, p.14).

Despite the various policy and procedural reforms that have been, and continue to be, implemented, and the determined practical efforts of (some) operational staff to take account of the specific needs of child prisoners, 'caring' for children in young offender institutions and sustaining effective child protection systems is an exceptionally complex, if not impossible, task. The very concept of 'safer custody' or the 'caring prison' (Prisons and Probation Ombudsman 2004, Ev. 68) is, in essence, an oxymoron; there is little or no evidence to suggest that the child protection reforms have succeeded in making prison custody any safer. Three factors are particularly significant in explaining why this might be so.

First, there are inherent tensions in values, roles and responsibilities. In the final analysis, the priority role of young offender institutions staff is to maintain discipline, order and institutional security. Set against this is the duty of care, which has a secondary status. This incongruous duality of controlling and caring functions is the source of conceptual ambiguity and operational difficulty. Second, limited resources and relatively low staffing levels tend to prohibit any meaningful engagement between staff and child prisoners beyond the basic routines of day-to-day operations. Third, staff training is generally inadequate. Expertly developed knowledge and skills, together with ongoing professional training, are required to meet the complex needs of child prisoners and to sustain an ethos of child protection. Although 'training' consistently features prominently within official discourse, policy statements and institutional 'mission statements', in reality its delivery is inconsistent and superficial. Her Majesty's Chief Inspector of Prisons (2005, p.59) has referred to 'concerns' with regard to 'the absence of sufficient training for staff' working with child prisoners and has observed that, although 'the Prison Service has now developed a training package…it lasts for only seven days and, even then, establishments are expressing concern about how they will facilitate this'. Furthermore, while 'some prisons keep up to date with training…others had done none in the previous year or failed to meet targets' (Her Majesty's Chief Inspector of Prisons 2005, p.18). In essence, staff in young offender institutions are required to fulfil a function for which they are neither professionally trained nor adequately equipped.

The complexities of providing protection within a context of punishment are compounded by prison overcrowding, a direct consequence of the excessive use of child imprisonment in England and Wales referred to earlier. When young offender institutions are pressured by overcrowding:

> services which have been put in place to support vulnerable [children] become overwhelmed with the result that some [children] cannot access support when they need it. Staff who are overstretched can fail to notice when [a child] is experiencing distress. (Mind 2004, Ev. 108).

It is inevitable, therefore, that many child prisoners continue to feel 'unsafe' (Challen and Walton 2004; Her Majesty's Chief Inspector of Prisons 2005), and progress in terms of advancing the child protection agenda remains 'patchy' (Her Majesty's Chief Inspector of Prisons 2005, p.56).

Concerns

The controversies and complexities that have been considered inevitably also raise concerns. In many respects locking up children is a sign of failure in earlier interventions, which is itself a source of concern. Furthermore, restricting children's liberty, within both child care and youth justice contexts, initiates a range of additional theoretical, conceptual and practical concerns.

Here it is not possible to address such concerns in their entirety, but two examples are offered by way of illustration. The first relates to the protection of children's emotional, developmental and psychological well-being, together with safeguarding their physical integrity and safety, in secure children's homes. The second applies to the same priorities within young offender institutions.

Secure children's homes: providing relief, precipitating danger?

Official representation, government guidance and professional discourse present secure children's homes as providing far more than a means of restricting liberty within the child care system. Indeed, they are conceived in terms of the 'added value' that they are thought to confer in respect of their civil application. They are presented as providing a specialist service that is not available elsewhere, for a constituency of particularly damaged, vulnerable and/or abused children. There can be little doubt that the adverse social circumstances of some children, and the perilous lives that they lead, place them at serious risk of significant harm. Despite the controversies raised with regard to the inconsistent and excessive application of locked institutional interventions, it is difficult to quarrel with the restriction of liberty per se as a 'last resort' and 'for the shortest appropriate period'. In cases where such interventions can relieve children from the most appalling maltreatment and, at the extremes, literally save lives, secure children's homes appear to fulfil an essential function (Goldson 2002).

The emphasis here is placed primarily upon the *immediate* benefits of secure children's homes. In this sense the secure children's home provides a sojourn facilitating temporary relief from the dangers of the street, a safe enclosure, an opportunity to attend to primary health needs, a 'pit-stop' for restoring a sense of 'childhood', a chance to rebuild emotional well-being and self-worth. The value of such tangible benefits should not be understated. However, in terms of the medium- to longer-term 'benefits' of secure children's homes far less is known.

In posing the question 'What is the effect of security on young people?', for example, Vernon (1995, p.2) could only conclude that, 'despite the importance of this question, the relative absence of long-term studies means that there is a dearth of conclusive research evidence in this respect'. This remains the case to this day. Furthermore, the evidence that is available raises a very important concern. Bullock and Little (1991, p.2), two of the most respected researchers in the field, have noted that, 'there is little doubt that secure accommodation is an effective damper on the immediate threat posed' and that, 'some observed improvements do seem to transfer to the outside world'. The same researchers, however, also point out that 'there are dangers of serious psychological and social damage being inflicted on children if placements are not managed well' (Bullock and Little 1991, p.2). In other words, secure children's homes may provide immediate benefits in certain circumstances, but they might equally make bad problems worse in others. It is of concern that the medium- to longer-term consequences of locked institutional interventions within the context of child care and child protection have been, and continue to be, neglected.

Young offender institutions: the pain of confinement

As noted earlier, there is little or no evidence to suggest that the various child protection initiatives that have been introduced within young offender institutions in England and Wales, have succeeded in making the 'jailhouse', however it is configured, a safer place for children (Goldson and Coles 2005). In fact, concerns relating to the damaging and corrosive nature of penal custody for children have been consistently expressed over time from some of the most authoritative sources.

A decade or more has passed, for example, since the United Nations Committee on the Rights of the Child (1995) first formally reported that the human rights of child prisoners in England and Wales were being routinely violated. Despite the serious concerns raised, little or no remedial action was taken. Indeed, in October 2002, the Committee again formally reported its 'deep concern' at 'the high increasing numbers of children in custody…in violation of article 37(b) of the convention', and its 'extreme concern' regarding 'the conditions that children experience in detention', including the 'high levels of violence, bullying, self harm and suicide' amongst child prisoners (United Nations Committee on the Rights of the Child 2002, para. 57). Similar concerns have also been expressed by a wide range of penal reform organisations and children's human rights agencies within England and Wales, together with the most senior personnel from eight major statutory inspectorates, who concluded that child prisoners 'face the gravest risks to their welfare' (Social Services Inspectorate *et al.* 2002, p.72). More recently, the Council of Europe's Commissioner for Human Rights noted that, 'one can only conclude that the prison service is failing in its duty of care towards juvenile inmates' (Office for the Commissioner for Human Rights 2005, para. 93).

In protecting the emotional, developmental and psychological well-being of locked-up children, together with safeguarding their physical integrity and safety, the size of the institution in which they are detained is particularly important. In comparing young offender institutions with secure children's homes and secure training centres, Her Majesty's Chief Inspector of Prisons (2002, pp.36–37) has explained:

> One of the most important factors in creating a safe environment is size. The other places where children are held – Secure Units and Secure Training Centres – are small, with a high staff–child ratio. The Prison Service, however, may hold children in what we regard as unacceptably high numbers and units. Units of 60 disturbed and damaged adolescents are unlikely to be safe... There are therefore already significant barriers to the Prison Service being able to provide a safe and positive environment for children; and the question whether it should continue to do so is a live one. Yet during the year the number of children has risen, to close to 3,000, and looks set to rise further. Promises to reduce unit size…are further than ever from being delivered.

The treatment and conditions experienced by many child prisoners in England and Wales is tantamount to institutional abuse. By way of illustration, the Children's Rights Alliance for England (2002) undertook a detailed analysis of the conditions and treatment experienced by children in penal custody, drawing on reports prepared by Her Majesty's Inspectorate of Prisons. The results showed widespread neglect in relation to physical and mental health; endemic bullying, humiliation and ill-treatment (staff-on-child and child-on-child); racism and other forms of discrimination; systemic invasion of privacy; long and uninterrupted periods of cell-based confinement; deprivation of fresh air and exercise; inadequate educational and rehabilitative provision; insufficient opportunities to maintain contact with family; poor diet; ill-fitting clothing in poor state of repair; a shabby physical environment; and, in reality, virtually no opportunity to complain and/or make representations.

Young offender institutions are corrosive places, therefore, in which children routinely suffer emotionally, developmentally, psychologically and physically (Goldson 2002). Most child prisoners suffer in silence. Some express their suffering by harming themselves. Between 1998 and 2002, for example, there were 1659 reported incidents of self-injury or attempted suicide by child prisoners in England and Wales (Howard League for Penal Reform 2005). Of greatest concern of all, are the children for whom the pain of confinement is literally too great to bear. Such is the depth of their suffering that death becomes preferable to life. Between July 1990 and January 2005, 28 child prisoners died in England and Wales, all but two of the deaths seemingly self-inflicted (Goldson and Coles 2005).

Conclusions

This chapter has engaged with a broad-based definition of child protection which has been taken to mean the protection of children's human rights, the protection of their emotional, developmental and psychological well-being, and the protection of their physical (including sexual) integrity. In many important respects the three dimensions overlap and intersect. Two discrete legal constituencies of children in England and Wales have been profiled: those who enter secure children's homes via the civil proceedings/child care route, and those who are detained within secure children's homes, secure training centres and young offender institutions under criminal proceedings/youth justice statute. Despite the legal differentiation, however, it has been argued that the circumstances, welfare needs and protection requirements of both constituencies are similar. By critically analysing the practices of restricting children's liberty through a child protection lens, a range of controversies, complexities and concerns has been raised and, here too, overlap and intersection is evident. The chapter illuminates some ways in which children's individual vulnerabilities, welfare needs and protection requirements can be exacerbated by the processes of institutional intervention. Closer critical exploration and more detailed research along similar lines is certainly required. In the meantime, perhaps sufficient ground has been covered to conclude that placing children in locked institutions can seriously compromise the spirit and practical imperatives of child protection.

References

Association of Directors of Social Services, Local Government Association and the Youth Justice Board for England and Wales (2003) *The Application of the Children Act (1989) to Children in Young Offender Institutions.* London: ADSS, LGA and YJB.

Aymer, C., Gittens, J., Hill, D., McLeod, I., Pitts, J., Rytovaata, M., Sturdivant, E., Wright, L. and Walker, M. (1991) 'The hard core – taking young people out of secure institutions.' In J. Dennington and J. Pitts (eds) *Developing Services for Young People in Crisis.* Harlow: Longman, 92–112.

Boswell, G. (1996) *Young and Dangerous: The Backgrounds and Careers of Section 53 Offenders.* Aldershot: Avebury.

Bullock, R. and Little, M. (1991) *Secure Accommodation for Children, Highlight No. 103.* London: National Children's Bureau and Barnardo's.

Challen, M. and Walton, T. (2004) *Juveniles in Custody.* London: Her Majesty's Inspectorate of Prisons.

Children's Rights Alliance for England (2002) *Rethinking Child Imprisonment: A Report on Young Offender Institutions.* London: Children's Rights Alliance for England.

Department for Education and Skills (2004) 'Safeguarding and Promoting the Welfare of Children and Young People in Custody.' *Local Authority Circular LAC (2004)26.* London: Department for Education and Skills.

Feilzer, M. and Hood, R. (2004) *Differences or Discrimination?* London: Youth Justice Board for England and Wales.

Goldson, B. (1995) *A Sense of Security.* London: National Children's Bureau.

Goldson, B. (2002) *Vulnerable Inside: Children in Secure and Penal Settings.* London: The Children's Society.

Goldson, B. (2004) 'Victims or threats? Children, care and control.' In J. Fink (ed) *Care: Personal Lives and Social Policy.* Bristol: The Policy Press, in association with the Open University, 77–109.

Goldson, B. and Coles, D. (2005) *In the Care of the State? Child Deaths in Penal Custody in England and Wales.* London: INQUEST.

Her Majesty's Chief Inspector of Prisons (1997) *Young Prisoners: A Thematic Review by HM Chief Inspector of Prisons for England and Wales.* London: Home Office.

Her Majesty's Chief Inspector of Prisons (2002) *Annual Report of HM Chief Inspector of Prisons for Engalnd and Wales 2001–02.* London: The Stationery Office.

Her Majesty's Chief Inspector of Prisons (2005) *Annual Report of HM Chief Inspector of Prisons for England and Wales, 2003–2004.* London: The Stationery Office.

Her Majesty's Prison Service (2003) *Prison Service Order 4950: Regimes for Under 18 Year Olds.* London: Her Majesty's Prison Service.

Her Majesty's Prison Service and the Youth Justice Board for England and Wales (2003) *Child Protection and Safeguards Review 2003 – Draft.* London: Her Majesty's Prison Service.

Hodgkin, R. (1995) *Safe to Let Out? The Current and Future Use of Secure Accommodation for Children and Young People.* London: National Children's Bureau.

Home Office (2002) *Criminal Statistics for England and Wales 2001.* London: Home Office.

Howard League for Penal Reform (2005) *Children in Custody: Promoting the Legal and Human Rights of Children.* London: Howard League for Penal Reform.

James, A. and Prout, A. (1997) *Constructing and Reconstructing Childhood: Contemporary Issues in the Sociological Study of Childhood.* London: Farmer Press.

Mind (2004) 'Memorandum submitted by Mind', written evidence to the House of Lords House of Commons Joint Committee on Human Rights *Deaths in Custody Interim Report: First Report of Session 2003–04.* London: The Stationery Office, Evidence 107–113.

Munby, The Honourable Mr Justice (2002) *Judgment Approved by the Court for Handing Down in R (on the application of the Howard League for Penal Reform) v. The Secretary of State for the Home Department,* 29 November. London: Royal Courts of Justice.

Muncie, J. (2004) *Youth and Crime.* London: Sage.

Muncie, J. and Goldson, B. (eds.) (2006) *Comparative Youth Justice.* London: Sage.

Nacro (2003) *A Failure of Justice: Reducing Child Imprisonment.* London: Nacro.

Nacro (2005) *A Better Alternative: Reducing Child Imprisonment.* London: Nacro.

Office for the Commissioner for Human Rights (2005) *Report by Mr Alvaro Gil-Robles, Commissioner for Human Rights, on His Visit to the United Kingdom 4–12 November 2004.* Strasbourg: Council of Europe.

O'Neill, T. (1999) 'Locking Up Children in Secure Accommodation: A Guardian ad Litem Perspective.' *Representing Children 11,* 4, 289–297.

O'Neill, T. (2001a) *Children in Secure Accommodation: A Gendered Exploration of Locked Institutional Care for Children in Trouble.* London: Jessica Kingsley Publishers.

O'Neill, T. (2001b) 'Secure Accommodation for Children in Trouble: Care or Custody?' Unpublished paper presented at the Nineteenth Annual Conference of the Howard League for Penal Reform – *Villains and Victims: Children and the Penal System.* New College, Oxford, September 2001.

Prisons and Probation Ombudsman for England and Wales (2004) 'Memorandum from Prisons and Probation Ombudsman for England and Wales', written evidence to the House of Lords House of Commons Joint Committee on Human Rights. *Deaths in Custody Interim Report: First Report of Session 2003–04.* London: The Stationery Office, Evidence 67–68.

Social Services Inspectorate, Commission for Health Improvement, Her Majesty's Chief Inspector of Constabulary, Her Majesty's Chief Inspector of the Crown Prosecution Service, Her Majesty's Chief Inspector of the Magistrates' Courts Service, Her Majesty's Chief Inspector of Schools, Her Majesty's Chief Inspector of Prisons and Her Majesty's Chief Inspector of Probation (2002) *Safeguarding Children: A Joint Chief Inspectors' Report on Arrangements to Safeguard Children.* London: Department of Health Publications.

United Nations Committee on the Rights of the Child (1995) *Eighth Session. Consideration of Reports Submitted by States Parties Under Article 44 of the Convention.* Geneva: Office of the United Nations High Commissioner for Human Rights.

United Nations Committee on the Rights of the Child (2002) *Concluding Observations of the Committee on the Rights of the Child: United Kingdom of Great Britain and Northern Ireland.* Geneva: United Nations.

United Nations General Assembly (1989) *The United Nations Convention on the Rights of the Child.* New York: United Nations.

Utting, Sir W. (1997) *People Like Us: The Report of the Review of the Safeguards for Children Living Away from Home.* London: The Stationery Office.

Valier, C. (2004) 'Litigation as a Strategy in Penal Reform.' *The Howard Journal of Criminal Justice 43,* 1, 15–26.

Vernon, J. (1995) *En Route to Secure Accommodation.* London: National Children's Bureau.

Youth Justice Board for England and Wales (1998) *Juvenile Secure Estate: Preliminary Advice from the Youth Justice Board for England and Wales to the Home Secretary.* London: Youth Justice Board for England and Wales.

Youth Justice Board for England and Wales (2004) *Strategy for the Secure Estate for Juveniles: Building on the Foundations.* London: Youth Justice Board for England and Wales.

Youth Justice Board for England and Wales (2005) *Youth Justice Annual Statistics 2003/04.* London: Youth Justice Board for England and Wales.

2

Trends in Child Protection and Youth Justice Policy

6

Developments in Child Protection

Jim Ennis

Introduction

During the second half of the twentieth century, most countries in western Europe and North America experienced growing policy and public awareness of child abuse, often accompanied by major criticisms of the responses by public agencies, which have come to be known as constituting the child protection system (Waldfogel 2001). The present chapter examines challenges facing the system in Scotland. Investigation and intervention here have followed many of the same trends as in England, the USA and some other countries, towards formalised and primarily legalised responses (Parton and Otway 1995), but the judicial process has been different. Even though the Children (Scotland) Act 1995 increased the role of sheriff courts in relation to emergency protection orders, the central body for most decisions has remained the Children's Hearings System outlined in the Preface.

Children's Hearings are the main forum for considering whether and what compulsory action should be taken in situations where children have been harmed within the family or are at risk of harm. When the Hearings started, most cases they dealt with concerned youth crime, but the proportion of cases involving issues of care and protection has grown markedly, to about half (Lockyer and Stone 1998). Not only has the volume of cases grown, but understanding of abuse and neglect has altered substantially over the same period. In the light of these developments, this chapter examines whether it is still appropriate to handle child protection cases in essentially the same way as offence-related and other kinds of case. The chapter asks whether highly specialist knowledge and training is needed to make key decisions about intervention, which can bring into question the role of lay people as decision-makers. The circumstances and evidence are largely reviewed within a Scottish context, but broader implications for other jurisdictions in working constructively with troubled and troubling children and young people are also identified.

The chapter will proceed by, first, outlining the evolution in approaches to the maltreatment of children in Scotland, before turning to the emotive issue of responses to child deaths. Thereafter it will assess the present condition of the Scottish Children's Hearings System from a number of perspectives, before advocating a thorough structural overhaul in order to address certain criticisms made of the system's procedures.

The unfolding story of the maltreatment of children

Fifty years ago decision-makers dealing with child abuse in Scotland, as elsewhere, mainly dealt with incidents of cruelty to children and severe neglect. Since then the range and scale of child maltreatment that comes to the attention of professionals and decision-makers has grown significantly.

Although there had long been concern about the vulnerability of children and their need for protective services, the modern phase of the discovery of child abuse is often attributed to the identification of 'battered baby syndrome'. New radiological techniques identified the fact that bodily injuries, hitherto seen as accidental, were the result of deliberate beatings by parents or carers (Kempe *et al.* 1962). Since the publication of that seminal paper, a steady accumulation of evidence and published material has served to 'lift the veil' on violent aspects of family life and suggest that considerably larger numbers of children are affected than was previously thought. Later research has illuminated both the causes of such ill-treatment and other forms of abuse, particularly sexual and emotional. This has continued to challenge social, political and institutional assumptions about services to children.

Surveys have shown that the risk of non-accidental child injury or death rises steeply with poverty. Also the likelihood of a child being injured or killed is associated with stress, and parental alcohol and substance abuse, which themselves are closely linked to poverty (Unicef 2001; Wedge and Prosser 1973). Thus anti-poverty measures need to be central in policies to prevent child abuse. The current UK government policy aims to lift an estimated one million UK children out of poverty (Horton 2005). This has met with some success, but figures for 2002/2003 show that 28 per cent of all children still lived in households with below 60 per cent of median income after housing costs (Bradshaw and Mayhew 2005).

The contemporary literature has identified further forms of abuse, which like 'battered babies' before the 1960s, went previously unrecognised. Researchers focusing on immediate post-birth experiences for healthy child development have concluded that the first three months of a baby's life are even more developmentally critical than was previously thought. Moreover, not only is good physical care required, but infants at this stage are also highly sensitive to the quality of their emotional care. This is illustrated by the concept of the trauma of absence, when very young babies are denied warm early engagement with adult carers (Hughes 1998; Perry 2001; Seigal 1999). Although the most extreme examples of the trauma of absence are derived from the 'warehouse' orphanages that came to world attention in the 1980s and 1990s in some post-Soviet eastern European countries and in China, there is evidence that similar problems for children are associated with particular circumstances in comparatively wealthy post-industrial countries (Shore 1997). That said, the work of Rutter *et al.* (2000) in tracking the developmental pathways of a sample of children from Romania indicates that even those children exposed to the most severe deprivation in early years can recover significant ground when moved at the earliest possible point to stable, richly nurturing family environments.

Awareness has grown too about the significance of neglect. Prolonged exposure to neglect seeps deeply into the very fibre of children and can imbue them with qualities of helplessness that can be very hard to shift (Katz 1992; Stevenson 1998). The rise and rise of parental substance misuse has been increasingly evident as a major contributing factor in child abuse and neglect, with some caregivers being so preoccupied with serving their addiction that they cannot attend consistently to the psychological needs of new-born children. Rodning, Beckwith and Howard (1991) reported that only one-fifth (18%) of infants exposed to serious drug misuse showed secure attachment to their biological parents at 15 months, compared with a 64 per cent rate for a matched sample of infants of parents who did not abuse drugs. Recent published work in the USA highlighted the 'conflicting time clocks' metaphor, where the young child's developmental needs are immediate, while the addicted parent's required recovery time may often be long (Ondersma, Simpson, Brestan and Ward 2000). Partly as a result, substance misuse is present in two of every three referrals involving concerns about the well-being of children (Ondersma and Chase 2003).

The literature also points to a phenomenon of parentification in very young children struggling to look after adults incapacitated by alcohol or drug misuse, or by mental health difficulties. In numbers of cases, the child's ability and willingness to parent the parents may become critical for the family to function, but at great cost to the child, often manifested in a failure to achieve developmental milestones (Chase 1999; Jurkovic 1997).

A major problem for decision-making in relation to neglect is that, often, the agencies most in contact with the families are adult-orientated, with a focus on substance misuse, mental health or offending. Just as the parents or carers may be too preoccupied with their own issues to attend to the needs of their children, so professionals without an explicit child protection remit may overlook or underestimate threats to safe and adequate care.

Recent figures suggest that 10 to 20 per cent of children are at risk of exposure to domestic violence (National Adoption Information Clearing-house (NAIC) 2003) and data continue to emerge about the profound impact on children of being brought up in a household characterised by domestic violence (Mullender and Morley 1994).

As Kempe and Kempe (1978) predicted, both professional and lay people have a struggle to fully acknowledge the existence of the sexual abuse of children by adults. The plausibility of exploitative adults can persuade other adults to disbelieve children, especially when the child's accusations are accompanied by a flatness of affect that appears inconsistent with the more exaggerated responses sometimes expected of children exposed to an abusive regime. Some sexual abuse perpetrators attach themselves to vulnerable families specifically to open opportunities for abuse. They may carefully cultivate a family culture of control and violence in order to commit abuse and to minimise the possibility of detection (Bentovim 2002; Salter 1995). Evidence is still emerging about the long-term impact and implications for people sexually abused as children, though the immediate negative impact is usually clear (Berliner and Elliott 2002). More is known about the capacity of exploitative adults to lie and cheat and cover up their activities. Even profes-sionally trained and closely supervised staff working with these issues can suffer secondary trauma (Conte 2001) and some will develop protective mechanisms that may at the same time prevent them from accepting and confronting the plight of children.

As with sexual abuse, it can be hard to believe that a small but significant number of adults deliberately inflict pain and injury on their offspring, causing physical and emotional trauma – and sometimes death – in the pursuit of their own needs (Dale, Green and Fellows 2002). A very experienced child care social work manager, Anne Black, co-led an independent review into the killing of a 13-month-old child in north-east Scotland. At the press conference publicly introducing the Review Report in September 2003, she said:

> The reality is that some parents do abuse their children seriously and some do kill them. We know it is very hard for any of us, and particularly the public, to accept that some parents can inflict that level of damage on their children. But they do. (Black and Burgham 2003)

Limitations in the quality of irrefutable medical evidence have caused controversy in a number of high-profile trial situations. For example, the concept of temporary brittle bone disease (TBBD) advocated by Paterson (1990) as a causal explanation for multiple fractures in infants has been discredited in British courts because no scientific basis was found for the claims. Similarly, controversy surrounds the evidential basis of alleged non-accidental brain injury detected in very young children, briefly labelled as 'shaken baby syndrome' in some professional circles. Much of the challenge to prosecutions involving this category of case situation has been based on one study (Geddes, Tasker and Hackshaw 2003) and it is clear that much further research is required. The impact of the controversies seems likely to be a contributory factor in the fall in numbers of practitioners applying to train in forensic paediatrics across the UK and a perceived reluctance to participate in the provision of expert witness testimony in cases.

Professionals and lay people working directly with these issues have to absorb the distress of victims and manage the capacity within us all to deny the degree of suffering caused to children, our most vulnerable citizens. The work places a premium on emotional toughness, on a broad and constantly updated knowledge base, on experience, and on a highly developed capacity to make sound and detailed assessments. Moreover, much of the new material points up a complexity and an interrelatedness that has profound implications for policy formulation, for service systems, and for the development of the knowledge and skills mixes required by professionals and others. In short, decision-makers dealing with child abuse cases need to be well informed, self-aware and emotionally strong. Later sections of this chapter consider how far this is possible within a system of lay decision-makers handling a wide variety of referrals, as in Scotland.

Responses to the deaths of children

Over a broadly similar period, there have been a number of high-profile events and inquiries in the United Kingdom and elsewhere, raising new questions and contributing to shifts in perception and procedure (Butler-Sloss 1988; Clyde Report 1992). In more recent times, there have been two significant policy responses to child deaths, one in England and one in Scotland. The death of Victoria Climbié in London in February 2000 led to a full inquiry chaired by Lord Laming, a former Director of Social Work. The Report of the Victoria Climbié Inquiry (Laming 2003), a coherent and detailed document, was published in early 2003 and made a total of 108 recommendations, a number of which were incorporated in a Green Paper published for consultation in September 2003 (*Every Child Matters* 2003). It is important to note that the legislative changes heralded in the Green Paper were intended only for England, Wales and Northern Ireland, and the document declared that Scotland would be keeping a watching brief on developments. Within a broad contextual framework pledging improvements in the quality and range of universal services for children and families, the central thrust of proposed changes included a raft of major organisational restructuring and harmonisation designed to clarify tasks and responsibilities. There was endorsement of the need for a common assessment framework to help standardise language and meaning across disciplines and professions, a recommendation for cross-professional training, an endorsement of the need for files to contain a chronology of significant events and a call for the policing of child protection cases to be conducted with the same degree of importance attached to the pursuit of any other crime. The Green Paper took forward the Laming Report recommendations for major change, leading to the Children Act 2004.

In Scotland, the Hammond Report into the death of Kennedy MacFarlane in Dumfries was closely followed by the launch of a review and audit of child protection, with the significant title 'It's everyone's job to make sure I'm alright' (Scottish Executive 2002). The public launch of the document was characterised by an unhelpful degree of threat and bluster, with professionals threatened with replacement if they did not reform their ways within three years. However, a key finding from the review and audit work was that, where social work was well conducted, the outcome was invariably good. Although cross-professional work was important at all points, good professional social work was central to good outcomes. Other pointers and recommendations bore similarities to the recommendations in the Laming Report, notably in relation to better record-keeping, the improved dissemination of good practice and the endorsement of the need for inter-agency assessment.

Decision-making

It is noteworthy that neither of these major review processes (like many earlier inquiries) gave much attention to courts or hearings. Given the degree of separation of youth justice processes from work with children in need in an England and Wales context, that lack of attention is perhaps less surprising. In Scotland, where responses to the two categories of child overlap and are dealt with together within the Children's Hearings System, it is a much more significant oversight. The more than three decades old Children's Hearings System is built on the Kilbrandon Committee Report (Kilbrandon 1964). The starting point of the deliberations of that Committee was the widespread dissatisfaction with court-centred procedures involving children in trouble with the law. At the heart of the Hearings System is an emphasis on co-operation among decision-makers, professionals, parents and children as the key weapon in promoting change. The recent reports have highlighted defects in communication and collaboration, as well as a lack of confidence on the part of the public in the care and protection system as a whole.

An original Committee member, Stone (1995) stated that the Committee anticipated that care and protection cases would come to the Children's Hearings and should be treated in the same way, but child abuse cases were in fact rare in the early years of operation, with fewer than 600 of 22,000 children referred solely because of maltreatment. Subsequently, the number of non-offence cases rose until they are now a clear majority (Scottish Children's Reporter Administration (SCRA) annual reports 2000–1 and 2001–2).

Although the proportion of time and work in the Hearings taken up by care and protection cases has grown markedly, it is arguable that concern about delinquency is still the principal preoccupation. Growing public anxiety about youth crime across the UK and elsewhere has led to pressures for tougher measures both to control criminal activity among young people and to curb behaviours perceived to be antisocial and threatening. England's policy responses have been categorised as retributive or punitive (Goldson 2002), with an estimated 800 per cent increase over ten years in the number of children in custody in England and Wales. Community-based measures introduced have included electronic tagging and curfews although, despite these and other novel approaches, dramatic increases in numbers of juveniles in custody are attributed to the increasing imposition of custodial sentences by courts rather than recorded increases in numbers of juveniles committing offences or general increases in the gravity of offence behaviours (see Chapter 8). In Scotland, public concern about the threat posed by youth has been expressed in a groundswell of concern about the contemporary relevance of the Children's Hearings System and criticisms that disposals were 'too soft' on crime. Other criticisms and complaints focused on perceived variations in decision-making, poor resourcing and an absence of detailed outcome data. It is significant that the most recent legal changes affecting the Children's Hearings have related to youth crime, including experimentation with fast-track procedures and youth courts, as well as the introduction of parenting orders and intensive support and monitoring.

Assessing the Hearings System today

The recent child protection review and ensuing programme in Scotland has focused mainly on service agencies, while changes in the Hearings as the key decision-making forum have mainly had a youth crime focus. Hence it is timely to consider the present condition of the Hearings System with respect to its care and protection functions. To do so, it is helpful to briefly examine three key structural and organisational design components of the system:

1. a broad level of political and societal support for the work, and a sympathy and tolerance for the underpinning social justice principles

2. a pool of concerned and informed citizens, interested in the work and willing and able to offer their time as volunteers

3. autonomous service-providing departments based in Local Authorities responsible for the assessment and help afforded to

children and families; these were originally planned to be social education departments, but in the event were social work departments, though nowadays social work services for children are provided in a range of structures.

Over time, there have been significant shifts in relation to all three of these key components. In light of the punitive approach to troublesome young people that has been apparent recently, it is increasingly difficult to perceive the 'broad level of political and societal support for the work and a sympathy and tolerance for the underpinning social justice principles' required by the Kilbrandon model.

A second vital component of the Children's Hearings System is that the main decision-makers (panel members) are trained volunteers (see Chapter 11). Thus the system is reliant on a 'pool of concerned and informed citizens, interested in the work and willing and able to offer their time as volunteers' (Kilbrandon 1964). Changing social and employment patterns have had a significant impact on this component. Some regions in Scotland have had to work very hard to attract and retain suitable people with available time. The shifting political and social attitudes towards older children and young people, and the sheer complexity of the case situations brought before panels may also be factors making it hard to recruit and retain panel members. Changing attitudes towards authority in general may have contributed to reducing parental compliance with the Hearings System of late. The Scottish Executive's Report of the Child Protection Audit and Review (Scottish Executive 2002, p.200) noted that in 80 per cent of cases referred to the Reporter for care and protection concerns, the matter was referred to the Sheriff because grounds were disputed either by the child or the parent(s).

Just like a court system, the Hearings are dependent on statutory and voluntary agencies to provide assessments on which to base decisions and to make available suitable help to children and families when carrying out compulsory measures required by a Hearing. In common with the wider United Kingdom, the front-line workforce in Scotland has been decimated as a result of overwork and stress, with diminishing numbers of key social workers with specialist child care knowledge able to perform to the required level. The percentage of vacant posts for qualified social workers in children's services across Scotland rose from 6.6 per cent in 2000 to 14.5 per cent in October 2002 (National Children's Homes (NCH) 2004). Figures for Edinburgh produced by the City Council record a vacancy rate in 2003 of 16 per cent, rising to 20.5 per cent by January 2004 (City of Edinburgh Council 2004). The Report also stated that the total number of unallocated cases had doubled during 2003. In front-line teams across Scotland and other parts of the UK, the most experienced practitioner may have just two years' post-qualifying experience and be struggling with work of great complexity. Although steps have been taken to increase the numbers of qualified social workers, the situation in the child care field seems far from resolution (McDougall 2005).

The concerns, misgivings and criticisms voiced in Scotland regarding the contemporary relevance of the Children's Hearings System led to the setting up of an inquiry by a leading voluntary child care organisation (NCH 2004). This took evidence and opinion from a good cross-section of stakeholders, including children and young people. Interestingly, the stated aim of the exercise was to 'inform and influence the post-devolution discussion in Scotland about the best way to deal with young people who offend' and made only indirect mention in statements of purpose of the service provided to the more than 50 per cent of cases referred to a Hearing on non-offence grounds. The final Report commented that there had been little evaluation of the Hearings System during its more than three decades of operation (see Chapter 10). However, the Report also noted that the most significant research undertaken (Hallett and Hazel 1998; Hallett *et al.* 1998; Waterhouse and McGhee 2000) found evidence of a lack of clarity about decision-making and a failure to prevent escalation in offending in a sample of young men at high risk of progression to adult courts and custodial sentences. The NCH Scotland Report noted weaknesses in the Hearings System in compiling and moni-toring outcome data, in the implementation of disposal decisions, and in relation to a perceived lack of imagination and investment in the range of available disposals. In addition, the exercise identified shortcomings in the recruitment and retention of panel members, in the absence of defensible data about the social profile of panel members and in the perceived lack of status attached to the panel member role. Despite these serious misgivings, the Report concluded that the Hearings System, with significant additional resources, was still a more cost-effective, humane and effective response to children in trouble with the law than the more punitive, court-based approaches favoured in other constituencies.

The Report also commented that the Hearings System had, by default, become almost the only route of access to services for children in need of care and protection because of deficiencies in systems intended to provide support for children in need. In other words, families and professionals often thought it unlikely that help would be provided unless the local authority was obliged to give support by a formal order of the Hearings. The Report concluded that the 'Hearings system was not designed for this purpose, so it is no surprise that it has been engulfed in a rising tide of care and protection cases that distract it from its primary purpose'. The implications of this reported difficulty for the Hearings in adjusting to the shift in the pattern of referrals to a majority of care and protection cases will be further explored later in this chapter, when the structure of the system is critiqued. First, however, it will be instructive to examine the issue of the resources available for putting into effect decisions made by hearings.

Service resources and finance

Just as the Scottish Executive Audit and Review identified many cases not receiving an adequate service, the NCH Report (2004) concluded that the Hearings System is foundering through a lack of resources. It appears that its capacity to respond well to those children who are victims (of abuse or poor care) is reducing, due to pressures to prioritise youth crime and focus on those most at risk, rather than 'merely' in difficulty or at an early stage of family stress or conflict. The arguments for retaining a social welfare model in Scotland for responding to the criminal and antisocial activities of children and young people are convincing in themselves. Placed alongside the outcome data from the increasingly punitive (and failing) court-based measures introduced in England and Wales, the arguments become overwhelming. However, finding a rationale and an organisational structure for the Hearings System's future work that fully incorporates the needs of children and young people who are victims of maltreatment is less easy to perceive.

The NCH Report pointed not only to non-implementation of Hearings' decisions in some cases, but also to a perceived lack of imagination and investment in the range of available disposals. Tensions in respect to decisions are not uncommon in work with children. In England, the work of guardians, appointed to report on children's best interests, has been criticised because a number have been seen to make unrealistic recommendations about the plans that should be made for children, suggesting the use of resources that are not available and causing disappointment for users and angst for service staff (Head 2002). In California, a major system overhaul was implemented because of concerns regarding the coherence of service responses in situations where serious parental substance misuse was reducing the life chances of young children. Judges, state child welfare and protection agencies, and specialist service providers now work together to address issues. Parents are faced with the reality of concerns about their children's development and the impact of continued drug use on them. The judge in the situation is able to require the parent(s) to attend drug treatment knowing that the facility is there, while the parent is also required to attend court monthly (before the same judge) to review attendance and progress, and the foster carer can update the court on the child's progress. The whole process can be managed within an agreed time frame known to all the stakeholders, and everybody is aware that parallel planning is progressing so there is no time lag in the provision of alternative arrangements for the child's future should the parent fail to progress towards agreed good-enough arrangements. Assessment, decision and disposal are integrated, timely and coherent.

The structure and nature of the Hearings

With this alternative view in mind, we may assess the structure of the Scottish Children's Hearings System and its consequences in terms of the quality of service provided. It may be argued that panel members become socialised into a certain way of approaching Hearings cases, and with it bring a certain mindset to bear on the cases they hear. However, the attitude and perspective required in a care and protection case must clearly differ from that appropriate to offending hearings. The historical legacy of the early years of the system, with its expectation that the panel would focus overwhelmingly on offending cases, may be problematic in view of the changed pattern of referrals over the subsequent period. Panel members may approach care and protection cases – now the majority of cases referred to the hearings – with an attitude ill suited to the issue at hand. In offending cases the panel members have to address themselves much more to the conduct and personal circumstances of the child concerned than to other parties. By contrast, excessive focus on the child is inappropriate in care and protection hearings, which must be concerned with the conduct of other actors and the consequences they have for the child.

Therefore, focusing primarily on the child, as panel members may habitually come to do in all cases, will not necessarily be fruitful in all hearings. Moreover, the knowledge base required is different for care and protection cases, compared with youth crime. Not only should the decision-makers be familiar with the complex and varied nature of the maltreatment of children outlined in the first part of this chapter, but they should also fully understand that different kinds of family dynamics are involved.

In the author's view, this divergence does not necessarily require a separation of decision-making systems and principles, but supports a case for panel member recruitment and training to become more specialised. Some would deal primarily *either* with care and protection *or* offending cases, not both, as currently happens. Panel member training would be adjusted to make this effective. The move towards a decoupling of the decision-making could be accompanied by a similar service specialisation, with the creation of a new multiprofessional agency with specific responsibility for the care and protection of the most vulnerable children. This would be multiprofessional, in contrast to the present set-up where, by and large, social workers have the lead role and other professions from different offices and agencies contribute on a case-by-case basis. The new agency would be staffed by selected social worker, police, health and education specialists, and work closely with a component of the Children's Hearings System dedicated specifically to children appearing before the Hearings on care and protection grounds. Rationalising the system along the lines proposed would enable panel members to have a more focused remit and, as a result, better meet the needs of the children referred to them.

In addition to the issue of institutional structure, there is a matching need for modernised, better resourced and more professional decision-making. It is most common in many countries for formal decision-makers to be either legally trained or lay people (see Chapter 11), but in my view the present situation in Scotland warrants panel members being offered a degree of child care professional status. This would not only give them the expertise required, but would encourage more people to undertake the role. Panel members would be selected with the specific task in mind, be given lengthy training and be paid, with an expectation that they all achieve a designated formal qualification. Appointments could of course be part-time and time-limited, and some employers could be encouraged to commit to secondment arrangements or sponsorship agreements.

To achieve even some of these aims, Scotland may need to rethink approaches and alter funding mechanisms, so that money follows children. Agencies would receive money only if and when they provided a service for the children referred to Hearings. The money would follow individual children and be wholly conditional upon the provision of specified services – letting the development of services follow the needs of the child rather than have the child's needs trailing along behind the organisational needs of the agency (Giuliani 2002).

There is a need also to address an anomaly in thinking that gets in the way of real progress. For a decade or more, academics and policy-makers have argued about whether emphasis should be placed on either preventive work versus investigative work (Parton 1997) as if there really is a case to be made for either one without the other. What is required are solid preventive and supportive services for all children, especially those categorised as vulnerable. But there is also need for the very best in investigative services, staffed by the best and most experienced professionals at our disposal. People and agencies with broad remits towards children tend to lose track of the most vulnerable, especially those children cared for by those who would deceive and mislead others (Laming 2003; O'Brien 2003).

Conclusions

This chapter has examined the key information emerging in recent decades in relation to the maltreatment of children and linked it to the evolution in approaches to the maltreatment of children in Scotland and elsewhere. The emotive issue of responses to child deaths has been explored, alongside the changing nature of knowledge and shifts in the capacity of both professionals and lay people to fully address the difficulties inherent in protecting vulnerable children from harm. The chapter concluded by assessing the present condition of the Scottish Children's Hearings System from a number of perspectives, before advocating changes in the selection, training, status and deployment of panel members in order to address certain criticisms made of the Hearing System's procedures.

References

Bentovim, A. (2002) 'Working with abusing parents.' In K. Wilson and A. James (eds) *The Child Protection Handbook*. London: Bailliere Tindall, 456–480.

Berliner, L. and Elliott, D.M. (2002) 'Sexual abuse of children.' In J.E.B. Myers, L. Berliner, J. Briere, C.T. Hendrix, C. Jenny and T. A. Reid (eds) *The APSAC Handbook on Child Maltreatment* (2nd edn). Thousand Oaks, CA: Sage, 55–78.

Black, A. and Burgham, A. (2003) *Child Review Report into the Life and Death of Carla Nicole Bone* London: NESCPC.

Bradshaw, J. and Mayhew, E. (eds) (2005) *The Well-being of Children in the UK* (2nd edn) London: Save the Children.

Brent, D., Oquendo, M., Birmaher, B., Greenhill, L., Kolko, D., Stanley, B. *et al.* (2002) 'Familial Pathways to Early-onset Suicide Attempt: Risk for Suicidal Behavior in Offspring of Mood-disordered Suicide Attempters.' *Archives of General Psychiatry 59*, 801–807.

Butler-Sloss, E. (1988) *Report of the Inquiry into Child Abuse in Cleveland 1987*. London: Her Majesty's Stationery Office, Cm 412.

Chase, N.D. (1999) *Burdened Children*. Thousand Oaks, CA: Sage Publications.

City of Edinburgh Council (2004) *Children and Families Social Work: Practice Team Staffing and Risk Management*. Report dated 18 March.

Clyde Report (1992) *The Report of the Inquiry into the Removal of Children from Orkney in February 1991*. Edinburgh: HMSO.

Conte, J. (2001) *Secondary Trauma*. Seminar paper (May). Stirling, Scotland (unpublished).

Dale, P., Green, R. and Fellows, R. (2002) *What Really Happened?* London: NSPCC.

DWP (2003) *Households Below Average Income Statistics 2001–02*. London: The Stationery Office.

Every Child Matters (2003) Government Green Paper. London: The Stationery Office.

Geddes, J.F., Tasker, R.C. and Hackshaw, A.K. (2003) 'Dural Hemorrhage in Nontraumatic Infant Deaths: Does it Explain the Bleeding in "shaken baby syndrome"?' *Neuropathology and Applied Neurobiology 29*, 14–22.

Goldson, B. (2002) *Vulnerable Inside: Children in Secure and Penal Settings*. London: The Children's Society.

Guiliani, R.W. (2002) *Leadership*. New York: Miramax Books.

Hallett, C. and Hazel, N. (1998) *The Evaluation of Children's Hearing's in Scotland Volume 2 – The International Context: Trends in Juvenile Justice and Child Welfare*. Edinburgh: The Scottish Office Central Research Unit.

Hallett, C. and Murray, C., with Jamieson, J. and Veitch, B. (1998) *The Evaluation of Children's Hearings in Scotland, Volume 1 – Deciding in Children's Interests*. Edinburgh: Scottish Office.

Head, A. (2002) 'The work of the guardian ad litem.' In K. Wilson and A. James (eds) *The Child Protection Handbook*. London: Bailliere Tindall 355–368.

Home Office (1999) *The Prison Population in 1998: A Statistical Review*. Research Findings No. 94. London: Home Office.

Horton, C. (ed) (2005) 'Working With Children 2004–05 Facts, Figures and Information.' *Society Guardian*.

Howe, D., Brandon, M., Hinings, D. and Schofield, G. (1999) *Attachment Theory, Child Maltreatment and Family Support*. Basingstoke: Macmillan Press.

Hughes, D.A. (1998) *Building the Bonds of Attachment*. Northvale, NJ: Jason Aronson, Inc.

Jurkovic, G.J. (1997) *Lost Childhoods – The Plight of the Parentified Child*. New York: Brunner/Mazel, Inc.

Katz, K. (1992) 'Communication Problems in Maltreated Children: A Tutorial.' *Journal of Childhood Communication Disorders 14*, 2, 147–163.

Kempe, C.H., Silverman, F.N., Steele, B.F., Droegemueller, W. and Silver, H.K. (1962) 'The Battered Child Syndrome.' *Journal of the American Medical Association 181*, 17–24.

Kempe, R. and Kempe, C. (1978) *Child Abuse*. London: Fontana.

Kilbrandon, L. (1964) *Children and Young Persons, Scotland,* Cmnd 2306, Edinburgh: Scottish Office, HMSO.

Laming, Lord (2003) *Report of the Victoria Climbié Inquiry* (2003) London: HMSO.

Lockyer, A. and Stone, F. (1998) *Juvenile Justice in Scotland: 25 Years of the Welfare Approach.* Edinburgh: P. & P. Clark.

McDougall, L. (2005) 'Social Work Crisis Leaves Children at Risk.' *Sunday Herald,* 2 October.

Mullender, A. and Morley, R (eds) (1994) *Children Living with Domestic Violence.* London: Whiting and Birch.

National Clearinghouse on Child Abuse and Neglect Information (2003) *Children and Domestic Violence* (at http://nccanch.acf.hhs.gov). Washington, DC: NAIC.

NCH (2003) *Factfile 2002–03. Facts and Figures about Children in the UK.* Glasgow: NCH.

NCH Scotland (2004) *Where's Kilbrandon Now? Reports and Recommendations from the Inquiry Panel.* NCH Scotland.

O'Brien, S. (2003) *Report of the Caleb Ness Inquiry.* Edinburgh and the Lothians Child Protection Committee.

Ondersma, S.J. and Chase, S.K. (2003) 'Substance Abuse and Child Maltreatment Prevention.' *APSAC Advisor 15,* 3, 8–11.

Ondersma, S.J., Simpson, S.M., Brestan, E.V. and Ward, M. (2000) 'Prenatal Drug Exposure and Social Policy: The Search for an Appropriate Response.' *Child Maltreatment 5,* 2, 93–108.

Parton, N. (ed) (1997) *Child Protection and Family Support: Tensions, Contradictions and Possibilities.* London: Routledge.

Parton, N. and Otway, O. (1995) 'The Contemporary State of Child Protection Policy and Practice in England and Wales.' *Children and Youth Service Review 17,* 5/6, 599–617.

Paterson, C.R. (1990) 'Osteogenesis Imperfecta and Other Bone Disorders in the Differential Diagnosis of Unexplained Fractures.' *Journal of the Royal Society of Medicine 83,* 72–74.

Perry, B.D. (2001) 'The neurodevelopmental impact of violence in childhood.' In D. Schetky and E. Benedek (eds) *Textbook of Child and Adolescent Forensic Psychiatry.* Washington, DC: American Psychiatric Press, Inc.

Ramsbotham, D. (2005) The death of Gareth Price Shames us All. *Guardian* (2 February).

Rodning, C., Beckwith, L. and Howard, J. (1991) 'Quality of Attachment and Home Environments in Children Prenatally Exposed to PCP and Cocaine.' *Development and Psychopathology 3,* 351–366.

Rutter, M., O'Connor, T., Beckett, C., Castle, J., Croft, C., Dunn, J., Groothues, C. and Kreppner, J. (2000) 'Recovery and deficit following profound early deprivation.' In P. Selman (ed) *Intercountry Adoption: Developments, Trends and Perspectives.* London: BAAF.

Salter, A.C. (1995) *Transforming Trauma.* Thousand Oaks, CA: Sage Publications.

Scottish Executive (2002) 'It's everyone's job to make sure I'm alright.' Report of the Child Protection Audit and Review. Scottish Executive.

Seigal, D.J. (1999) *The Developing Mind: Towards a Neurobiology of Interpersonal Experience.* New York: Guildford Press.

Shore, R. (1997) *Rethinking the Brain.* New York: Families and Work Institute.

Stevenson, O. (1998) *Neglected Children: Issues and Dilemmas.* Oxford: Blackwell Science.

Stone, F. (1995) 'Children's Hearings: The Second Kilbrandon Child Care Lecture.' Glasgow University, 12 October.

Travis, A. (2005) 'Opinion.' *Guardian* (2 February).

Unicef (2001) *Poverty and Children: Lessons of the 90s for Least Developed Countries.* New York: Unicef.

Waldfogel, J. (2001) *The Future of Child Protection.* Cambridge, MA: Harvard University Press.

Waterhouse, L. and McGhee, J. (2000) *The Evaluation of Children's Hearings in Scotland, Volume 3 – Children in Focus.* Edinburgh: Scottish Executive.

Wedge, P. and Prosser, H. (1973) *Born to Fail?* London: Arrow Books.

7

The Relationship between Youth Justice and Child Welfare in England and Wales

Anthony Bottoms and Vicky Kemp

Introduction

In a recent analytical survey of youth justice in Great Britain, it was argued that 'the differing structural relationship between what used to be called the "criminal" and the "care" jurisdictions [of the juvenile court] is now probably the most profound way in which the systems in England and Scotland diverge' (Bottoms and Dignan 2004, p.124). In this chapter, focusing on the situation in England and Wales,[1] we attempt two tasks. The first is historical: to explain how this Anglo-Scottish divergence came to occur, bearing in mind that in the late 1960s – the time of the genesis of the Scottish Children's Hearings System – there were marked commonalties between official policies in the two jurisdictions. Our second task is more contemporary: to explain how the relationship between the youth justice system and the child welfare system now operates in England and Wales, and how this relationship might be changing in the light of recent policy proposals.

The Children and Young Persons Act 1969

In 1968, the UK Parliament passed the Social Work (Scotland) Act, the founding statute for the new Scottish Children's Hearings System. A year later, though with much more political controversy, the Children and Young Persons Act 1969 was enacted for England and Wales (see Bottoms 1974). At this time, as in Scotland, the youth justice and child welfare systems closely converged in English policy thinking. However, this was for only a brief period, followed by growing separation over the next two decades. As we shall explain, elements of the 1969-enacted policy vision were not implemented, and others were later discarded.

The procedures envisaged by the 1969 Act are most easily understood, in the first instance, in relation to children under 14. Their central feature was the concept of *care proceedings*, a civil procedure that required two separate criteria to be met before the juvenile court could make an order. The first criterion (the 'primary condition') could be met by any of a number of factual situations, if satisfactorily proved; these included parental neglect, the child being beyond control, school truancy, or *the commission of an offence*. The second criterion (the 'care/control test') required the juvenile court to be satisfied that the child was 'in need of care or control which he is unlikely to receive unless the court makes an order' (Section 1(2)).

The 1969 Act provided that, except in cases of homicide, no child under 14 could be subject to a criminal prosecution. A child aged 10 and under 14 who had committed an offence should, instead, be considered for care proceedings, using the offence as the ground for the primary condition.[2] As already noted, however, proving an offence (or any other primary condition) would not, in care proceedings, justify the juvenile court in making an order; the court *also* needed to satisfy itself that the child was in need of compulsory care or control, taking into account his/her own welfare needs. There was therefore a strong resemblance between this system and that enacted in the late 1960s in Scotland (Bottoms 2002, pp.425–433), though with the difference that in England the juvenile court was retained.

In the 1969 Act, the focus on welfare, and the commonality between the 'offence' and 'care' aspects of the work of the juvenile court, was evident not only with regard to procedures, but also for outcomes after successful care proceedings. Thus, in offence-based cases, possible outcomes after such proceedings did not include 'punitive' disposals such as fines. Instead, it was intended that the two main orders would be the supervision order and the care order – and both were available in both offence-based and non-offence-based cases. Again, this was very similar to the Scottish Children's Hearings, whose main disposals then and now involve home supervision and supervision with a requirement to live away from home, applicable to all types of reason for referral. A further similarity was that, in both jurisdictions, the primary role in supervising such cases was to be given to a new unified Local Authority social work agency – in Scotland known as Social Work Departments, and in England as Social Services Departments (SSDs).[3]

A special word is necessary about the care order, since it was to be the subject of much controversy in England in the 1970s and 1980s. The effect of this order was to give the local authority (or, in practice, the SSD) most of the legal powers of a parent over the child in question, so that, even if both natural parents were alive and mentally competent, in law the child's parent became for most purposes the Local Authority. Unless discharged, a care order once made would run until the child's 18th birthday; and once a child was subject to a care order, he or she could be placed by the Local Authority wherever it saw fit. As with a Scottish supervision requirement, therefore, placements under a care order could range widely – from allocation to a residential school to allowing the child to live with his or her natural parents. Under the Children and Young Persons Act 1969 – unlike the previous law in England – the intention was that the care order would in time become the only way in which young offenders, and others coming before the juvenile courts, could be placed in residential institutions. With that goal in mind, quite ambitious plans were developed for reshaping, in a more welfare-orientated direction, the content of programmes in residential institutions run by Local Authorities or voluntary bodies, to be known as 'community homes' (Home Office 1970; Sparks and Hood 1969).

Turning now to older children (aged 14 and under 17), the intention of the 1969 Act was that in this age range those who were alleged to have committed offences would again normally be dealt with in care proceedings, though in restricted categories of cases a criminal prosecution would be possible. After a successful prosecution, the juvenile court could continue to impose one of a range of familiar sentences such as a fine or attendance centre order. In addition, the care order would be available as a disposal following criminal proceedings, as well as after care proceedings. Custodial sentences (served in Prison Service establishments) were initially retained, but the intention was that these should eventually be phased out in favour of care orders and the new welfare-orientated 'community homes'.

Implementation of the 1969 Act

So much for the theory of the 1969 Act. In practice, however, for 20 years after 1969 England had a complex system based on only partial implementation of the Act.

On the 'child welfare' side, the 1969 Act was fully implemented in 1970 (i.e. 'care proceedings' were put in place for all primary conditions except the offence-based condition). By contrast, on the 'crime' side, matters were very different. In 1970 a new Conservative government was elected, which rapidly put the brakes on the gradualist implementation of the Act that had been planned by the previous Labour government. Reflecting the more traditional policy preferences that the Conservative front bench had enunciated in opposition to the 1969 Act during its passage through Parliament, the new government introduced the following changes.

- No order requiring the use of care proceedings in offence-based cases for any age group was issued by the government, nor was there to be any restriction of juvenile prosecutions. Care proceedings in offence-based cases were allowed, if the police wished to use them, but criminal prosecutions were also freely permitted for all age groups over the age of criminal responsibility. In practice, therefore, from 1970 onwards the police virtually never used care proceedings in offence-based cases, instead employing criminal prosecution. Thus, in England from 1970, care proceedings were effectively confined to non-offence cases, though both care and criminal proceedings continued to be dealt with in the same juvenile court.

- The intention to phase out custodial sentences for older juveniles was initially postponed and eventually abandoned.

This emasculation of the 1969 Act had some complex and unintended consequences for the relationship between the 'crime' and the 'care' elements of English youth justice policy.

Care order controversies

The care order became a major target of controversy in England in the years after 1969. There were two main sources of opposition: first, juvenile court magistrates; and, later, some influential voices in academic social science and in the social work profession.

Especially for younger children, the main order that the care order replaced was the 'approved school order', whereby the juvenile court could send a young offender (or a child deemed in need of care and protection) to a reform school for an indeterminate period of up to three years. Significantly, whereas an approved school order made by the court guaranteed an institutional placement, under a care order the Local Authority (in practice the SSD of the authority) had full discretion to decide the child's placement, and was not obliged to remove him or her from home to an institution. Hence, decision-making power in this kind of case shifted to a considerable extent from the juvenile court magistrates to the SSDs.[4] This proved extremely unpopular with magistrates. Claims were made in influential contexts that in some cases magistrates had made a care order intending placement in a residential institution, but then the Local Authority had immediately sent the child home (for various possible reasons, including a deliberate treatment decision or simply the need to wait for a suitable residential placement). Although the data that were available on this matter indicated that cases where the child was sent home were fairly rare, and created little risk of reoffending (see Zander 1975), in political terms such cases were of great importance. In this rather tense atmosphere, it certainly did not help matters that decisions as to a child's placement under the care order were the sole preserve of the new SSDs, whereas juvenile magistrates made it unequivocally clear at this time that they greatly preferred the probation service, with which they were much more familiar as the traditional providers of social work services to juvenile courts.

As a result of these developments, during the 1970s there was a significant decline in the use of care orders in offence-based cases. By contrast, custodial sentences for older juveniles increased, since in the eyes of the courts these guaranteed an institutional placement (see Bottoms 2002, Table 15.4).

Notwithstanding the numerical decline of the care order, research at the end of the 1970s suggested that care orders after criminal proceedings were, in the main, being made on the recommendation of social workers, and that rather than the care order being a remedy of last resort (as had been, in general, the approved school order) not a few recommendations for care orders were being made for first offenders (Giller and Morris 1981). These and similar findings then led to a substantial critique of the welfare assumptions of the 1969 Act from social scientists who espoused a more justice-orientated (or deserts-based) perspective – that is, who believed that court interventions in offence-based cases should above all be proportionate to the severity of the crime and the length of the criminal record (Morris *et al.* 1980; Taylor, Lacey and Bracken 1979). From these and other sources was born the 'juvenile justice movement', to which we now turn.

The 'juvenile justice movement': offence focus and minimum intervention

An important element in the 1969 Act was the concept of 'intermediate treatment' (IT). IT was, from the outset, intended to offer interventions intermediate between residential and ordinary supervision, as a requirement of a supervision order, and hence to act as an 'alternative to custody or care'. However, the term 'intermediate treatment' was also given a wider connotation, not necessarily linked to court orders but having a 'preventive' function. In the early 1980s, it was defined by the then government as available for identified offenders, *and* children at risk of offending, 'including where appropriate those who may be the subject of care proceedings' and available also on both a compulsory and a voluntary basis (see Bottoms *et al.* 1990, Appendix A).

When a comprehensive national survey of IT was undertaken in the mid-1980s (Bottoms *et al.* 1990), it was found to be widespread, and wide-ranging in its scope. However, a strong movement was also under way to redefine it. This movement had much in common with the social-scientific critique of 'welfare'-based decision-making, but it was mounted from within the social work profession, especially by academics at Lancaster University (e.g. Thorpe *et al.* 1980) and like-minded practitioners. They suggested that two negative unintended consequences were occurring as a result of the development of 'preventive IT'. First, 'net-widening' meant that, it was claimed, young people who were only on the fringes of trouble were being drawn into the formal system by welfare-based interventions like IT. Second, 'up-tariffing' was said to occur because courts were inclined to use institutional disposals if and when the preventive welfare-based treatment eventually failed; and, it was argued, the more intrusive the welfare-based intervention, the more likely it was that this would happen, as the court went 'up tariff' in search of an appropriate solution.[5] From beliefs of this kind, three policy consequences were thought to follow: first, preventive IT should no longer be offered; second, only an offence could justify IT interventions; and, third, where an offence had been committed, then the minimum possible intervention on the current occasion should be argued for, in order to avoid future custody or residential care (a policy that was taken as paramount). These became some of the key axioms of the so-called 'juvenile justice movement', which, from an uncertain beginning, rapidly acquired a position of ideological dominance in English youth justice during the 1980s and early 1990s. This movement developed especially in SSDs, thus effectively marginalising the probation service contribution to English youth justice from the mid-1980s onwards.

One celebrated consequence of the 'juvenile justice movement' was to achieve a significant reduction in the use of custodial sentences and care orders in criminal cases in the 1980s (Allen 1991). Another consequence, of more immediate relevance to the present discussion, was to help create among middle managers within SSDs a strong preference for a separation between *offence-based* and *needs-based* interventions. Haines (1996) has provided a good case study of the implementation of this approach in one Local Authority area (Cambridgeshire) circa 1989–91. One key feature of both policy and practice in this county was an attempt to *draw clear organisational boundaries* between the work of the specialist juvenile justice teams and the generic Area Teams within the SSD, illustrated by this extract from an interview with a juvenile justice worker:

> We take a very pure justice approach...I've got a case at the moment...a [post-school age] kid who's got tremendous welfare problems – a mental age of about 10, his mum has kicked him out, he's got no job or money. In a sense he would respond ever so well to [a] Supervision [Order], you could do such a lot of work with that kid on supervision but it wouldn't be about his offending it would be about his social skills, his ability to work, and my recommendation to court is attendance centre.[6] [If that recommendation is accepted] I will make a referral to the Area Team and say will you look at doing something with him [on a voluntary basis]. (Haines 1996, p.108)

Within the same county, however, it was acknowledged by front-line workers that, if they worked with young offenders for any length of time, it could be very difficult to maintain these kinds of boundaries:

> The juvenile justice issues are all in relation to the court issues and [the kids] complying with the Supervision Order. But...if the family has fallen apart at the seams, then you get hauled in to that, going in to try and calm things down because at the end of the day that can backfire onto the Supervision Order and they will get into more trouble... So I think it [maintaining boundaries] is difficult. (Haines 1996, p.109)

It is, of course, not at all surprising that maintaining a strict justice/welfare boundary proved to be very difficult in practice, because criminal careers research has consistently shown that young offenders have a disproportionate incidence of family and social problems (Farrington 2002; Waterhouse *et al.* 2000).

In most local areas, SSD juvenile justice teams retained into the 1990s a separate identity from teams handling child care and protection. This organisational separation was radically different both from the Scottish system (Bottoms 2002) and from the English policy espoused only 20 years earlier in the Children and Young Persons Act 1969.

The Children Act 1989

We briefly pause in the chronological story relating to criminal justice to take a look at a parallel set of developments relating to children in need. Important research on this topic was completed in the early 1980s, which in turn led to a wide-ranging review of child care law, a White Paper and, eventually, the Children Act 1989, which significantly remodelled the whole framework of the law relating to child protection and children in need (Bainham 1990; Eekelaar 2002).

Two features of the Children Act 1989 are of special interest for present purposes. First, the 'care order' was replaced by new provisions. As part of this process, the power to impose such an order (a welfare measure) following criminal proceedings was abandoned (though by 1989 care orders were in any event rarely used in criminal cases). Second, it was decided to separate the long-standing dual crime and care jurisdictions of the juvenile court. Henceforth, care cases were to be dealt with in the 'family proceedings court' (a civil section of the magistrates court). The juvenile court thus became, for the first time since its creation in England in 1908, exclusively a *criminal court*; it was subsequently renamed the 'youth court' and given a higher upper age for initial jurisdiction (18th birthday rather than 17th birthday) in the Criminal Justice Act 1991. Once again, therefore, though for different reasons than in the case of the 'juvenile justice movement', a policy of separation between the child care and juvenile justice systems was being applied in England, in radical contrast to the 1969 policies.

Ironically, these developments happened at a time when recent evidence was available highlighting the close interconnection between care issues and offending. A study by Packman (1986) examined the characteristics of both those admitted to care and those seriously considered for care but not admitted in two towns in the south of England. In over half these 'care and protection' cases both parents and social workers identified significant behaviour issues (mainly delinquency, truancy, runaways, aggressive behaviour and unmanageability/disruptiveness). By contrast, only one policy document was encountered in the two Local Authorities that referred to troublesome behaviour among those being considered for care. In other words, troublesome behaviour was a reality in the care and 'considered for care' populations, but was not acknowledged as such in official thinking. Once again, the cross-over between the kinds of cases dealt with in the parallel English jurisdictions was being demonstrated.

The post-1998 youth justice system

The Labour Party came to power in May 1997, and reform of the English youth justice system was a priority for the new government (Bottoms and Dignan 2004; Gelsthorpe 2002). Proposals for reform were strongly influenced by the Audit Commission's (1996) report *Misspent Youth*, which criticised the youth justice system for being inefficient and ineffective. The report argued that little was being done with the majority of young offenders identified by the police (for example, three-fifths of young offenders apprehended by the police received a caution without intervention, and many court proceedings ended in a discharge). It also suggested that too much money was being spent on procedural matters (for example, repeated court appearances before a final disposal), instead of focusing on effective interventions to reduce future reoffending. Recommendations in the report therefore included the adoption of a more interventionist approach when working with young offenders and better co-operation between youth justice agencies to achieve greater efficiency and effectiveness. Necessarily, the new government's acceptance of this approach entailed a conscious rejection of the formerly influential approach of 'minimum intervention' espoused by the 'juvenile justice movement'.

The centrepiece of the new government's approach to youth justice was the Crime and Disorder Act 1998. An important feature of this was that, for the first time, it set out a 'principal aim of the youth justice system', namely 'to prevent offending by children and young persons' (Section 37) – though since the reference here is to the 'youth justice system', the focus is actually on the prevention of reoffending by persons who have already offended. However, despite the strong research evidence on the extent of family and social problems among young offenders, the government's 1997 White Paper, on which the Act was based (Home Office 1997), made virtually no reference to the child welfare system.

An important feature of the post-1997 reforms is a 'stepwise' or 'progressive' approach to reoffending, sometimes called the 'automaticity principle'. Thus, the old cautioning scheme for young offenders was abolished, and a new system of pre-court reprimands and warnings introduced. Under the new scheme, for a first minor offence a formal reprimand is recorded,[7] while for a second offence (or a first offence that is relatively serious but does not require prosecution) a final warning is given. A feature of final warnings is that the young offender must be referred to the Youth Offending Team (see below), who must consider an intervention, or 'change package', with the expectation that such packages will normally be part of the final warning approach. On the commission of a further offence in the two years after a final warning, the scheme requires the offender to be prosecuted.

On a first appearance in the youth court, a young offender must be given a 'Referral Order', unless the offence is minor or very serious. This involves referral to a separate and more informal panel, the 'Youth Offending Panel', consisting of lay community representatives, and with the victim invited to participate. The expectation is that an 'offending behaviour contract' will be entered into; that is to say, the young offender engages with the panel to construct a tailor-made 'package' to reduce reoffending (see Crawford and Newburn 2003). (The referral order is also intended as a version of 'restorative justice', with an emphasis on young offenders making amends to their victims for the offence committed.) For second and subsequent offences dealt with at court, the offender can be given a community sentence or a custodial sentence. Thus, the *automaticity principle* anticipates that offences by juveniles will, in sequence, trigger particular criminal justice responses; as a consequence, there is limited room for discretionary consideration of welfare needs in taking decisions on individual cases.

In addition to these changes in intervention strategies, the 1998 Act also created a new organisational framework, presided over by the national Youth Justice Board (YJB) and with each Local Authority required to co-ordinate the delivery of youth justice services through the setting up of a local multi-agency Youth Offending Team (YOT). The membership of YOTs must by statute include, at minimum, a police officer, probation officer, social worker, a health authority representative and a person nominated by the education department. (YOTs thus differ significantly from the pre-1998 'juvenile justice teams', which were intra-SSD teams comprised mainly of social workers, though often with seconded probation representatives.) The composition of the YOTs has been deliberately framed to take a wide-ranging view of offending and its prevention, including health and education issues, and this evidently requires some inclusion of both 'justice' and 'welfare' considerations.

Initial evidence on welfare/justice links

While it is clear that the reforms have been effective in encouraging an interventionist approach (Bailey and Williams 2000; Burnett and Appleton 2003; Holdaway *et al.* 2001), the evidence is more patchy on the extent to which welfare issues are addressed by YOTs. Empirical research suggests there was some initial resistance to the reforms by former youth justice workers, but this slowly dissipated. The inclusion within YOTs of representatives from other agencies has come to be accepted, and collaborative work with young offenders is generally positively embraced (Bailey and Williams 2000; Burnett and Appleton 2003; Holdaway *et al.* 2001).

For some commentators (Goldson 2000; Pitts 2001), 'punishment' rather than 'welfare' was intended to be the dominant theme within the youth justice reforms. In carrying out an in-depth study of a YOT, Burnett and Appleton (2003) considered the extent to which punishment was the dominant philosophy. Having reflected on this, their 'overwhelming impression' was that the new legislation had resulted in joined-up services that increased the range of help and opportunities extended to young offenders. In particular, they state that faced with the 'chaotic lives and often desperate social circumstances of their young charges, the provision of a supportive relationship and attention to welfare needs were the assumed essentials of the job' (Burnett and Appleton 2003, p.132). As we have seen, this contrasts sharply with the assumptions of some former juvenile justice teams (Haines 1996).

There remains evidence, however, of sometimes fragmented service delivery across the crime/welfare divide. In 2002, for example, a joint Chief Inspectors' report on the safeguarding of children commented that the work of the YOTs was detached from other services. Furthermore:

> The focus of [YOTs'] work with young offenders was almost exclusively on their offending behaviour, and did not adequately address issues addressing their needs for protection and safeguarding. (Chief Inspectors 2002 para. 8.20)

The Chief Inspectors (2002) also found that in just one area was a YOT represented on the Area Child Protection Committee (ACPC).

In a later inspection HM Chief Inspector of Probation (2004, p.26) indicated that he was surprised 'at the apparent lack of communication between [YOTs and SSDs], with liaison occurring with social services in only 61% of cases of "Looked After Children"'.[8] On a more optimistic note, the Chief Inspector found that, at their best, YOTs were managing the tensions between the youth justice and child welfare agendas successfully.

More recent inspections show that YOTs have improved co-operation (Chief Inspectors 2005; HM Chief Inspector of Probation 2005). They 'now view relationships with their key partners as a strength and have a much higher profile on Area Child Protection Committees' (Chief Inspectors 2005, p.80). These improvements, however, are particularly at a senior level and 'the challenge is to embed this commitment into practice' (Chief Inspectors 2005, p.79).

Not dissimilar concerns have been raised by academics. When reviewing two books dealing with social work assessments, for example, Piper (2004) finds only brief reference to YOTs in one and none at all in the other. She states, 'It is a sad reflection of the separate bureaucracies and professional cultures of the child protection and youth justice systems...that these texts do not make more obvious their relevance to youth justice' (Piper 2004, p.63). Bottoms and Dignan (2004) comment on the paradox that the Crime and Disorder Act 1998 had brought the health and education services within the

YOT framework, in an imaginative multi-agency partnership approach to youth offending, yet there too often seemed to be 'a continuing sharp divide between the activities of the YOTs and the child protection teams' (p.127). The origin of this divide lies in the continuing influence of pre-1997 practices; initially, the 'social work' members of YOTs were, in most local areas, members of former specialist SSD youth justice teams.

A recent Audit Commission (2004) report on youth justice in England found significant variability in the relationship between YOTs and SSDs. According to a 2003 YOT Census, for instance, fewer than 40 per cent of YOTs consider that they are 'always' or 'mostly' able to gain 'timely and appropriate' practical help from SSDs, while 30 per cent said they could do so 'rarely' or 'never' (Audit Commission 2004, p.127). The reasons for this, however, are not simply lack of communication between the agencies, but also the fact that in many areas SSD child protection teams are overstretched, with substantial workloads. In order to improve matters, the Audit Commission (2004) proposed seconding a SSD social worker who deals with child care and protection to the YOT, so that he/she can help to access action in individual cases from the department, just as the police, education and health members of the YOT may already do in appropriate cases.

One of the present authors carried out an observational study of a YOT at a time of transition from the pre-1998 to the present youth justice system (Kemp 2003). Contrasting the approach taken by YOT workers in two criminal cases where there were complex welfare issues involved helps to highlight some of the difficulties in practice where different agencies are dealing with crime and welfare matters.

In the first case, Kelly, a 16-year-old, was referred for her first offence of common assault, the victim being Kelly's assistant care worker, with whom she resided. While Kelly was eligible for an informal action (a reprimand under the post-1998 scheme) her case was referred by the police to the YOT for a 'caution plus' (now a final warning) because there were complex welfare issues involved. The case was managed by a YOT worker who adopted a pure justice approach, seeking to focus solely on the offence, though the victim's reluctance to engage in reparation limited the offence-based work that could be undertaken.

Kelly was, however, keen for the YOT worker to become involved in wider welfare issues, involving the safety of her child, given that Kelly's partner was shortly due to be released from serving a term in prison as a Schedule One sex offender. The YOT worker stressed the need for boundaries between the offence and complex welfare issues (cf. Haines 1996). This meant that her involvement in the welfare issues was limited to making contact with the social worker assigned to Kelly and ascertaining details of the child protection case conference and the social work procedures involved. The YOT worker resisted Kelly's request to attend the case conference and YOT involvement was terminated.

The second case, of Malcolm, a 14-year-old referred for a 'caution plus' (the equivalent of a final warning) for his second offence, provides an interesting contrast to Kelly's case. The offence in this case (theft of a bicycle) was straightforward, because the bike had been returned and the victim did not want to engage with the YOT.

The YOT worker had great difficulty in communicating with Malcolm, whose replies were mainly monosyllabic. Nevertheless, she sought to get involved in the welfare issues, which included concerns over Malcolm's poor physical and mental health and also the possibility of his taking drugs. The worker also offered to talk about a serious sexual assault that Malcolm had experienced, which was the subject of a forthcoming Crown Court trial, but Malcolm declined this offer. The worker did, however, act as an advocate on Malcolm's behalf by engaging with a multidisciplinary network group that was meeting to discuss concerns over Malcolm's health and welfare.[9]

The contrast between these two cases helps to highlight the difficulties, in 'mixed' cases, of deciding on appropriate action from the perspective of a YOT worker. The cases also highlight the fact that the 'stepwise' approach to youth justice, previously discussed, has been formulated with no reference to welfare issues. Thus, had the post-1998 system been in full force, Malcolm would have been prosecuted (because he had already received a 'caution plus' and committed this offence within two years of the earlier disposal), while in Kelly's case – a minor first offence – the formal framework would suggest that a reprimand would have been issued by the police, with no reference to the YOT.

In Kemp's (2003) research, seven out of the twenty unselected pre-court cases observed involved complex welfare issues so these two cases cannot be described as isolated incidents, as other research confirms (Farrington 2002; Waterhouse *et al.* 2000). In real life, therefore, 'offenders' and 'children with welfare needs' are not discrete categories. Where, as in England, there are separate agencies dealing with these issues, tricky cross-agency problems are almost bound to arise.

Children's Trusts: the future?

Recent developments within children's services in England appear to have the potential to bring the justice and welfare systems closer together. In particular, an inquiry into the death of Victoria Climbié (resulting from neglect and abuse while in the care of her great-aunt) found there to be a comprehensive failure in a number of agencies to co-ordinate their services to protect her (Department of Health and the Home Office 2003). The subsequent Children Act 2004 is intended to improve outcomes for children and young people by requiring agencies to work together in order to provide services to safeguard vulnerable children and, more generally, to promote children's well-being through universal preventive services.

Under the 2004 Act, each local authority must set up a Children's Trust. SSDs, education departments and health authorities are *required* to be members of these Trusts; YOTs are one of two other services that *may* be included (Department for Education and Skills 2003). It is intended that all local authorities will have a Children's Trust by 2006, but, in the meantime, 35 Pathfinder Children's Trusts are being evaluated by the University of East Anglia (UEA). As YOTs can decide locally how much, or how little, they are involved in the Children's Trusts it is not surprising that the evaluators found there to be varying degrees of integration at the front line. In July 2004, just six of the thirty-five Pathfinder Children's Trusts formally included YOTs as members of their boards (University of East Anglia 2004).

Informal discussions with government officials and some YOT managers indicate that significant developments have occurred in some areas since July 2004, not only in the Pathfinder areas but also in other areas where Children's Trusts are now being set up. One YOT manager, for example, estimates that around half of Children's Trusts now formally include YOTs.

In response to the report on the Climbié case, the Home Office (2003) set out further proposals for reform of the youth justice system in its so-called *Next Steps* document. The government was criticised by some for producing a separate publication on this topic, which was said to imply that children with social needs were separate from young offenders. *Next Steps*, however, makes it clear that the Home Office expects the youth justice system to continue to be distinct from the child care system. In this way, it claims, the youth justice system can complement more general supportive and preventive work 'by ensuring a particular focus on those who despite all efforts do become offenders in their teens – which damages not only their and their families' interest but also the wider community' (Home Office 2004, p.9). These are in many respects wholly unexceptionable remarks, but they do not necessarily fit all cases well. In the case of Malcolm described above, for example, the government's comments appear to require something of a 'particular focus' on the bicycle theft. At a seminar held in 2004 with very senior police officers, however, Malcolm's case was discussed and a unanimous view expressed that Malcolm's welfare needs, and the need to support him emotionally so that he could give good evidence at the Crown Court trial, were significantly more important than the theft.

The Youth Justice Board has also issued guidance to YOTs in the new context. It states that 'YOTs must not be so embedded within the child welfare system that the confidence, support and contribution of criminal justice agencies and the public is lost' (echoing concerns from the 1970s), but it then goes on to state that, equally, 'YOTs must not be dominated by criminal justice services so that they are too distanced from other children's services and cannot access the services needed to address the risk factors faced by young offenders' (Youth Justice Board 2004, p.6). To ensure that YOTs retain their distinct identity, the guidance states elsewhere that 'if a YOT is located within a Children's Trust, it is essential that it remain a discrete team with a dedicated steering group/ management board and has clear links with the Youth Justice Board and local Crime and Disorder Partnerships' (Youth Justice Board 2004).

The setting up of Children's Trusts appears to provide an important opportunity for establishing a more integrated approach. Separation between the 'family' and 'youth' courts in England means that formal 'justice' and 'welfare' decisions are dealt with in different jurisdictions, yet there appears to be a convergence occurring at the service delivery stage, with some YOTs tending to work in conjunction with welfare services, as appropriate. It is early days in the creation of Children's Trusts, but there seems to be the potential to create a vehicle through which to integrate children's services more closely within a single organisational focus. Within the youth justice system, however, the automaticity principle continues to be dominant, limiting the attention that might be given to any welfare considerations that may arise. How this improved integration will work out in practice, therefore, remains to be seen.

Notes

1. Following the usual convention, throughout this chapter we often use the terms 'England' and 'English' instead of the more technically correct 'England and Wales' or 'English and Welsh'.

2. The age of criminal responsibility remained at ten; below that age, care proceedings using an offence as the primary condition were not permitted.

3. An important difference, however, was that in England the probation service remained separate from the SSDs, whereas in Scotland it was incorporated into the Social Work Departments.

4. By contract, in Scotland the Children's Hearing retains the power to decide whether or not a supervision requirement includes a residential component.

5. Although members of the 'juvenile justice movement' strongly believed in the existence of up-tariffing as a phenomenon, solid empirical evidence supporting this belief was thin on the ground (see Nellis 1987).

6. The reason for this recommendation is the 'minimum intervention' principle, linked to the avoidance of 'up-tariffing'; attendance centres were seen as less intrusive (and hence lower on the tariff) than supervision orders.

7. Previously, some police areas used informal warnings quite extensively; official guidance now strongly recommends that this practice be restricted to 'non-recordable' (i.e. very minor) offences (Home Office 1999).

8. 'Looked After Children' is a statutory term embracing children in the care of the Local Authority and those provided with Local Authority accommodation for special purposes.

9. The main aim of the network group was to try to encourage the SSD child protection team to hold a case conference, but this was resisted, partly because the SSD did not regard Malcolm to be at a high risk of future serious harm and particularly – and ironically – because a number of agencies were already involved in the case.

References

Allen, R. (1991) 'Out of Jail: The Reduction in the Use of Penal Custody for Male Juveniles 1981–88.' *Howard Journal of Criminal Justice 30*, 30–52.

Audit Commission (1996) *Misspent Youth: Young People and Crime.* London: Audit Commission.

Audit Commission (2004) *Youth Justice 2004: A Review of the Reformed Youth Justice System.* London: Audit Commission.

Bailey, R. and Williams, B. (2000) *Inter-agency Partnerships in Youth Justice: Implementing the Crime and Disorder Act 1998.* Sheffield: University of Sheffield Joint Unit for Social Service Research.

Bainham, A. (1990) *Children – The New Law: The Children Act 1989.* Bristol: Jordan & Sons.

Bottoms, A. (1974) 'On the decriminalisation of the English juvenile court.' In R. Hood (ed) *Crime, Criminology and Public Policy.* London: Heinemann.

Bottoms, A. (2002) 'The divergent development of juvenile justice policy and practice in England and Scotland.' In K. Rosenheim, F. Zimring, D. Tanenhaus and B. Dohrn (eds) *A Century of Juvenile Justice.* London: University of Chicago Press.

Bottoms, A. and Dignan, J. (2004) 'Youth Justice in Great Britain.' In M. Tonry and A. Doob (eds) *Youth Crime and Youth Justice: Comparative and Cross-national Perspectives.* London: University of Chicago Press.

Bottoms, A., Brown, P., McWilliams, B., McWilliams, W. and Nellis, M. (1990) *Intermediate Treatment and Juvenile Justice: Key Findings and Implications from a National Survey of Intermediate Treatment Policy and Practice.* London: HMSO.

Burnett, R. and Appleton, C. (2003) *Joined-up Youth Justice.* Lyme Regis: Russell House.

Chief Inspectors, England and Wales (2002) *Safeguarding Children: A Joint Chief Inspectors' Report on Arrangements to Safeguard Children.* (A joint report by the Chief Inspectors of Social Services, Health, Police, Crown Prosecution Service, Magistrates' Courts' Service, Schools, Prisons and Probation.) London: Department of Health.

Chief Inspectors, England and Wales (2005) *Safeguarding Children: The Second Joint Chief Inspectors' Report on Arrangements to Safeguard Children.* (A joint report by the Chief Inspectors of Social Services, Health, Police, Crown Prosecution Service, Magistrates' Courts' Service, Schools, Prisons and Probation.) London: Department of Health.

Crawford, A. and Newburn, T. (2003) *Youth Offending and Restorative Justice.* Cullompton: Willan Publishing.

Department for Education and Skills (2003) *Every Child Matters.* Cm. 5860. London: Department for Education and Skills.

Department of Health and the Home Office (2003) *The Victoria Climbié Inquiry* (The Laming Report). Cm. 5730. London: The Stationery Office.

Eekelaar, J. (2002) 'Child endangerment and child protection in England and Wales.' In K. Rosenheim, F. Zimring, D. Tanenhaus and B. Dohrn (eds) *A Century of Juvenile Justice.* London: University of Chicago Press.

Farrington, D. (2002) 'Developmental criminology and risk-focused prevention.' In M. Maguire, R. Morgan and R. Reiner (eds) *The Oxford Handbook of Criminology* (3rd edn) Oxford: Clarendon Press.

Gelsthorpe, L. (2002) 'Recent changes in youth justice policy in England and Wales.' In I. Weijers and A. Duff (eds) *Punishing Juveniles: Principle and Critique.* Oxford: Hart Publishing.

Giller, H. and Morris, A. (1981) *Care and Discretion: Social Work Decisions with Delinquents.* London: Burnett Books.

Goldson, B. (ed) (2000) *The New Youth Justice.* Lyme Regis: Russell House.

Haines, K. (1996) *Understanding Modern Juvenile Justice.* Aldershot: Avebury.

HM Chief Inspector of Probation (2004) *Joint Inspection of Youth Offending Teams.* London: The Stationery Office.

HM Chief Inspector of Probation (2005) *'From Arrest to Sentence': The Role of YOTs in the Safeguarding of Children.* London: Home Office.

Holdaway, S., Davidson, N., Dignan, J., Hammersley, R., Hine, J. and Marsh, P. (2001) *New Strategies to Address Youth Offending: The National Evaluation of the Pilot Youth Offending Teams.* Home Office Occasional Paper No. 69. London: Home Office.

Home Office (1970) *Care and Treatment in a Planned Environment: A Report on the Community Homes Project.* London: HMSO.

Home Office (1997) *No More Excuses: A New Approach to Tackling Youth Crime in England and Wales.* Cm. 3809. London: HMSO.

Home Office (1999) 'Guide to the Final Warning Scheme.' *Circular 9/1999: Guides to the Crime and Disorder Act 1998.* London: Home Office.

Home Office (2003) *Youth Justice – The Next Steps.* London: Home Office.

Home Office (2004) *Consultation Response to Youth Justice – The Next Steps,* at www.homeoffice.gov.uk/justice/sentencing/youthjustice/indx.html.

Kemp, V. (2003) *Youth Justice Reform: Pre-court Decision-making and Multi-agency Functioning.* Unpublished PhD thesis, University of Cambridge.

Morris, A., Giller, H., Szwed, E. and Geach, H. (1980) *Justice for Children.* London: Macmillan.

Nellis, M. (1987) 'The Myth of Up-tariffing in IT.' *AJJUST: The Journal of the Association of Juvenile Justice 12,* 7–12.

Packman, J. (1986) *Who Needs Care?* Oxford: Basil Blackwell.

Piper, C. (2004) Book review of Calder, M. and Hackett, S. (eds) (2003) *Assessment in Child Care, Using and Developing Frameworks for Practice,* and Walker, S. and Beckett, C. (2003) *Social Work Assessment and Intervention.* In *Youth Justice 4,* 63.

Pitts, J. (2001) *The New Politics of Youth Crime: Discipline or Solidarity.* Basingstoke: Macmillan.

Sparks, R. and Hood, R. (1969) *The Residential Treatment of Disturbed and Delinquent Boys.* Cambridge: University of Cambridge Institute of Criminology.

Taylor, L., Lacey, R. and Bracken, D. (1979) *In Whose Best Interests? The Unjust Treatment of Children in Courts and Institutions.* London: Cobden Trust/MIND.

Thorpe, D., Smith, D., Green, C. and Paley, J. (1980) *Out of Care: The Community support for Juvenile Offenders.* London: Allen & Unwin.

University of East Anglia (2004) *Children's Trusts: Developing Integrated Services for Children in England.* Available at www.everychildmatters.gov.uk/strategy/childrenstrustpathfinders/nationalevaluation.

Waterhouse, L., McGhee, J., Whyte, B., Loucks, N., Kay, H. and Stewart, R. (2000) *The Evaluation of the Children's Hearings in Scotland: Children in Focus.* Edinburgh: Scottish Executive.

Youth Justice Board (2004) *Sustaining the Success: Extending the Guidance.* London: Youth Justice Board.

Zander, M. (1975) 'What Happens to Young Offenders in Care?' *New Society,* 24 July, 185–187.

8

Change, Evidence, Challenges: Youth Justice Developments in Scotland

Bill Whyte

Introduction

Scotland has had a distinctive approach to youth justice for more than 30 years in the shape of its Children's Hearings System, which attempts to integrate measures for protecting children and dealing with their criminal behaviour within a single system. Research evidence on youth crime highlights that many children and young people who become involved in crime are themselves victims of abuse and neglect and in need of protection. This raises serious challenges across jurisdictions about the interplay and overlapping responsibilities between systems of child welfare, protection and youth justice.

Many positives have already come from the Scottish Executive Review of Youth Crime of 2000. These include substantial investment in specialist multidisciplinary staffing and dedicated strategic resources to build the capacity for effective provision within a developing framework of national objectives and service standards. Indeed more has been done in a few years than in the previous decade (Scottish Executive 2000a, 2002b). However, with change come opportunities, risks and challenges.

Youth Justice has become highly politicised in all UK jurisdictions. After 30 years of relative stability in which a significant degree of distinctiveness in the Scottish approach was maintained, some recent proposals for change suggest signs of some convergence in youth justice policy across the UK (Bottoms and Dignan 2004).

Government commitment to reviewing Scotland's system of Children's Hearings in 2004, alongside ongoing changes in youth justice provision, suggests that Scotland may be at a crossroads likely to direct the shape and effectiveness of youth justice for many years to come. The Scottish reviews afford an opportunity to scrutinise rigorously the evidence, principles and values that ought to shape the direction and effectiveness of any youth justice system if the result is to be a more effective and ethical approach to dealing with children and young people who offend. It raises issues relevant to all jurisdictions in attempting to find a balance between welfare and justice for children. These issues, discussed in this chapter set an agenda for all jurisdictions committed to effectiveness in youth justice provision.

Youth justice policy in Scotland

It's a Criminal Waste: Stop Youth Crime Now, Scotland's youth crime review report (Scottish Executive 2000) provided a thorough re-examination of youth justice provision. It concluded that while the principles underpinning the Children's Hearings System were fundamentally sound, practices and the resources to support them had fallen behind the times and that change was overdue. To some extent the detailed findings of Audit Scotland's report (2002) confirmed this conclusion, highlighting inconsistencies in decision-making and resources across the country and expressing concern that two-thirds of financial resources were being used up in legal and administrative processes rather than on direct provision for young people. The Scottish Executive review makes the case that any jurisdiction seriously attempting to bring about positive change in youth crime would require a range of responses, which it categorised under the following headings.

- *Prevention* – to increase effective universal provision for all children and their families to reduce or compensate for conditions that expose children to harmful behaviours of all kinds; with particular attention to drugs- and alcohol-related risks for those below 16 and to school exclusion.

- *Early Intervention* – quick targeted assistance for individual children whose behaviour or family circumstances indicate vulnerability towards offending and other problems.

- *Diversion* – from formal processes (both Hearings and criminal courts) to allow immediate action to address problems and re-equip children and young people for more positive citizenship.

- *Intervention* – only when necessary and at the right time and right level.

- *Participation* – of young people and families; more joint action between voluntary and statutory agencies, communities and the commercial and business sectors to create safer communities, in which individual needs, responsibilities and rights are respected and in which restorative justice features; better information on factors that contribute to youth crime and its reduction.

Policy and practice for persistent offending by young people

The Scottish review highlighted that young people persistent in their offending were being failed by the system. Since 1991 national guidance for criminal justice social work (adult probation services) had recommended the need for special planning for 15–17-year-olds as part of integrated social work planning. The reason for this was that 'experience has shown a tendency for offenders in this category to progress fairly rapidly to custody once they enter the criminal justice system' (Social Work Services Group (SWSG) 1991: General Issues, para. 134).

Little progress was made in this respect throughout the decade. One small study of Social Enquiry Reports (SERs) on young people aged 16 and 17 found that summary criminal courts were seldom alerted either to criminal justice policy supporting diversion from formal prosecution, or to the special legal provision available for this age group. SERs seldom recommended the use of provisions under the legislation permitting summary courts to take the advice of a Children's Hearing or indeed to transfer 'risky' young people back to the Hearings System under Section 44 of the 1995 Act (Johnstone 1995).

In a two-year follow-up study of jointly reported young people – young people reported simultaneously to the adult criminal justice system and to the Children's Hearings System – 46 per cent of these young people had experience of custody by age 18. All had been subject to supervision in the Hearings previously and most were discharged at the recommendation of child care social workers only to reappear in criminal proceedings within a matter of months (Waterhouse *et al.* 2000; Whyte 2004). Hallett *et al.* (1998) identified a degree of ambivalence among Children's Panel members and professionals about dealing within the Hearings System with young people who persistently offend. Young people heavily caught up in crime seemed, in effect, to be transferred out or up to the adult criminal system. Scotland is now the only UK country and one of few in western Europe where young people aged 16 and 17 are routinely dealt with in adult criminal proceedings. Changes are clearly required.

The youth crime review report (Scottish Executive 2000) acknowledged the paradox of this, given research evidence that those most likely to make the transition to the adult court under the age of 18 are also those who are most likely to:

- be immature and impulsive risk-takers
- reoffend on deferred sentence if not given support, to default on fines, to fail to keep appointments for supervised attendance orders and to breach their probation, and to find themselves in custody
- lead chaotic lives that lack constructive home supports
- be at greatest risk of substance abuse and violence
- have been victims of offences themselves
- have had limited education.

(Scottish Executive 2000, Annex C)

The Children's Hearings System was designed specifically to deal with such young people persistent in offending. Despite this, Scotland's First Minister expressed the view in 2003 that the system was designed in the 1970s and is unable to cope with persistent young offenders aged 15–17. Failing to deal effectively with this age group is not the same as being unable to deal with them effectively and it could be argued that practice and service failings have created a self-fulfilling situation. Given the complex difficulties of such young people there is little evidence to suggest that a criminal court, even a specialist youth court, would provide a more effective way of dealing with them without the necessary services available.

Integrated responses

Scotland's youth crime review demonstrated the need for change, and a central factor in this was the insufficient resources allocated to the Hearings System. Equally, however, some routine practices raised serious questions about the expertise and training of staff for maintaining and challenging young people in the community. The review also raised questions about the meaning, in practice, of the statutory duty placing responsibility on the 'whole authority' for children in need under the 1995 Act in respect to children and young people who offend. The role of education, housing, leisure and recreation, cultural and other community services in assisting the most difficult young people in desistance did not seem to feature strongly in the work with young people who offend. The review suggested that the 'whole person' approach is, however, 'no less valid for the 16 or 17 year old offender than it is for the 15 year old' (para. 13) and suggested that there needed to be 'a unified approach at a practical level, combining care and protection with the public's concerns over the need to address offending behaviour' (para. 14).

Changes and challenges in youth justice policy in Scotland

On the basis of the review's recommendations, an ambitious 'Action Programme to Reduce Youth Crime' was announced in 2002 encompassing the following wide-ranging set of aims:

- increasing public confidence in Scotland's youth justice system
- giving victims an appropriate place in the youth justice process
- encouraging all children and young people to thrive
- easing the transition between the youth justice and adult criminal justice systems
- effective early intervention.

The Action Programme made a number of commitments, which we will now examine in fuller detail.

The first target outlined in the Action Programme was that of 'increasing public confidence in Scotland's youth justice system'. There were a variety of aspects to this aim, which was to be realised through:

- the development of a framework of national standards and objectives

- the development of a common information and assessment framework within better integrated children's services

- strengthening the role and work of youth justice teams, and

- improving outcome measurements and evaluation proposals for programme accreditation.

National Standards for Youth Justice Services were introduced in 2002, setting a target of 2006 for full implementation. These stress the importance of delivering youth justice provision within the context of integrated children's services. Each Local Authority has appointed dedicated and specialist staffing, in some case multidisciplinary, and a designated youth justice co-ordinator. Strategic planning groups are active in establishing baseline data through youth crime audits and service mapping exercises. For 'persistence' – five episodes of offending within a six-month period – a structured and standardised assessment (ASSET, Roberts *et al.* 2001; or Youth Level of Service/Case Management Inventory (YLS/CMI), Hoge and Andrews 2002) is required for all young people meeting the criterion.

Other identified priorities in the action programme included violent offenders, female offenders, drug misuse and offending, and the involvement of and support for parents and families with a view to reducing the number of placements in secure accommodation. A National Community Justice Accreditation Panel was established to promote and accredit structured programmes for adult criminal and youth justice provision. These changes, if implemented effectively, will reflect a step-change in youth practice in Scotland.

The second target outlined in the Action Programme concerned the need to 'give victims an appropriate place in the youth justice process'. It sought to achieve this by improving information and services to victims. The 2000 Scottish Crime Survey (Scottish Executive 2000c) showed that young people who admitted to committing offences were themselves more likely to be a victim of crime (65%) than non-offenders (41%). Recent findings from the Edinburgh Study of Youth Transitions confirmed what practitioners see daily

– the strong association between being the victim of crime by age 12 and later offending (Smith *et al.* 2001). A major challenge will be to ensure that services in this area are available to victims including young people who are both victims and offenders.

Substantial investment has been provided to support the extension of restorative justice approaches across Scotland. Restorative justice measures have captured worldwide attention but have been a major omission from Scottish practice. These involve helping children and young people to understand the consequences of their criminal behaviour, to appreciate the harm done and, where possible, to have the positive experience that can be gained from making good the wrong done. It may be thought that this is inconsistent with a welfare-based approach, but knowledge of social and moral development indicates this is in the best interests of the child who offends, as well as the victim. From April 2005, all police cautions to juveniles will take the form of a restorative police caution. This is a meeting facilitated by a trained police officer based around a structured dialogue about the offence and its implications. This change in practice assumes that restorative cautioning is likely be a more effective approach to policing than traditional cautioning, though the evidence is, as yet, inconclusive (Wilcox, Young and Hoyle 2004). Nonetheless there is promising evidence that a sensitive restorative approach can give families an opportunity to take and share responsibility with and for their young people, and to do something positive about offending. Care needs to be taken, however, to ensure that the value of restorative measures is not overstated and that they do not become an end in themselves. Any movement that captures the imagination of the political right and left in Australia, New Zealand, the USA and the UK has to be introduced with a critical mindset. It is important that restorative cautioning by police or other restorative approaches do not result in more young people being drawn unnecessarily into formal systems as a result of political pressure to be seen to be doing something early. In some jurisdictions relatively minor first offences are receiving restorative cautioning without giving families an opportunity to resolve the matter first, with assistance if necessary. This is not only poor restorative practice, it is likely to use scarce resources unnecessarily and runs the risk of net-widening intervening in the lives of young people who are unlikely to reoffend in any case.

Many of the more than 30 studies about the effects of restorative justice examined by Braithwaite (1999) showed reduced offending, and only one revealed an increase. However the evidence of reduced offending, specifically for young people, remains very modest. The Canberra Re-integrative Shaming Experiments (RISE) (Sherman *et al.* 2000) found no difference in offending rates compared to controls when using restorative measures specifically for juvenile property offences and offences against personal victims on the basis of one-year before/after changes. The Indianapolis Restorative Justice Conferencing Experiment (McGarrell *et al.* 2000) replicated a Canberra-type experiment with very minor first offenders under the age of 14. Rearrest rates at 12 months for those who had successfully completed a programme found that only 23.2 per cent had been rearrested at 12 months compared with only 29 per cent for the controls. The results were not statistically significant.

Commentators suggest that when community members are asked to help, plan and become involved in an intervention, they develop a sense of ownership (Graham 1998). Involving the community can also make it easier to obtain resources and volunteers to carry out long-term support. There is very little research on how best to assist neighbourhoods to take constructive responsibility for their difficult young people. Developments through Communities that Care in Scotland and community projects, such as Family Action in Rogerfield and Easterhouse (FARE) in Glasgow, may provide models for the future. A large investment in street wardens is under way in Scotland. In Denmark community safety programmes such as School, Social Agencies and Police (SSP) programmes provide trained street youth workers, not to move young people on, but to engage with them on the streets, to link with their families, to respond to the concerns of local residents and to report to SSP co-ordination groups to assist in the targeting of help and support.

A major challenge facing community safety initiatives in Scotland is to find effective non-criminalising mechanisms to promote neighbourhood safety.

The third target outlined in the Action Programme was concerned with 'encouraging all children and young people to thrive'. This was to be achieved in the following ways:

- linking youth justice strategies more closely with other strategies supporting young people
- developing the role of youth work

- making stronger connections between youth justice and education
- reviewing access to mental health services, and
- enhancing the role of sport, the arts and cultural opportunities in building young people's self-esteem.

These are ambitious and very positive objectives but significant developments in these areas have still to be delivered. It remains to be seen, for example, if the recommendation to have a designated member of school staff take daytime responsibility for the care, welfare and tracking of progress of 'looked after' children will apply equally to young people 'looked after' because of their offending in the same way as to others. Outcomes from the investment of the New Opportunities Fund Active Steps programme (£24 million) are not yet available to show if local authorities took the research findings seriously that sport and physical exercise are unlikely to have a positive impact on youth crime without associated social assistance (Coalter with Allison and Taylor 2000).

Turning now to the fourth target of the Action Programme, 'easing the transition between the youth justice and the adult criminal justice systems', we should note that a major commitment of the Action Programme is to create a more integrated welfare and justice system for 16 and 17 year olds. The government decided to establish a criminal youth court and to drop a previously accepted proposal for a bridging pilot to deal with more young people aged 16 and 17 in the Hearings System. This change in policy was signalled by the growth of populist punitive rhetoric demonising difficult and vulnerable young people. The same kind of political rhetoric has been associated by some commentators with a 'new youth justice' in England and Wales (Goldson 2000) where the commitment to be 'tough on the causes of crime' seems increasingly overshadowed by the imperative to be seen to be 'tough on crime'.

As yet there are no coherent guiding principles or philosophy outlined to direct the youth court process in Scotland, as distinct from an adult court in 'youth's clothing' or one that meets the terms of the Beijing rules to be 'different from adult proceedings' (United Nations 1985). The pilot youth court has the same range of powers of disposal as the adult sheriff summary court, including the power to refer young people to a Children's Hearing. There are some positive modifications to the adult proceedings. These include requiring criminal prosecutors (Procurators Fiscal) to consult with the Children's Reporter to discuss the possibility of diversion from prosecution.

Guidance stresses that no young person should be dealt with by the youth court who could otherwise be dealt with by a Children's Hearing. Disappointingly, the fiscal has no power to refer a young person directly to a Children's Hearing. This is a long-standing anomaly that the now abandoned bridging pilot was intended to resolve. The youth court has dedicated youth court sheriffs and provides continuity of judicial oversight in dealing with issues relating to community supervision; it is subject to regular judicial reviews and has the capacity to take into account additional outstanding charges in a single court hearing; it can also 'fast track' breach procedures. These are all welcome developments, as is the appointment of a youth court co-ordinator to improve multidisciplinary co-operation. In practice the success of this venture may depend on the commitment and skill of the youth court personnel. More significantly, substantial additional resources have been committed to ensure that new and extended supervisory programmes are available as a matter of routine. The main vehicle for community supervision through the youth court is a probation order, which attracts an adult criminal conviction under existing legislation. It is too early yet to comment on the impact of these developments until the evaluations of both fast-track hearings and the youth court are complete.

Scottish Executive policy developments show a determination to improve youth justice. The re-establishment of a youth court may provide a welcome complement to the existing Children's Hearings System and may be a significant improvement on adult criminal courts. If new resources result in more young people being retained in the Hearings System until the age of 18, the role of the youth court should remain limited for this age group. It would be a much more positive step to see youth courts extended to more serious offenders appearing on indictment, and to older youth up to 21 (as in some European countries) rather than to see them extended downwards. Despite a clear policy statement that there is no intention to net-widen, a major challenge for any well-resourced youth court is to ensure it does not, unintentionally, draw young people more readily into its criminal jurisdiction rather than divert them.

Of all the proposed developments in the Action Programme, it is the fifth target, concerned with the promotion of 'effective early intervention', that presents the greatest opportunities, challenges and risks. It was intended from the outset of the Children's Hearings System that entry would be premised on the possibility of early intervention. The legal test for entry is the need for 'compulsory' measures. It is difficult to justify the need for compulsion if no relevant provision has previously been offered or refused; or if young people have not failed to co-operate or comply; or if their situation does not present such high risk that compulsion alone can safeguard others or themselves. Anecdotal evidence suggests that few young people have, in the past, been subject to well-structured and multidisciplinary provision of any sort before being made subject to compulsory measures.

Generally speaking, the practice model on offer in Scotland for many years seems to have been one dominated by diversion without service – in effect, radical non-intervention (Schur 1973). While there continues to be a place for diverting many young people on the assumption that they will simply 'grow out' of crime with minimal intervention, others simply will not. Doing nothing may well be a missed opportunity to provide positive help at an early stage. This, of course, has to be weighed against the unintended consequences of early intervention.

Research on young people who offend has highlighted at least two distinctive groups, identified by Moffitt (1993) as 'adolescent limited' and 'life course persistent' offending. For some young people, personal difficulties combined with early involvement in offending may be a stepping stone on a pathway to more serious, violent and persistent offending (Loeber and Farrington 1998). Studies have suggested that the risk of becoming involved in persistent offending is two to three times higher for a child who starts offending aged under 12 than for a young person whose onset of delinquency is later (McGarrell 2001). However, because children tend not to commit particularly serious or violent offences, and because they usually have not acquired an extended pattern of criminal behaviour, they often receive limited appropriate attention for this behaviour (Snyder and Sickmund 1995). A major challenge is to provide effective, non-stigmatising and age-appropriate interventions. This presents major challenges to Reporters, who act as gatekeepers to formal systems, and to those who decide whether or not compulsion is likely to be required.

Protecting communities

It is the arena of early intervention in particular that has highlighted tensions in current government policy. The evidence of high levels of disadvantage among young people who offend is well established. Labour-led administrations, at UK and Scottish levels, have expressed a commitment to tackling child poverty 'within a generation'. A substantial investment has been made in child poverty measures in what essentially has to be a long-term strategy. In the shorter term, antisocial behaviour is a major concern for communities and needs to be taken seriously. However, in the context of increasingly punitive rhetoric, implementation of the Anti Social Behaviour (Scotland) Act 2004 runs the risk of creating parallel pathways for young people in trouble and of separating early prevention strategies for youth crime from strategies for better integrated social and educational provision for children and families and from any framework of children's rights. This makes provision for antisocial behaviour orders, intensive supervision and monitoring (including electronic tagging) and community reparation orders for young people under 16 years old.

Early interventions relating to antisocial behaviour reflect, for the first time in Scotland, a shift in the political discourse away from the language of children in need and from welfare-orientated strategies towards a language of correctionalism, personal responsibility and punishment that has dominated debates in other jurisdictions. Experience in England suggests that practice responsibilities for early intervention for behavioural difficulties are increasingly being transferred to youth crime professionals outwith a child welfare and child protection framework through parallel legal provisions. To date in Scotland's dual system, criminal pathways are seldom used for under 16s. These new early intervention measures under antisocial behaviour legislation, unless routed through the Reporter and the existing child care system, could create a new range of parallel pathways for children. The introduction of antisocial measures will test the capacity of local authorities to co-ordinate provision and operate in a multisystemic way across the 'whole authority' as required by child care legislation.

Greater political emphasis on the personal responsibility of children and parents has to be matched with service resources and equal leverage on service providers to guarantee the quality of assistance. Local co-ordination is required to ensure that mainstream services are directed by principles of effectiveness and subject to meaningful quality assurance measures. The establishment of strategic planning groups in each local authority and the appointment of youth justice co-ordinators in Scotland are valuable developments intended to assist in this. These issues, more than any, challenge Local Authorities to deliver well-co-ordinated provision to deal with antisocial behaviour effectively within an integrated framework for vulnerable children and families.

Learning from other jurisdictions

There is some promising evidence from England and Wales that early voluntary intervention approaches can be implemented positively. Data from the safety Partnerships in London until March 2003 had produced only 50 Anti-Social Behaviour Orders (ASBOs) and 40 per cent had been breached. However, over 700 voluntary agreements (Acceptable Behaviour Contracts – ABCs) had been put in place, with only 11 per cent broken (Home Office 2005). The facility for voluntary agreements has been available for 25 years under Scottish legislation. The challenge is to make them relevant and effective by ensuring that agreements that are binding on young people and families are equally binding on all parties, including service providers. *A Failure of Justice* (Nacro 2003) presents a cautionary tale from England and Wales. It reports that the custody rate for young people under 15 has risen substantially, in recent years – a 100 per cent rise overall since 1992; a 400 per cent rise for females and an 800 per cent rise for children aged 12–14 – leading to a general condemnation by the UN Committee on the Rights of the Child (Harvey 2002). Nacro makes a direct association between this increase and the punitive rhetoric dominating political discourse. It argues that 'the apparent determination to be seen as tough on youth crime' (p.28) has to some extent been counterproductive, with the result that 'an increasingly punitive environment for all those who offend has been combined with a particularly reduced tolerance for children who break the law' (p.11). The report warns that

> In a period of rapid change…it is sometimes difficult to retain a clear overview…keeping abreast of new initiatives may leave little space for critical reflection…the dynamic of reform may divert attention from specific areas of concern'. (p.28)

In the Scottish context, to spend large amounts of money to see a reduction in minor offences while at the same time failing to halt the progression to custody or secure accommodation of those at risk of serious and persistent offending will, in the long run, provide communities with limited comfort, important though the reduction in minor offending may be. This is emphasised by the fact that early criminalisation and detention of young people is as good an indicator of progression of criminality and the associated harm to future victims as is available. One US review concluded that:

> If there is one clear finding to be gleaned from the research on juvenile justice programming in recent decades, it is that removing youthful offenders from their homes is often not a winning strategy for reducing long-term delinquency. Most juvenile…facilities…suffer very high recidivism rates. Intensive community-based supervision programs typically produce recidivism rates as low or lower than out-of-home placement (at a fraction of the cost), while intensive family-focused or multi-dimensional intervention programs have produced the lowest recidivism rates of all. (Mendel 2000, p.16)

A fundamental challenge for Scottish policy has been refocusing on the issue of youth crime and its reduction. A major challenge for practitioners is to recognise the importance of understanding the nature of crime as a social phenomenon as well as understanding the developmental needs and social characteristics of those who commit it. To fail to address these issues with young people is to fail the young people and the community whose welfare interests in this regard should be mutually inclusive. Models of practice need to adopt an offence focus, when appropriate, without abandoning a focus on the wider and related social and welfare needs of children, young people and their families.

Issues of providing structured assistance within a framework of positive authority and control will always be a major challenge for service providers when working with troubled and troublesome young people. Responses to youth crime equally need to be set within a child protection framework, building on whatever strengths the young person has. Parents who are seen as part of the problem need also to become part of the solution, and partnership and direct work with families, rather than coercion, are likely to be crucial. The responsibility of parents, while important to stress, has to be supported and shared by state agencies.

Conclusions

The developments in youth justice in recent years in Scotland have been significant and have been backed by substantial resources. This kindles optimism that a quality service suited to the twenty-first century and consistent with the principles of the United Nations Convention on the Rights of the Child (CRC) (1989) can be established. They reflect the challenges faced by all jurisdictions.

The landscape is changing fast and it is too early to judge the outcomes of changes and proposed changes. More recent proposals, creating parallel legal processes, whether civil or criminal, have the capacity to increase criminalisation and undermine effectiveness unless they are part of a coherent system of youth justice and child protection. It may be important for the Scottish Parliament to look for inspiration beyond England and North America and towards northern European countries, given the original Scandinavian influence on setting up the Children's Hearings System. In any case, while international comparisons can provide interesting data, they can equally be misleading if set outside their social and cultural context – in particular attitudes to young people, issues of community tolerance and the sense of community responsibility for young people's welfare in general. If Scotland is to borrow ideas from other jurisdictions then it is important to examine the evidence for effectiveness critically to avoid recycling old ideas in new presentations and to avoid abandoning existing philosophies unnecessarily.

Like parents trying to work out how best to raise their children, states wrestle with the question of how best to respond to troubled and troublesome children and young people. While core features vary greatly, systems in western jurisdictions reflect a belief that children and young people should be treated differently from adult offenders and in many circumstances require protection of some sort. Many different models exist; few are completely satisfactory; compromises abound. Most are searching for new and better ways. Few are comfortable with the distinction or separation between justice and welfare, which results in variations in the balance of the shared 'ingredients' of prevention, early intervention, diversion, social treatments, and sanctions or punishments. The manner in which each country has responded cannot be understood in isolation from its historical development, which makes comparisons problematic.

In this regard Scottish policy-makers would do well to heed Donald Dewar's vision for the Scottish Parliament, which was to find 'Scottish solutions to Scottish problems'.

References

Audit Scotland (2002) *Dealing with Offending by Young People.* Edinburgh: Auditor General Accounts Commission.

Bottoms, A. and Dignan, J. (2004) 'Youth justice in Great Britain.' In *Youth Crime and Youth Justice: Comparative and Cross-national Perspectives in Crime and Justice. A Review of Research. Volume 2.* Chicago: University of Chicago.

Braithwaite, J. (1999) 'Restorative justice: assessing optimistic and pessimistic accounts.' In M. Tonry (ed) *Crime and Justice: A Review of Research.* Chicago: University of Chicago Press.

Buist, M. and Whyte, B. (2004) *International Evidence to Scotland's Children's Hearing Review: Decision Making and Services Relating to Children and Young People Involved in Offending.* Edinburgh: Scottish Executive.

Coalter, F. with Allison, M. and Taylor J. (2000) *The Role of Sport in Regenerating Deprived Areas.* Edinburgh: Scottish Executive Central Research Unit.

Francis, J. and Whyte, B. (eds) (2004) *European Youth involved in Public Care and Youth Justice Systems: A Collection of Papers from Three European Symposia.* Edinburgh: University of Edinburgh, at www.ensayouth.cjsw.ac.uk.

Goldson, B. (ed) (2000) *New Youth Justice.* Lyme Regis: Russell House Publishing.

Graham, J. (1998) *Schools, Disruptive Behaviour and Delinquency: A Review of Research.* London: Home Office.

Hallett, C. and Murray, C. with Jamieson, J. and Veitch, B. (1998) *The Evaluation of Children's Hearings in Scotland, Volume 1: Deciding in Children's Interests.* Edinburgh: Scottish Executive Central Research Unit.

Harvey, R. (2002) 'The UK before the UN Committee on the Rights of the Child. *ChildRIGHT 190* October. London: Children's Legal Centre.

Hoge, R.D. and Andrews, D.A. (2002) *The Youth Level of Service/Case Management Inventory Manual and Scoring Key.* Toronto: Multi-Health Systems.

Home Office (2005) *Young People, Crime, and Anti-Social Behaviour.* London: Research and Statistics Directorate.

Jackson, P. (2004) 'Rights and representation in the Scottish Children's Hearing System.' In J. McGhee, M. Mellon and B. Whyte (eds) *Addressing Deeds: Working with Young People who Offend.* London: NCH.

Johnstone, H. (1995) *Interface of the Children's Hearings System and the Criminal Justice System.* Edinburgh: University of Edinburgh (unpublished MSc thesis).

Loeber, R. and Farrington, D. (1998) *Serious and Violent Juvenile Offenders: Risk Factors and Successful Interventions.* Thousand Oaks, CA: Sage.

McGarrell, E. (2001) 'Restorative Justice Conferences as an Early Response to Young Offenders.' *OJJDP Juvenile Justice Bulletin,* August. Washington, DC: US Department of Justice.

McGarrell, E.F., Olivares, K., Crawford, K. and Kroovand, N. (2000) *Returning Justice to the Community: The Indianapolis Juvenile Restorative Justice Experiment.* Indianapolis: Hudson Institute.

Mendel, R. (2000) *Less Hype More Help. Reducing Youth Crime: What Works and What Doesn't?* Washington, DC: American Youth Policy Forum.

Moffitt, T. (1993) 'Adolescent-limited and Life-course-persistent Adolescent Behaviour: A Developmental Taxonomy. *Psychological Review 100,* 674–701.

Muncie, J. (2004) 'Youth justice: globalisation and multi-modal governance.' In T. Newburn and E. Spark (eds) *Criminal Justice and Political Cultures.* Devon: Willan.

Nacro (2003) *A Failure of Justice: Reducing Child Imprisonment.* London: Nacro.

Roberts, C., Baker, K., Jones, S., Merrington, S. *et al.* (2001) *Validity and Reliability of ASSET: Interim Report to the Youth Justice Board.* Oxford: University of Oxford Centre for Criminological Research.

Schur, E. (1973) *Radical Non-intervention: Rethinking the Delinquency Problem.* Englewood Cliffs, NJ: Prentice Hall.

Scottish Executive (2000) *It's a Criminal Waste: Stop Youth Crime Now.* Edinburgh: Scottish Executive.

Scottish Executive (2002a) *Statistical Bulletin: Criminal Proceedings in Scottish Courts, 2001.* Edinburgh: Scottish Executive.

Scottish Executive (2002b) *Scotland's Action Programme to Reduce Youth Crime.* Edinburgh: Scottish Executive.

Scottish Executive (2002c) *The 2000 Scottish Crime Survey: An Overview.* Edinburgh: Scottish Executive Central Research Unit.

Scottish Law Commission (2002) *Report on Age of Criminal Responsibility.* Scottish Law Commission Report No. 185. Edinburgh: The Stationery Office.

Sherman, L.W., Strang, H. and Woods, D. (2000) *Recidivism Patterns in the Canberra Re-integrative Shaming Experiments (RISE).* Australian National University Centre for Restorative Justice.

Smith, D., McVie, S., Woodward, R., Shute, J., Flint, J. and McAra, L. (2001) *Edinburgh Study of Youth Transitions and Crime: Key Findings at Ages 12 and 13.* Edinburgh: University of Edinburgh.

Snyder, H.N. and Sickmund, M. (1995) *Juvenile Offenders and Victims: A National Report.* Pittsburgh, PA: National Center for Juvenile Justice.

SWSG (1991) *National Objectives and Standards for Social Work in the Criminal Justice System.* Edinburgh: Scottish Office.

United Nations (1985) *Standard Minimum Rules for the Administration of Juvenile Justice* [The Beijing Rules]. Geneva: United Nations.

United Nations (1990a) *Guidelines for the Prevention of Juvenile Delinquency* [The Riyadh Guidelines]. Geneva: United Nations.

United Nations (1990b) *Standard Minimum Rules for Non-custodial Measures* [The Tokyo Rules]. Geneva: United Nations.

Waterhouse, L., McGhee, J., Whyte, B., Loucks, N., Kay, H. and Stewart, R. (2000) *The Evaluation of Children's Hearings in Scotland, Volume 3: Children in Focus.* Edinburgh: Scottish Executive Central Research Unit.

Whyte, B. (2004) 'Responding to Youth Crime in Scotland.' *British Journal of Social Work 34*, 395–411.

Wilcox, A., Young R. and Hoyle, C. (2004) 'An Evaluation of the Impact of Restorative Cautioning: Findings from a Reconviction Study.' *Research Findings 255.* London: Home Office.

3

Issues in Evaluation

9

Assessing How Well Systems Work: The Example of Scottish Children's Hearings

Sally Kuenssberg

Introduction

In their book on juvenile justice in Scotland published in 1998, Lockyer and Stone (1998) commented that the changes introduced in the Children (Scotland) Act 1995 had 'a dual potential which will allow the core principles and institutions of the children's hearings system to be either maintained and strengthened or undermined'. Its future, they predicted, would depend 'on what support there continues to be from politicians and the public for the welfare approach to children in trouble'. One important consideration in harnessing support involves evidence about how well the system is working.

The context

Despite demographic, political, economic, social and legislative changes over the last 30 years, affecting all aspects of Scottish life, the fundamental principles and operation of the Hearings System have remained remarkably unchanged since its inception in 1971. However, following the establishment of the Scottish Parliament in 1999, it has like many other institutions been under scrutiny, with major reviews of juvenile offending (Scottish Executive 2000) and child protection (Scottish Executive 2002) and, in 2004, the first phase of a wide-ranging review by the Scottish Executive of the Hearings System itself (Scottish Executive 2004b).

Debates about juvenile justice and welfare have been played out in increasingly strident newspaper headlines, deploring in tones of equal outrage the failure both to punish and to protect children and young people. However paradoxical such newspaper comments appear, the cumulative effect is inevitably to undermine public confidence in the Hearings System, which deals with the children subject to these comments. Add to that a political drift towards a more punitive approach to offending, and there is no doubt that the fundamental principles of the system, including its integrated approach to child protection and youth crime, are under serious challenge.

It must be acknowledged that the Hearings System was slow to recognise the changing political culture that now requires all UK public agencies to be rigorously accountable for the efficiency and effectiveness of the services they provide. There is a general expectation that the activities of all public agencies should be subject to audit and evaluation, often as a condition of ongoing funding. A trend towards central regulation dictates that their performance and service quality are measured against an ever increasing number of standards and targets, which in turn become yardsticks of political success. National standards are being introduced for many areas of activity that affect children's lives, including youth justice, child protection, education, and care services.

This chapter is written from the point of view of an 'insider' with long experience of the Hearings System, but its message was prompted by a stark realisation that if these challenges are to be confronted, there are some hard questions to answer. The most fundamental – and the most difficult – is a perennial and legitimate question that has never been satisfactorily addressed: 'Does the Hearings System work?'

At one time, vague assertions about the distinctive 'Scottishness' of the Hearings System and the benevolent motivation of its welfare ethos might have been sufficient to justify it as 'a good thing'. But over the last decade such uncritical self-satisfaction has been rendered increasingly unacceptable in the face of a series of high-profile child protection inquiries (Scottish Executive 2002), severe pressure on front-line services in some parts of the country, and rising political and public unease about the ability of the current system to address offending.

Much has been written about the difficulties of evaluating public services. Newman (2003) has argued that the 'audit explosion' that took place during the 1980s and early 1990s in an attempt to assess the performance of public and welfare services often undermined confidence rather than the reverse, and 'the increase in regulation, inspection and audit can be viewed as filling the resulting trust vacuum'. Since 1997 the Labour government has continued this trend by extending the regulatory role of government. Whether we like it or not, standards, targets and 'key performance indicators' are the currency of the time and in answering the question 'Does the Hearings System work?' a vague commitment to children's welfare is no longer enough.

This chapter argues that in order to respond to such challenges, the Hearings System must be prepared to adopt means of demonstrating its effectiveness that are more in keeping with prevailing practice. It identifies a number of problems in assessing the effectiveness of such a complex system and then moves on to suggest some possible criteria by which this might reasonably be judged.

Barriers to assessment of the Hearings System's effectiveness

So what evidence do we need in order to judge the Hearings System's effectiveness? It is reasonable to assume that a meaningful assessment would be based, at the minimum, on accurate and timely data, an accumulated body of research, and clear aims and standards against which to measure its achievements. However, deficiencies in each of these categories have up to now created barriers to a comprehensive assessment of the system.

Lack of data

First, there has been a lack of up-to-date integrated information systems to collect comprehensive and speedily available data on which to base analysis. The complexity of the process, with multiple agencies involved at different stages, has made it difficult to collate even the existing data into a coherent picture.

In terms of available data, however, there has been a major step forward since the Scottish Children's Reporter Administration (SCRA) took over national responsibility for producing and publishing annual statistics about the Hearings System. Its electronic case management system should now make it possible to access records, track cases, manage data, analyse referral patterns and identify trends, giving greater potential than ever before to assess and demonstrate what is really happening. An example is the report by

Bradshaw (2005) on young people who persistently offend. Also, there is now widespread acceptance of the need to share the mass of information collected separately by all the different agencies involved in the system, including the police, the SCRA, Crown Office and the Scottish Courts Service, Local Authorities, the National Health Service and the voluntary sector.

An increase in easily accessible data does not, however, come without its own risks – of simply drowning in numbers and not seeing the wood for the trees; of drawing oversimplified conclusions about very complex processes; of confusing short- and long-term time perspectives; of drawing unjustified general conclusions from individual cases; of using statistics selectively to support partisan conclusions; of failing to recognise that figures may reflect demographic, societal or policy changes rather than illustrating the results of intervention by the Hearings System. In addition, despite recent advances in information technology, data protection issues and professional sensitivities still inhibit the sharing of information. There are further risks that pressure on organisations to comply with targets as the benchmarks of their success may actually distort practice. Publishing statistics about complex services will almost inevitably run the risk of misinterpretation by individuals who lack the necessary understanding for informed analysis or may distort the figures to support a biased point of view.

Dearth of research

In addition to the collection of data recording activity, there is obviously a place for the depth and rigour of academic research to provide broader objective analysis. While sporadic studies over the years have focused on discrete aspects of the system, there was until very recently no large-scale systematic approach and their conclusions were rarely drawn together into a comprehensive picture. However, major research studies by a number of Scottish universities have begun to fill this gap – for example, *The Evaluation of the Children's Hearings In Scotland*, published by the Scottish Executive between 1998 and 2000 (Hallett and Hazel 1998; Hallett and Murray 1998; Waterhouse *et al.* 1999) and *The Edinburgh Study of Youth Transitions and Crime*, a wide-ranging longitudinal study co-directed by Professor Smith and Dr McAra of Edinburgh University School of Law, begun in 1998 with the intention of following a single year group of 4300

Edinburgh school pupils from the age of 12 through their teens and twenties (Smith and McAra 1998 onwards).

One obvious problem here is that research takes a long time. Politicians, while genuinely committed to improving the quality of life for children in Scotland, demand quick results to illustrate the effectiveness of their policies, and may be unwilling to await the outcomes of major longitudinal studies or to embrace conclusions that appear at odds with their policies. Murray (1998), who devoted many years to research into the Hearings System, was realistic about its likely impact:

> Through studies designed to illuminate the workings of justice systems it may be possible to achieve greater self-awareness and more thoughtful and effective practice on the part of the lay and professional participants. At the same time we should not harbour any illusions that research-based knowledge will necessarily prevail over emotional convictions and ideological prejudice. (Murray 1998)

Finding appropriate methods to evaluate the effectiveness of complex public services such as the Hearings System is currently the subject of much debate. Despite a laudable desire to evaluate the effectiveness of the system on an objective basis to provide a basis for replicating 'what works', it is not necessarily helpful to transfer the concept of 'evidence-based practice' beyond scientific areas such as clinical practice to other areas of public policy such as justice, social welfare and education. Trinder (in Trinder with Reynolds 2000) has pointed out the risks of 'an overly simplistic and reductionist approach, which fails to do justice to the inherent complexity of practice situations, and may mislead in the search for certainty'. While numerical data will be important, there are limitations in a purely quantitative approach: the selection of outcomes that are measurable at the expense of more qualitative aspects and 'the focus on scientifically defined interventions appears to shift the focus away from the caring, emotional and supportive aspects of professional work' (Trinder with Reynolds 2000). This view is backed up by Hill (1999), who comments that 'theoretical critiques doubt the wisdom of applying a natural science method to complex human interactions'.

Hence, a comprehensive and reliable assessment of the quality of the service and impact of interventions by many different agencies on the complex problems faced by individual children and families within the

Children's Hearings System must be based on a much wider range of approaches, including the reflections of practitioners, the views of service users and judgements by commissioners of the services about such aspects as value for money.

Lack of clear aims

More significant barriers to assessment have been raised, however, by the multiple and often loosely defined aims of the Hearings System, as well as the divergent expectations of the many stakeholders involved. Moreover, intervention via the Children's Hearings System is seeking to influence a range of circumstances and behaviour (including children's care and safety, youth crime, school non-attendance), which are affected by a variety of social pressures. This will inevitably make it very difficult to track the specific results of interventions with certainty.

So what *is* 'the System' actually trying to achieve? In answering this question, it is illuminating to return to its roots in the Kilbrandon Report (Kilbrandon 1964). The members of that Committee were quite clear when proposing their radically new approach to juvenile justice that 'the object must be to effect, so far as this can be achieved by public action, the reduction, and ideally the elimination, of delinquency'. In short, the broadest aim of the system should be to work itself out of a job.

In clearly defining this ambitious general aim, the Committee also proposed that the broad social problem of juvenile offending should be tackled through an individualised approach to changing the behaviour of each child. And in recognising that many offending children were also victims, it also emphasised that its 'preventive' approach could be applied only through considering children and their problems in the context of their life circumstances as a whole. The Committee was wise enough to acknowledge that the kind of 'social education' it was proposing would not be a quick fix but a subtle long-term process requiring continuous assessment and a flexibility of approach to take account of an individual child's changing needs. The final outcome would depend on multiple influences and might not be apparent for many years.

From the beginning, then, judgements about the success of the system would require assessment at two levels: its impact on the life of an individual child and, in aggregate, its success or otherwise in reducing the level of juvenile offending on a national scale. Over the years the situation has become even more complex, with a shift in the balance of the system to an ever increasing percentage of children being referred on care and protection rather than offence grounds. In these circumstances, assessment of the effectiveness of the system becomes more difficult: though it may be possible to evaluate the intervention in terms of reduction of risk to the child, is it fair to attribute success or failure when this will depend on its ability to change the behaviour of the adults over whom the system has no direct control?

Different perspectives

Another difficulty is that the question 'Does the Hearings System work?' automatically begs a further question: 'Work for whom?' Here there are many different perspectives. For the child and family, panel members, the Reporter, social workers and others involved in a case, the primary focus will be on identifying and implementing measures that will address the problems and needs of that individual child. On the other hand, for the police making efforts to arrest and refer offending children, a 'no formal action' decision by the Reporter or discharge by a hearing may be a discouraging indication that the System is a soft option. Professionals responsible for the management of children's cases within Local Authorities, the Crown Office or the courts are likely to focus on *process*, being judged by the demands of a performance culture that looks at activity levels, time targets and the complexities of inter-agency communication rather than outcomes for children. Victims and communities on the receiving end of offending by children and young people are unlikely to admire a system that adopts a welfare rather than a punishment approach and appears to ignore their interests. The system is clearly not working for a shopkeeper who has his window broken for the fifth time in a month. Members of the Scottish Parliament, tired of receiving complaints about the behaviour of 'neds' (a young hooligan, a disruptive adolescent) in their neighbourhoods, may join in the chorus of criticism. 'Society', outraged by reports of the barbaric treatment of children by those responsible for their welfare, naturally seeks a scapegoat within 'the system' that has failed to protect them from harm.

A further barrier to open and objective assessment is that the confidentiality that governs Children's Hearings proceedings (a welcome protection for children and families) means that the only cases reported by the media tend to be those that enter the public domain when something goes wrong. By definition, these are the most extreme cases, which lend themselves to the most sensationalised reporting. The impact of negative reports about this small number of cases thus colours public perception of the Hearings System as a whole.

Views of service users

An indispensable facet in any modern assessment of a public service is feedback from its users, variably described as 'clients', 'customers' or 'consumers'. Unfortunately a genuine desire to involve children and their families in expressing views about their experiences of the Hearings System and how it has worked for them tends to be hampered by the constraints of confidentiality and by their understandable reluctance to engage in dialogue about their experiences of a system in which they were compulsorily involved. Efforts by voluntary organisations have filled some of the gaps here – for example the report by NCH Scotland (2004) on a wide-ranging consultation exercise, which gave prominence to comments by young people on their experiences of the Hearings System.

But this is not enough: it should surely be incumbent upon a system founded on the principle of participation by children and families routinely to seek and take seriously their views about the quality of the service they receive and the effectiveness of the intervention in addressing their problems.

How should we measure the Hearings System's 'success'?

First of all it is essential for any system under scrutiny to develop appropriate criteria by which its performance can be judged. The risk of not doing this is that (as experienced in other parts of the public sector) unsuitable and oversimplistic measurements will simply be imposed, and practitioners will spend time and precious resources counting things that will give very little evidence of the true quality or effectiveness of their work. In face of the varied perspectives already described, it becomes all the more important for the agencies involved in the Hearings System to define collectively and very clearly what it is trying to achieve and to agree some 'key performance indicators' to demonstrate its effectiveness.

A comprehensive evaluation will entail examination of the multifaceted aspects of both the process and the outcomes of the Hearing, including compliance with its underlying principles, the efficiency of complex administrative processes, the performance of both professionals and panel members, the effectiveness of different interventions in addressing the problems of individual children and the success of the System in fulfilling its broad general aims for communities and for Scotland.

Evaluating the process

One consideration in the formal processing of concerns about children is the time taken, since victims of abuse or offences usually want a quick response, while a long gap between offence and response may weaken the connection. In 1997 a multi-agency working group was set up by the Scottish Office to devise ways of reducing delays in the Hearings System (Time Intervals Working Group 1997). It found evidence of delay, duplication and lack of communication between the many agencies involved in the management of children's cases. Over the next three years, after wide consultation, it produced a *Blueprint for the Processing of Children's Hearings Cases* (Scottish Office 1999) containing an inter-agency Code of Practice based on a step-by-step analysis of actions undertaken by all agencies involved, and an integrated series of standards and performance targets designed to provide the Hearings System with a national framework for self-evaluation and continuous improvement. The original 14 standards highlighted particular steps in the process where problems had been identified, and set agreed time targets for the agencies concerned. Data produced from the Scottish Children's Reporter Administration (SCRA) database system described earlier has shown that improvements in overall timescales have occurred since this approach was introduced (SCRA 2005).

In our consumer-orientated society it has become common practice for public agencies to define and publish the standards of service their 'customers' are entitled to expect. One of the most innovative aspects of the Hearings System was the introduction of a distinctive decision-making *process* that, while conforming to legal procedures, also embodied a number of principles and values in keeping with its welfare-based approach to care and justice for children. With the best interests of the child as a paramount principle, the process is designed to be as 'informal' as possible to encourage children and families to participate in reaching decisions. As well as protecting children's rights, it is assumed that such involvement in the process should encourage a positive attitude towards co-operation with the disposal. An important aspect of evaluation of the system, therefore, is to see how far the process lives up to these aims.

First steps have been taken as part of the *Blueprint* programme. Though originally concentrating on the government priority to reduce delay, this was extended to other more qualitative aspects of the service that children and families should have a right to expect, including effective communication, participation, inter-agency co-operation and facilities that meet the needs of all service users. Importantly, it also proposed a system for monitoring compliance with the standards and reporting at Local Authority and national level.

'Performance' by agencies

While assessment of the performance of a single agency against activity targets, professional standards, protocols for practice and budgets is relatively straightforward, this is much harder to achieve in an environment like the Hearings System, which, crucially, depends on joint working among many organisations. As Newman points out:

> the challenge here is that networks are diffuse and complex, with many reporting lines and relationships cutting across each other. The complexity of the emerging relationships produces a lack of transparency that makes it difficult for government, service users or citizens to hold actors to account. (Newman 2003, p.278)

It is also important to recognise that performance indicators appropriate for one agency may be irrelevant or actively unhelpful for another. For example, as the Consultative Group pointed out during the recent Child Protection Review by the Scottish Executive:

> a successful child protection *agency* might be one that generates high levels of child protection referrals while a very successful national child protection *strategy* might reduce overall levels of abuse and neglect and referrals to agencies. (Scottish Executive 2002)

To avoid such confusion it is essential to involve practitioners in attempting at least to align the aims by which they will be judged, though it is important to acknowledge that establishing a totally combined set of objectives may not be possible.

Panel members

While assessment of the performance of professionals within the system will come within the ambit of management, the Hearings process is of course crucially dependent on the availability and competence of its volunteer panel members (see Chapter 11), which may raise further issues. Checks on this are currently provided by the involvement of the local Children's Panel Advisory Committees in the recruitment and monitoring of panel members. In addition, ratification of their appointment depends on satisfactory completion of a nationally approved but locally delivered training programme, and further training is mandatory throughout their period of service.

While these structures provide a built-in quality assurance framework for the panel system, it could be argued that greater emphasis should be placed on the principle of consistency within the national system of juvenile justice, which could lead to the development of a more national approach to the recruitment and training of panel members. Alternatively, it might be maintained that the extent to which the volunteer panel members are 'representative' of their communities and how far the selection process takes account of the current political aims for social inclusion and diversity might be taken as a measure of the system's 'legitimacy' as part of the justice system in Scotland. The current review of the system will provide an opportunity to examine such issues.

Outcomes for the individual child

A separate and urgent need is to develop ways of evaluating the Hearings System in terms of the outcomes it achieves for children. The report mentioned earlier, which prompted attention to time intervals and delays, warned that

> while speed of case processing might be seen as an indicator of how *efficiently* a child has been dealt with, this need not necessarily produce the best outcome …The effectiveness of a child's treatment within the system can only be measured…by an 'outcome' much further down the line that the original 'disposal' by a hearing… Arguably the most important time interval is that between the decision by a hearing of what is best for a child and the achievement of beneficial change in the child's life. (Time Intervals Working Group 1997, Section 2.4)

In this connection it is impossible to overstate the importance of a clear plan approved by the Hearing to define the intended outcomes of any supervision requirement imposed and the steps that will indicate progress towards them.

Unfortunately in recent times, owing to shortages of social work staff and pressures on other services such as health and education, timely and complete implementation cannot be taken for granted. This leads to disillusionment among children and families, panel members and other agencies, and without this most vital link between the process and the outcome, it will be impossible to claim that the system is working either for particular children or in general. The Scottish Executive (2002) has acknowledged the importance of this aspect by proposing that the new Children's Services Inspection System should have responsibility to examine the extent to which Hearings' decisions are implemented.

From an individual point of view, 'successful' intervention by the Hearings System will be when key necessary changes take place: the child stops offending, returns to school or is protected from exposure to a previous risk. The importance of monitoring progress towards this was recognised at the start by the Kilbrandon Committee, which required all cases under an existing supervision requirement to be regularly reviewed by a Hearing to monitor the young person's progress and the impact of the measures put in place. If supervision was to consist of 'preventive' measures based on a child's needs, it advised, 'the application of what is essentially an educational process in this way demands both a flexibility of approach and a continuing oversight and scrutiny of the actual measures being applied' (Kilbrandon 1964, Section 88).

Through the review process the Hearing itself should thus become the initial and arguably the most important monitor of the effectiveness of its own decision.

Effectiveness of 'the System'

For a broader assessment of the System, we also need to look beyond individual cases to assess the results of supervision and the effectiveness of different interventions in children's lives. The data therefore need to expand from simply monitoring activity to collating the outcomes achieved by different kinds of intervention and considering trends. To gain insights into what remedies work, we will need to keep track of repeat offenders and the measures put in place to try to break their cycle of offending, making links where necessary across their transition into the adult criminal justice system. In child protection cases, we need to assess rigorously what measures have effectively supported families in providing the kind of care that reduces risk to their children.

As a control mechanism and to evaluate the 'minimum intervention' approach enshrined in the Children (Scotland) Act 1995, Section 16(3), it would also be instructive to monitor what happens to children who have been diverted from the system by police warning or some kind of non-compulsory measure, though there are ethical questions about maintaining records about children who have not formally been brought within the system.

A good system for Scotland?

In order to judge how well the Hearings System operates nationally we need to be very clear about its overall goals. This would require wide consultation among all stakeholders to agree objectives and desired outcomes. It would seem logical for these to relate to reasons why children are brought into the system in the first place (i.e. the grounds for referral).

Some key questions to ask might include the following.

- Is offending by children and young people reducing?
- What are the risks to children and are they being protected?
- How many children are not attending school?
- What are the outcomes for 'looked after' and accommodated children leaving care?
- What is the incidence of drinking and drug-taking among young people, and what measures are being tried to reduce this?

Data to answer such questions – much of it already collected by individual agencies – could provide a fair and measurable set of indicators to combine into an overall picture by which to judge the system's success.

Compliance with 'softer' aims about how the system safeguards the rights and interests of children could be assessed against the aspirations of the Scottish Executive's 'vision for children' or the Charter for Child Protection (2004a), drawn up by young people themselves.

Public accountability

Another feature of evaluating public services is the obligation on them to account publicly for how they have discharged their responsibilities. In a system as complex as the Children's Hearings System this will take place at several levels. New models of integrated working mean that as well as monitoring achievement of their own internal objectives, agencies are now increasingly being assessed against goals shared by a number of organisations with whom they are working in partnership. Within the Hearings System, this is likely to take place at Local Authority level, possibly within the context of the Children's Services Plan and, at national level, through an annual report by the Scottish Executive drawing together information about how the system is performing as a whole.

There are obvious difficulties in this. Newman describes 'the current shift towards attempting to set goals and targets relating to broad policy outcomes, rather than organizational outputs', but accepts that 'the assessment and evaluation of broad outcomes, rather than organizational outputs, presents a number of challenges that currently remain unresolved'. However, this kind of proactive reporting would help raise the profile of the surprisingly little-known system and increase public awareness of how Scotland deals with its children in trouble.

Greater public understanding might also help to counteract the current blame culture, which, when things go wrong, leads to well-intentioned professionals and volunteers themselves becoming scapegoats for the damage caused by children and young people or done to them as victims of adults. Such an outlook inevitably leads to a general undermining of confidence in the effectiveness of the system.

Conclusions

This chapter has tried to suggest some pointers to how we might overcome barriers, clarify expectations and establish shared criteria to judge the success of the Children's Hearings System, both its processes and the outcomes it achieves for children. This will rely on the development of common systems of data collection and protocols for sharing information, and the combination of different approaches through informed, objective analysis of both quantitative and qualitative data to build up a composite picture. In keeping with modern ideas of accountability, this information should then be reported at individual, local and national level to demonstrate success, identify room for improvement and disseminate good practice.

Despite the many difficulties in this challenging task, it is encouraging to note that one of the key areas explored by the Scottish Executive's current review of the Children's Hearings System was the need to evaluate it. A significant number of respondents to the first phase of consultation felt that the objectives of the System needed to be more focused and explicitly linked to delivering effective outcomes for children, and agreed that there was a need for better evaluation of the impact of interventions on children who have been involved in the System. There was also strong support for giving the Children's Services Inspection System a role in this process. It is to be hoped that these ideas will be further developed in the proposals that emerge in the second phase of the review. Such an approach has the potential to increase the confidence of participants, politicians and public in a system of which Scotland can be justly proud.

References

Bradshaw, P. (2005) *On the Right Track, a Study of Children and Young People in the Fast Track Pilot.* Stirling: SCRA.

Hallett, C. and Hazel, N. (1998) *The Evaluation of the Children's Hearings: The International Context.* Edinburgh: The Scottish Office Central Research Unit.

Hallett, C. and Murray, C. with Jamieson, J. and Veitch, B. (1998) *The Evaluation of Children's Hearings in Scotland: Deciding in Children's Interests.* Edinburgh: The Stationery Office.

Hill, M. (ed) (1999) *Effective Ways of Working with Children and Their Families.* London: Jessica Kingsley Publishers.

Kilbrandon, Lord (1964) *Report of the Committee on Children and Young Persons, Scotland* (Kilbrandon Report), cmnd 2306. HMSO, paras 12, 88.

Lockyer, A. and Stone, F. (1998) *Juvenile Justice in Scotland, Twenty-five Years of the Welfare Approach.* Edinburgh: T&T Clark, 253.

Murray, K. (1998) 'The Contribution of Research'. In A. Lockyer and F. Stone (eds) *Juvenile Justice in Scotland, Twenty-five Years of the Welfare Approach.* Edinburgh: T&T Clark, 225.

NCH Scotland (2004) *Where's Kilbrandon Now?* Edinburgh: NCH.

Newman, A. (2003) *Accountability for Welfare.* In P. Alcock, A. Erskine and M. May (eds) *The Student's Companion to Social Policy.* Oxford: Blackwell Publishing.

Scottish Executive (2000) *It's a Criminal Waste: Stop Youth Crime Now.* Report of the Advisory Group on Youth Crime. Edinburgh: Scottish Executive.

Scottish Executive (2002) *It's Everyone's Job to Make Sure I'm Alright.* Report on Child Protection Audit and Review. Edinburgh: The Stationery Office, Section 7.59.

Scottish Executive (2004a) *Protecting Children and Young People: Charter and Framework for Standards.* Edinburgh: Scottish Executive.

Scottish Executive (2004b) *Getting it Right for Every Child.* Review of the Children's Hearings System, Consultation Document, Section 2, Issues and Questions, 5, and Report, Key Findings, ii.

Scottish Office (1999) *Blueprint for the Processing of Children's Hearings Cases.* Edinburgh: The Stationery Office.

SCRA (2005) *Performance Review 2004–05.* Scottish Children's Reporter Administration.

Smith, D.J. and McAra, L. (directors) (1998 onwards) Longitudinal study: *The Edinburgh Study of Youth Transitions and Crime.* Multiple publications 1998 onwards. Scottish Executive and Nuffield Foundation, at www.law.ed.ac.uk/cls/esytc.

Time Intervals Working Group (1997) *Just in Time.* Report on Time Intervals in Children's Hearings Cases, Section 2.4.1-2. Edinburgh: The Scottish Executive.

Trinder, L. with Reynolds, E. (eds) (2000) *Evidence-based Practice, A Critical Appraisal.* Oxford: Blackwell Science, 218.

Waterhouse, L., McGhee, J., Loucks, N., Whyte, B. and Kay, H. (1999) *The Evaluation of the Children's Hearings System in Scotland: Children in Focus.* Edinburgh: The Scottish Office Central Research Unit.

10

The Scottish Children's Hearings System: Thinking about Effectiveness

Lorraine Waterhouse

Any child welfare and youth justice system needs to be judged so far as possible by evidence about how well it is working and its impact. The Children's Hearings System has come under increasing political scrutiny. How robust is evidence to judge its success or failure? This chapter begins by outlining key features of the Children's Hearings and discussing current political interest in Scotland to reform the system. The nature of evidence required for assessing the Children's Hearings and any system of youth justice and child protection is considered.

Key features of the Children's Hearings System

Most western systems for dealing with children who offend use formal courts and have sought to combine welfare considerations with punishment. On the recommendations of the Kilbrandon Committee (Kilbrandon 1964), children and young people in Scotland were to be dealt with by a tribunal of lay people in a single forum integrating decision-making for two groups of children: children who offend and children in need of care and protection. It was contended that there were more similarities than differences in the lives of these two groups. Offending was seen largely as the result of failures in the upbringing of the child. The utility of punishment was questioned for children who offended (although not ruled out in grave cases) when the underlying circumstances were taken into account.

Over the past 30 years, Children's Hearings have dealt with all cases referred using a similar format and with the same range of disposals (mainly variants of compulsory supervision), with decisions made to promote the child's welfare. Small changes were made in the mid-1990s, but the over-arching commitment to a welfare principle remains.

Over this same period, many western jurisdictions have witnessed an erosion of youth justice systems and the philosophies that underlie them. Sprott (1998) found public concern about the ability of the youth justice system in the province of Ontario (Canada) to accomplish anything beyond imprisonment. Doob and Tonry (2004) compared recent youth justice developments in England, Canada, New Zealand and northern Europe. They identified a move away from the principle of concentrating on the child's welfare to concentrating on the offence, use of punishment measures and treating youths more like adults. By comparison the Children's Hearings System is seen as 'a relatively rare surviving example of a full-fledged, welfare-oriented system, and an assessment of its contemporary functioning is of great theoretical interest' (Bottoms 2002, p.454).

Current political interest to reform the Hearings

Scotland has not been immune to the doubts found elsewhere about a welfare approach. Recent concerns in Scotland are twofold. First, it is feared that undue leniency is exercised by the Children's Hearings System towards young people who offend. Second, politicians have expressed alarm at the harm caused to local communities by the system's apparent failure to prevent reoffending. Their continuing vulnerability is not in question (Wallace and Henderson 2004; Waterhouse et al. 2000).

Some 30 years on, the Children's Hearings System is under threat with the growing politicisation of youth crime in Scotland and the criminalisation of the young, resulting in new 'punitive' measures (Scottish Executive 2002). The Scottish Executive introduced a bill on Anti-Social Behaviour to allow for the implementation of Anti Social Behaviour Orders and electronic tagging for young people under 16. In 2003 a youth court was reintroduced on a pilot basis in one Scottish town (Hamilton) (Scottish Executive 2004). It was established to deal with alleged offenders aged 16 and 17 years (and some

15-year-olds) who met the eligibility conditions, including three separate offence incidents in the previous six months resulting in a criminal charge.

The reintroduction to Scotland of the pilot youth court in Hamilton not only represents a significant shift back towards a court-based system, but also highlights that policy decisions about continuity or change are not based on good evidence. Significant changes in the philosophy and architecture of the Hearings System are being considered, yet there has been patchy and inter-mittent evaluation for most of its existence.

A national voluntary agency instigated a public inquiry (National Children's Homes (NCH) Scotland 2004) into dealing with offending by young persons. The purpose was to gather evidence that might inform political and professional debate on the fitness and relevance of the Children's Hearings System in twenty-first century Scotland. The inquiry could be seen as a counterpoint to formal mechanisms of policy development. The report (published in 2004) identified the need to develop a view about the future of the Children's Hearings System based on evidence rather than apparent public anxiety and shifting attitudes of public opinion about social disorder.

The nature of evidence on the Children's Hearings System

The distinctiveness of the Children's Hearing as a non-court-based system remains just as important now as when the idea first took root. The continuing difference of the Scottish system (at least as it currently stands) offers a natural experiment for carrying out comparative evaluation in the UK and interna-tionally. This is important when account is taken of the fact that some of the most vulnerable children, their families and their communities will bear whatever the social and personal consequences are of policy differences and changes. With these potential costs at stake it might be expected that any policy changes would be predicated on evidence of two kinds: first, what is likely to do the most good and, second, to cause the least harm?

There is rarely a single way of understanding evidence about a complex social and political institution like the Children's Hearings. Interpreting evidence involves bringing multiple levels of information together. Often no single explanation fits all the evidence. This is understandable when so many different factors are involved. For example, Waterhouse and McGhee (2002) in their study of children placed on supervision by a Children's Hearing found that children involved on a compulsory basis were likely to come from more disadvantaged households, poverty and adverse housing conditions compared with those dealt with on a voluntary basis. This echoes the conclusion of Bebbington and Miles (1989) in their study of children admitted to public care in England.

But what does this association mean when the majority of children referred to the Children's Hearings System (like many children referred to discretionary welfare-orientated systems (Bebbington and Miles 1989; Farrington 1996, 1995b; Fergusson, Harwood and Nagin 2000; Packman and Hall 1998)) come from families facing multiple adversities? Virtually all children and young people who come to the attention of the authorities for welfare or offending reasons have a background of disadvantage, but those who are then processed and considered to be in need of compulsory measures of care and protection tend to have an even higher amount of disadvantage.

First, the distinction is between disadvantaged and somewhat less disadvantaged children and not between advantaged and disadvantaged children. Second, it is possible that an association between disadvantage and compulsory interference reflects higher levels of surveillance and regulation of children growing up in the more distressed areas. Third, it could be that children may be in need of compulsory measures of supervision in part at least because they come from the more distressed environments.

The key point is that evidence on so profound a system will not easily be interpreted without painstaking and sustained study. The Children's Hearings System is dependent on other agencies to provide services to children and their families who come before a Hearing and are made subject to compulsory (or voluntary) supervision. The efficacy of decision-making affecting children and young people dealt with has to be disentangled from what happens following decisions reached.

The research base on the Children's Hearings System is not extensive. The main studies have been conducted at very different times. There is no systematic evidence of how the public view the Children's Hearings System. The majority of studies focus on children offending rather than offended against. In effect these two groups of children, normally treated separately in different systems, are also mainly researched separately according to different academic disciplines.

There was in fact a fair amount of very early research about the Children's Hearings, including three key empirical evaluations. Morris and McIsaac

(1978) found that, despite the welfare principle, the offence was of continuing importance as the primary criterion of decisions about intervention. A more comprehensive examination of the workings of the Children's Hearings System in relation to juvenile offenders highlighted a range of influences on decision-making that sought to balance the seriousness of the offences committed against the strengths and weaknesses of the home and school circumstances (Martin, Fox and Murray 1981). This study also found variation in decision-making between and within geographical areas across Scotland.

Two analyses of the occupational backgrounds of the lay people making decisions at Hearings revealed that a great majority had professional or managerial backgrounds, even though they were meant to represent the whole community (Mapstone 1973; Moody 1976). Bruce and Spencer (1976) identified considerable uncertainty in the early operation of the System among these tribunal members as to the extent of their powers. It is interesting to note that, writing in 1976, Bruce and Spencer saw the latent capacity of the Hearing to use its powers to have a child make voluntary restitution.

Asquith (1983) completed the only empirical study to compare aspects of English and Scottish juvenile justice systems. He found greater consensus among Scottish tribunal members than English magistrates on the importance of welfare factors in decision-making.

Lockyer (1988) examined the relationship between social work recommendations to Hearings and the decisions taken, finding widely different policies and practices between different regional localities throughout Scotland.

There have also been some studies of the views of children and families involved with the System (Petch 1988; Willock 1972, 1973). Erickson (1981) reported on interviews with 105 young people aged between 12 and 15 referred to a Hearing on offence grounds. Many young people considered that the process was fair and that the aim of the hearing was to assist them. Adverse reactions from parents was rare (Bruce and Spencer 1976). This has remained a consistent finding in later studies (Hallett *et al.* 1998; Waterhouse *et al.* 2000).

Audit Scotland (2003) completed an influential study looking into the practices of all 32 Scottish councils and eight police forces for dealing with children and young persons who offend. A key finding points to the shortage of voluntary preventive services for children and families, which the Kilbrandon

Committee (Kilbrandon 1964) took as a given. The findings also show that the imposition of compulsory measures of supervision does not guarantee that children and their families will receive social work supervision or other specialist services. Thus the system is not operating as intended, because the provisions necessary to fulfil decisions are often not in place.

Kilbrandon's propositions in the twenty-first century

Although empirical evidence about the functioning of the Hearings has been sparse, the intervening years have yielded considerable amounts of data relevant to the underpinning principles of the Hearings System, derived from the Kilbrandon Report. The first three have stood the test of time, the fourth has not.

The first proposition was that most offending by young people is transitory. This has, in the main, been supported by subsequent research (Hagell and Newburn 1994). Second, youth offending was believed to be rooted in family and community circumstances. Research evidence consistently points to social disadvantage as a risk factor in child delinquency. Prospective longitudinal surveys seeking to identify the developmental origins of juvenile offending suggest a complex interaction of factors. Farrington (1990), in the Cambridge Study in Delinquent Development, concluded that low family income and poor housing were predictive of official and self-reported offending, juvenile and adult. Fergusson et al. (2000), in their study of a New Zealand birth cohort, divided the children into four predictive groups based on their probability of offending from low to high when age was taken into account. They concluded that between-group differences were influenced by the extent to which the individual child was exposed to adverse social, family and individual factors.

A third proposition concerned the irrelevance of legal categorisation for the children according to offence and non-offence referrals, because young people who offended usually also evoked concern about their care or safety (Kilbrandon 1964, para. 13, p.12). This appears to be largely upheld for the majority of children but not all. Analysis of changes in the legal categories of the referral records of 482 children (Waterhouse and McGhee 2004) found two-thirds of them were referred on both offence and non-offence grounds at different times in their contact with the System.

Fourth, it was expected that the relatively small numbers of care and protection cases in the 1960s would continue. In fact there has been a huge rise in non-offence referrals to the Children's Hearings. Over a ten-year period (1989–99) the number of non-offence referrals far more than doubled (167% increase), whereas offence referrals rose by a quarter (26.5%), (Scottish Children's Reporter Administration (SCRA) 2001, Statistical Bulletin no. 24, p.4). A partial explanation for the proportionately significant increase in non-offence referrals may lie in the rudiments of child care policies and practices.

In the last 30 years, child care policy in Scotland, as elsewhere in the UK, has been firmly concentrated on the social problem of child abuse and developing systems for the identification and management of children at risk of physical, sexual or emotional harm. The Department of Health (1995) identified in England and Wales that many of the children who are referred to social services where there are child protection concerns are children in need, only some of whom require formal protective measures. Fiscal restraint since the early 1980s is probably leading to a greater targeting of services to children seen as at risk of abuse. Tunstill (1996) argues that 'children in need' has become the modern filter through which the flow of demand for family support services must pass. She also suggests that this concept will be vulnerable to professional priorities, fiscal constraint and political will (p.156). Identifying child protection concerns was found to be 'the key to unlocking services' (Department of Health 2001, para. 3.39). Similarly in Scotland, the NCH Report (NCH 2004) makes the point that the Hearings have become almost the only route of access to services for children in need of care and protection although, this was not the original intention for the System.

A second reason why the Hearings System has seen a significant increase in non-offence referrals may involve the 'recycling' of children found more widely in child care systems. Gibbons (1995) showed in a study of children placed on child protection registers in England that most of the children (65%) had previously been known to social services and a prior investigation had been undertaken in 45 per cent of the 1888 cases (Department of Health 1995, p.25). Likewise, out of 1155 children referred to the Reporter across Scotland in the first two weeks of February 1995, 822 of them (74%) had a prior history of involvement in the Hearings (Waterhouse and McGhee 2002).

Evaluating success: outputs and outcomes

Doob and Tonry (2004) argue that no agreement has been reached among relatively similar western societies on how best to respond to youth crime. Even when, as in England, policy has a single clear aim to prevent offending by children and young people, it has been difficult to show clearly which overall approaches have been successful. This is even more complex for a system such as the Children's Hearings, which has multiple objectives. The importance of considering the harm and the good done by public policies (intentional or not) is compellingly drawn by Tonry (1995).

The basis for compulsory intervention under the Children's Hearings System is to improve the child's welfare, not only through tackling the immediate reason for referral but by considering the 'underlying unsatisfactory situation' (Asquith and Docherty 1999, p.30). As Asquith (1998b) has argued, an initial test for any discretionary welfare system is what measures of help have been provided, voluntarily or compulsorily. This is the first element on which to evaluate a system. Next must be considered whether the children have benefited as intended. Further assessment must be made of any collateral damage resulting to the children and their families in relation to the protection afforded others. This should include consideration of the potential for net-widening leading to high levels of intervention on welfare grounds, and issues of not harming individual children and young people who are engaged with a system.

Marshalling evidence on providing efficient help and limiting collateral damage to children and their families sets the compass.

Numerically the most likely result for children referred to a Hearing not already under a supervision requirement is the imposition of supervision (72% of boys and 78% of girls) (SCRA 2001). Two-thirds of children under formal supervision live at home. Once on supervision, children should receive help from Local Authority social work services. Both research and audit reports shed light on these. Murray *et al.* (2003), analysing documentary evidence, examined 189 social work case files of children on home supervision. They found that over half (58%) of social work files were unspecific in their aims and objectives for supervision, especially in relation to offending. This is important for defining and gathering evidence about effectiveness because it is impossible to judge the success or otherwise of interventions if the intention is unclear from the outset. It will also restrict the development of mutual understanding of what constitutes progress between children under supervision, their families and social workers.

Audit Scotland (2002) found in a review of 612 case files of children on a supervision requirement that in around 20 per cent of cases children were seen more than twice a month by social workers. Half, however, were seen less than once a month. Shortages of social workers qualified to supervise children was one explanation given for this low frequency of contact. If some children are not seen, some seen rarely and some frequently then the service provided is something of a lottery (Audit Scotland 2002). Evaluation becomes difficult unless these differences are controlled for. Like needs to be compared with like. Differences in outcomes may be an artefact of the amount of contact between child and social worker. Furthermore the information available in the case files was very patchy, limiting the evidence available for making any kind of judgement about progress.

The findings above, taken together, suggest that raising standards in practice and in the resources and professional time available to children and young people on supervision is important for two reasons. First and foremost these would improve services to them and their families. Second, the conditions would be better for gathering meaningful evidence about help provided under the rubric of the Children's Hearings System. The Children's Hearings System itself cannot be evaluated in isolation from the social work, police and other specialist services on which it depends to meet the requirements of supervision.

There are three reasons for paying attention to the harm side of the equation, limiting collateral damage. First, we would never knowingly accept for any child medical intervention that was known to cause more harm than good. This would be a breach of trust and contrary to the principles of all UK child care legislation. Second, if it can be known that the Children's Hearings System is causing no harm then, on a rational basis, those in a hurry for change can legitimately slow down before the System is irreversibly altered. Third, if on the other hand real harms are being caused, reforms should be speeded up.

There is not much evidence to support an assumption that the System is extending social control into normal populations (net-widening) (Bottoms and McWilliams 1979; Bottoms *et al.* 1990; Sutton 1988). Kilbrandon sought to avoid this by diverting children and young people from formal processes where they were unlikely to be necessary. As noted earlier, nearly all children referred come from backgrounds with factors associated with social adversities. The System, therefore, is dealing mainly with children some of whom are less disadvantaged than others rather than drawing a line between advantaged and disadvantaged children.

Diversion from formal processing continues to be a major component of the System. Over a period of a decade there was a sharp increase in the number of 'no action' decisions, from 50 per cent in 1989 to 66 per cent of referrals in 1999/2000 (SCRA 2001, Statistical Bulletin No. 24, Table 9, p.11). Waterhouse and McGhee (2002) similarly found three-fifths of all referrals attracted a 'no action' outcome. They also found that no action probably means just that. Only a small proportion of the children given a 'no action' decision were receiving educational and social work services (6% had learning support, 5% educational psychology and 6% social work).

Offending children were less likely than their non-offending counter-parts to have supervision imposed (53% of non-offenders compared to 45% of offenders, p.6) (Waterhouse and McGhee 2002). National data also show that offence referrals were as likely to result in 'no action' decisions as were non-offence referrals (SCRA 2001, Statistical Bulletin No. 24, Table 9, p.11).

The number of children under 16 years and prosecuted in the criminal court has steadily fallen since 1994 from 246 to 105 in 1999 (Scottish Law Commission 2002, p.20). However, rates of formal processing for 12–15-year-olds who offend have reduced in England and increased in Scotland, especially in the 1990s (Bottoms 2002, p.482). This is the opposite to crime rates, which have increased in England and declined in Scotland. Between 1981 and 1995 recorded crime and survey crime rates in England had risen by over 80 per cent compared with less than 40 per cent in Scotland (see Bottoms 2002, pp.481–484). Bottoms is careful to argue that causal links between these differences and the existence of Children's Hearings cannot be drawn. The trends point to various hypotheses for testing, which include the possibility that a higher rate of processing in Scotland may have a deterrent effect on potential offenders.

Audit Scotland (2002) concluded that it takes on average five and a half months for a child to reach a Hearing and seven and a half to eight and a half months on average to get a court decision on a young person. These delays represent more of a child's life than an adult's. If a child is one year old and waits nearly six months then they have waited half their life. Unless voluntary measures are already in place, delays compromise the preventive principle on which the System was built.

These different sources provide evidence both for and against the Children's Hearings System limiting collateral damage to children, their families and their communities. Of particular importance is the evidence on declining criminal court prosecutions. This factor could be compared with other jurisdictions, taking into account wherever possible different categorisations and processes that may exist. Delays in seeing children may fail to optimise the potential capacity of the System to ward off further harm being done to the child or young person or their causing harm to others. Overly interventionist the System clearly is not. Harm seems most likely to arise in the Children's Hearings System by limited rather than excessive intervention and the consequences of not doing something rather than doing too much.

Observations

It is hardly surprising that the Children's Hearings System is highly complex to evaluate, bridging two separate policy domains dealing with offences of a criminal nature by children and young people and welfare concerns, including offences of a criminal nature against them. Like other youth justice and child welfare systems the Children's Hearings System is also concerned with two types of justice affecting children dealt with by the system: legal justice and social justice. A system predicated on acting in the child's best interests can ignore neither of these concepts in its processes and outcomes.

Goldson (2002, p.690) identifies two competing ideologies when comparing legal/criminal justice and social justice agendas. In the latter, the primary construct is the 'child in need' associated with welfare-orientated approaches in child care and antipoverty policies. In criminal justice 'punitive correctionalism' (Goldson 2002, p.690) has been central to youth justice policies where need is replaced by individual responsibility, reparation and a push towards adulthood. In addition to this thematic independence between the ideologies, they are moving in opposite directions: juvenile justice policy is moving away from a welfare orientation towards retributive justice (McGarrell 1989); child care policy is trying to shift from a narrower concept of child protection towards a child welfare orientation in practice (Spratt and Callan 2004). In child care and child protection there appears to be growing policy support and evidence for the importance (if not yet an established effectiveness) of prevention and family support for vulnerable and distressed children and their families (Thoburn 2002). At the same time, however, the importance of not drawing young children unnecessarily into formal child welfare mechanisms but responding to their need for advice, guidance and family support to foster a child's development appears to be widely accepted. In Scottish law there is a concept of 'minimum intervention', expressed as the 'no order' principle (Sections 11 (70(a) and 16(3) Children (Scotland) Act 1995). In practice the resulting presumption must be that a compulsory measure of supervision should not be made unless it would be better for a child not to have one made.

The Children's Hearings System crosses this policy divide. This makes sense when so many children come from significantly disadvantaged backgrounds and when no clear-cut divide exists in reality between children who commit offences and who have offences committed against them. A division comes about because institutional systems in most western jurisdictions separate responses for these two groups of children. The Crime and Disorder Act 1998 in England and Wales established youth offending teams that are accountable to the Youth Justice Board (YJB) for England and Wales and through it to the Home Office. Since these legislative changes, youth justice has been conceptually and institutionally set apart from local government social services departments and child care provision (Goldson 2004).

There is an urgent need for empirical comparative studies between the Children's Hearings System and alternative models in other jurisdictions before it is too late. Comparative evaluations need to focus on evidence for and against limiting collateral harm as well as the effectiveness of core aspirations. There is a good reason for this. In youth justice policies in most other western jurisdictions the concepts of need and help are being replaced by the concepts of guilt and punishment. When punishment fails, however, there is little recourse other than inflicting progressively harsher punishments and penalties. This in turn increases the risk of bringing further harm into already troubled and disadvantaged lives as a direct consequence of the intervention. Tonry (2004, p.35) concludes that the evidence for the effectiveness of harsher treatment in deterring future offending in adult criminal justice is not supported. Even if the Children's Hearings System were to be found to be no more effective than youth courts in the rates of reconviction, for example, if it causes less harm by providing services rather than responding punitively to children referred then it could be said to be the more effective. Evidence of the least detrimental approach is as important as evidence of effectiveness in a narrower sense.

The Children's Hearings System came about in an era when welfare-orientated systems were more favoured in criminal justice policies. As poverty widens, it is conceivable that youth justice policies and child care policies are both seeking new ways of responding to changing expectations. In child care the threshold for defining need can be raised while still retaining a disposition to a welfare orientation. Referrals to the Children's Hearings System continue to rise but there is a limit to how often compulsory measures of supervision can legitimately be invoked. The Children's Hearings System was never intended as a welfare system on its own despite a welfare-orientated philosophy. It is a welfare-orientated system dealing with children who offend and are offended against. The test is whether compulsory measures of supervision are necessary. The evaluation of its success is inextricably linked with the success of other welfare systems in dealing with the material and social circumstances of children referred.

In looking at evidence on outcomes a distinction can be made between service delivery on the one hand and impact on children and young people individually or collectively, on the other. It cannot be ruled out that children referred to the Children's Hearings System are helped or hindered as a class of people as well as what happens to individual children caught up in the system. Asquith (1998a) makes the point that many of the approaches considered appropriate for children who offend are largely designed to deal with boys. It follows that the impacts on different groups of children, not only males and females but also, for example, children with learning difficulties and children from different ethnic groups need to be taken into account when assessing effectiveness.

The Audit Commission drew attention to the extent to which requirements of the Hearings are carried out by service agencies, mainly social work. This interdependence will be similar in other jurisdictions whereby court orders may be carried to differing extents by service agencies. Measuring outcomes needs to go further than whether or not the children (and their families) received the services they were supposed to. Outcomes need to consider whether these made any difference to concerns that brought the children to the attention of the authorities in the first place, whether this be child protection concerns, offending or school attendance. In other words, outcomes do need to embrace some indication of changes in family circumstances and/or behaviour to be consistent with a system's welfare-orientated philosophy.

Finally, the retention of national annual statistics providing information on broad trends in referral patterns and outcomes is of vital importance. There have been changes in the categories used and the classification of grounds over the years, limiting to some extent comparisons over time. Nevertheless they provide comparatively objective information on the patterns of children's involvement over time, allowing a longitudinal perspective. The longer the system continues, the more important a source of information this thread provides.

More recently the management of statistical data on the Children's Hearings System has undergone further changes, including changes in the categories used. The complexity of the statistical data that is based on referrals rather than on individual children may not have been sufficiently appreciated following the transfer of the database from the Scottish Executive to the Scottish Children's Reporter Administration's Referral Administration Database. There is no one-to-one correspondence between referrals, children and disposals, with offence and non-offence grounds always reported on separate returns. Some questions have arisen over the reliability of the data in recent correspondence between the Scottish Executive and the Reporter Administration. The reliability of the data is critical for evaluating the effectiveness of the System over time, for determining valid trends in referral patterns and disposals, and for evaluating current pilot projects, an example of which was given at the outset of this chapter.

Conclusions

Paradoxically the Kilbrandon Committee (Kilbrandon 1964) appears to have made only limited use of evidence in forming the recommendations that led to the introduction of the Children's Hearings System in Scotland. Instead the emphasis was on the articulation of some core principles, which emanated from doubts about the effectiveness of punishment for dealing with childhood delinquency, the necessity to attribute moral blame and the appropriateness of the state sanctioning the punishment of children. Throughout the Children's Hearings' lifetime, research has had a chequered history, limiting the evidence on which to evaluate their effectiveness. Perhaps there has always been some ambivalence to large-scale investigations of the System lest the findings fail to meet expectations in the two politically sensitive policy areas of juvenile justice and child care and protection. It is remarkable when most other western jurisdictions have increasingly moved towards ideas of crime, responsibility and punishment in their responses to delinquency that the Children's Hearings System has remained relatively steadfast in its commitment to a welfare-orientated approach. The piloting of the Hamilton youth court, while bringing a welcome emphasis on empirical enquiry, marks a major departure from the underlying philosophy of the System and arises in the absence of longitudinal data on outcomes for children and the consequences of disposals in their subsequent histories.

Since its inception much of the relevant research and to some extent policy have been concerned with children and young people who commit offences, especially those who offend persistently. This chapter points to an urgent need to look more closely at children in need of care and protection in the Children's Hearings System. This would reflect more accurately the significant shift in the pattern of referrals towards non-offence-based referrals. It would also capture the distinctive nature of the System integrating decision-making for two groups of children: children who offend and children in need of care and protection.

There is a need to evaluate evidence according to the objectives and principles of the Children's Hearings System. This suggests the importance of evaluating the impact of any services provided to children individually and collectively. The Children's Hearings System itself cannot be evaluated in isolation from the social work, police and other specialist services on which it depends to meet the requirements of supervision. There is also a need to evaluate collateral damage by considering evidence for and against harm caused to children and young people by the Children's Hearings System vs protection of the public from harm caused by the behaviour of children appearing before the System. This in turn should be compared with outcomes associated with other youth justice and child welfare systems. The Children's Hearings System is dealing with a very small percentage of children in the

Scottish population where disproportionate inequality is found in the lives of children referred. This compounds the challenge of disentangling cause and effect when evaluating evidence of providing help.

The Children's Hearings System operates in two publicly and politically contentious areas of policy that, in many other western jurisdictions, involve separate formal systems of youth justice and child care. This is why it is so important that institutional changes in the Children's Hearings System are formulated on the basis of evidence. Changes in one sphere may have consequences for the other. In most other jurisdictions these connections may remain largely invisible. Evidence takes time to mature. Without it, however, there is a serious risk of bringing mischief to a system before there has been time for it to be sufficiently well understood. This is especially important when the Scottish Children's Hearings System is rapidly becoming one of the few remaining welfare-orientated institutions dealing with children and young people in trouble in northern Europe. This serves to make comparison across systems essential for understanding what the Children's Hearings System is trying to achieve. In so doing it is necessary, but not always easy, to stand back and see the System as clearly as evidence permits now and in the future. Time is of the essence.

References

Asquith, S. (1983) *Children and Justice: Decision-making in Children's Hearings and Juvenile Courts.* Edinburgh: Edinburgh University Press.

Asquith, S. (1998a) 'Children's Hearings in an international context.' In A. Lockyer and F.H. Stone (eds) *Juvenile Justice in Scotland.* Edinburgh: T&T Clark.

Asquith, S. (1998b) 'Scotland.' In J. Mehlbye and L. Walgrave (eds) *Confronting Youth in Europe; Juvenile Crime and Juvenile Justice.* Copenhagen: AKF Forlaget.

Asquith, S. and Docherty, M. (1999) 'Preventing offending by children and young people in Scotland.' In P. Duff (ed) *Criminal Justice in Scotland.* Aldershot: Ashgate.

Audit Scotland (2002) *Dealing with Offending by Young People.* Edinburgh: Audit Scotland, at www.audit-scotland.gov.uk.

Audit Scotland (2003) *Dealing with Offending by Young People, A Follow-up Report.* Edinburgh: Audit Scotland, at www.audit-scotland.gov.uk.

Bebbington, A. and Miles, J. (1989) 'The Background of Children who Enter Local Authority Care.' *British Journal of Social Work 19*, 5, 349–368.

Bottoms, A. (2002) 'The divergent development of juvenile justice policy and practice in England and Scotland.' In M.K. Rosenheim, F.K. Zimring, D.S. Tanenhaus and B. Dohrn (eds) *A Century of Juvenile Justice.* Chicago: University of Chicago Press.

Bottoms, A. and McWilliams, W. (1979) 'A Non-treatment Paradigm for Probation Practice.' *British Journal of Social Work 9*, 159–202.

Bruce, N. and Spencer, J. (1976) *Face to Face with Families. A Report on the Children's Panels in Scotland.* Loanhead: Macdonald Publishers.

Department of Health (2001) *The Children Act Report 2000*. London: Department of Health.

Doob, A.N. and Tonry, M. (2004) 'Varieties of youth justice.' In M. Tonry and A.N. Doob (eds) *Youth Crime and Youth Justice: Comparative and Cross–national Perspectives*. Chicago: University of Chicago Press.

Erickson, P.G. (1981) 'The client's perspective.' In F.M. Martin, S.J. Fox and K. Murray (eds) *Children Out Of Court*. Edinburgh: Scottish Academic Press.

Farrington, D.P. and West, D.G. (1990) 'The Cambridge Study in Delinquent Development: a long-term follow-up of 411 London males.' In H.J. Kerner and G. Kaiser (eds) *Criminality, Personality, Behaviour and Life History*. Heidelberg: Springer-Verlag, 115–138.

Fergusson, D.M., Harwood, L.J. and Nagin, D.S. (2000) 'Offending Trajectories in a New Zealand Birth Cohort.' *Criminology 38*, 2, 525–551.

Gibbons, J., Conroy, S. and Bell, C. (1995) *Operating the Child Protection System: A Study of Child Protection Practice in English Local Authorities*. London: HMSO.

Goldson, B. (2002) 'New Labour, Social Justice and Children: Political Calculation and the Deserving–Undeserving Schism.' *British Journal of Social Work 32*, 683–695.

Goldson, B. (2004) 'Differential justice? A critical introduction to youth justice policy in UK jurisdictions.' In J. McGhee, M. Mellon and B. Whyte (eds) *Meeting Needs, Addressing Deeds – Working with Young People who Offend*. Glasgow: NCH Scotland.

Hagell, A. and Newburn, T. (1994) *Persistent Young Offenders*. London: Policy Studies Institute.

Hallett, C. and Murray, C. with Jamieson, J. and Veitch, B. (1998) *The Evaluation of Children's Hearings in Scotland. Vol. 1 Deciding in Children's Interests*. Edinburgh: Scottish Office Central Research Unit.

Kilbrandon, Lord (1964) *Children and Young Persons, Scotland, Cmnd 2306*. Edinburgh: Scottish Office/HMSO.

Lockyer, A. (1988) *Study of Children's Hearings Disposals in Relation to Resources. Children's Panel Chairman's Group*. Edinburgh: Macdonald Lindsay.

Mapstone, E. (1973) 'The Selection of the Children's Panel for the County of Fife.' *British Journal of Social Work 3*, 4.

Martin, F.M., Fox, S.J. and Murray, K. (1981) *Children Out Of Court*. Edinburgh: Scottish Academic Press.

McGarrell, E.F. (1989) 'The Ideological Bases and Functions of Contemporary Juvenile Law Reform: The New York State Experience.' *Contemporary Crises 13*, 163–187.

Moody, S.R. (1976) *Survey of the Background of Current Panel Members*. Edinburgh: Scottish Home and Health Department, Mimeo.

Morris, A. and McIsaac, M. (1978) *Juvenile Justice?* London: Heinemann.

Murray, C., Hallett, C., McMillan, N. and Watson, J. (2003) *Children (Scotland) Act 1995: Home Supervision*. Unpublished report. Stirling: University of Stirling, Department of Applied Social Science.

Murray, K. (1998) 'The contribution of research.' In A. Lockyer and F. Stone (eds) *Juvenile Justice in Scotland: Twenty-five Years of the Welfare Approach*. Edinburgh: T&T Clark.

National Children's Homes (NCH) Scotland (2004) *Where's Kilbrandon Now? Report and Recommendations from the Inquiry*. Glasgow, at www.nch.org.uk/kilbrandonnow.

Packman, J. and Hall, C. (1998) *From Care to Accommodation: Support, Protection and Control in Child Care Services*. London: The Stationery Office.

Petch, A. (1988) 'Answering Back: Parental Perspectives on the Children's Hearings System.' *British Journal of Social Work 18*, 1–24.

Scottish Children's Reporter Administration (SCRA) (2001) *Statistical Bulletin No. 24, Referrals of Children to Reporters and Children's Hearings. 1999/00*. No. SCRA/MJH 2000/24. Stirling: Scottish Children's Reporter Administration.

Scottish Executive (2002) *It's a Criminal Waste: Stop Youth Crime Now. Report of the Advisory Group on Youth Crime*. Edinburgh: Scottish Executive.

Scottish Executive (2004) *The Hamilton Sheriff Youth Court Pilot: The First Six Months.* Research Findings, No. 77, Edinburgh: Scottish Executive.

Spratt, T. and Callan, J. (2004) 'Parents' Views on Social Work Interventions in Child Welfare Cases.' *British Journal of Social Work 34,* 199–224.

Sprott, J.B. (1998) 'Understanding Public Opposition to a Separate Youth Justice System.' *Crime & Delinquency 44,* 3, 399–411.

Sutton, J.R. (1988) *Stubborn Children: Controlling Delinquency in the United States.* Berkeley: University of California Press.

Thoburn, J. (2002) 'Social work with children and families.' In M. Davies (ed) *The Blackwell Companion to Social Work.* Oxford: Blackwell Publishing.

Tonry, M. (1995) *Malign Neglect: Race, Crime and Punishment in America.* New York: Oxford University Press.

Tonry, M. (2004) *Punishment and Politics, Evidence and Emulation in the Making of English Crime Control Policy.* Devon: Willan.

Tunstill, J. (1996) 'Family Support: Past, Present and Future Challenges.' *Child and Family Social Work 1,* 13, 151–158.

Wallace, K. and Henderson, G. (2004) *Social Backgrounds of Children referred to the Reporter: A Pilot Study.* Stirling: Scottish Children's Reporter Administration.

Waterhouse, L. and McGhee, J. (2002) 'Children's Hearings in Scotland: Compulsion and Disadvantage.' *Journal of Social Welfare and Family Law 24,* 279–296.

Waterhouse, L., McGhee, J. and Loucks, N. (2004) 'Disentangling Offenders and Non-offenders in the Scottish Children's Hearings: A Clear Divide?' *Howard Journal of Criminal Justice 43,* 2, 164–179.

Willock, I. (1972) *Inquiry into Parental Involvement in the Work of Children's Hearings.* Dundee: University of Dundee, Mimeo.

Willock, I. (1973) *Dundee Children's Panel Parental Attitudes Survey.* Dundee: University of Dundee, Mimeo.

Further reading

Adler, R. (1985) *Taking Juvenile Justice Seriously.* Edinburgh: Scottish Academic Press.

Bottoms, A. and Dignan, J. (2004) 'Youth Justice in Great Britain.' In *Crime and Justice, A Review of Research 31,* 21–183.

Cowperthwaite, D.J. (1988) *The Emergence of the Scottish Children's Hearings System: An Administrative/Political Study of the Establishment of Novel Arrangements in Scotland for Dealing with Juvenile Offenders.* Southampton: University of Southampton.

Curran, J.H. (1983) 'The Relevance of Research to the Working of the Juvenile Justice System in Scotland.' Paper presented at a Scottish Office Central Research Unit seminar, 24 March.

Dartington Social Research Unit (1995) *Child Protection: Messages from Research.* London: HMSO.

Farmer, E. and Owen, M. (1995) *Child Protection Practice: Private Risks and Public Remedies – Decision-making, Intervention and Outcome.* London: HMSO.

Feld, B.C. (1999) *Bad Kids: Race and the Transformation of the Juvenile Court.* New York: Oxford University Press.

Finlayson, A. (1992) *Reporters to Children's Panels. Their Role, Function and Accountability.* Edinburgh: Social Work Services Group/Scottish Office/HMSO.

Fox, S. (1991) 'Children's Hearings and the International Community.' The Kilbrandon Child Care Lecture. Edinburgh: HMSO.

Garland, D. (2001) *The Culture of Control: Crime and Social Order in Contemporary Society.* Oxford: Oxford University Press.

Graham, J. (1996) 'The organisation and functioning of juvenile justice in England and Wales.' In S. Asquith (ed) *Children and Young People in Conflict with the Law. Research Highlights in Social Work 30*. London: Jessica Kingsley Publishers.

Griffiths, A., Kandel, R.F. and Jay, J. (2000) 'Hearing Children in Children's Hearings.' *Child and Family Law Quarterly 12*, 3.

Hallett, C. and Hazel, N. (1998) *The Evaluation of Children's Hearings in Scotland. Vol. 2. The International Context: Trends in Juvenile Justice and Child Welfare*. Edinburgh: Scottish Office Central Research Unit.

Howarth, C., Kenway, P., Palmer, G. and Miorelli, R. (1999) *Monitoring Poverty and Social Exclusion 1999*. York: Joseph Rowntree Foundation.

Howells, L.A.L., Furnell, J.R.G., Puckering, C. and Harris, J. (1996) 'Children's Experiences of the Children's Hearings System: A Preliminary Study of Anxiety.' *Legal and Criminological Psychology 1*, 233–250.

Kearney, B. (2000) *Children's Hearings and the Sheriff Court*. London: Butterworth.

Kennedy, R. and McIvor, G. (1993) *Young Offenders in the Children's Hearing and Criminal Justice Systems: A Comparative Analysis*. Unpublished report for Tayside Regional Council.

Lockyer, A. and Stone, F.H. (1998) *Juvenile Justice in Scotland. Twenty-five Years of the Welfare Approach*. Edinburgh: T&T Clark.

Martin, F.M. (1983) 'Regions Caesar Never Knew.' *The Hearing: Bulletin of the Panel Training Resource Centre 9*.

Norrie, K.M. (1995) *Greens Annotated Acts. Children (Scotland) Act 1995*. Edinburgh: W. Green/Sweet & Maxwell.

Norrie, K.M. (1997) *Children's Hearings in Scotland*. Edinburgh: W. Green/Sweet & Maxwell.

Pitcairn, T., Waterhouse, L., McGhee, J., Secker, J. and Sullivan, C. (1996) 'Evaluating parenting in child physical abuse.' In L. Waterhouse (ed) *Child Abuse and Child Abusers, Protection and Prevention*. London: Jessica Kingsley Publishers.

Scottish Children's Reporter Administration (SCRA) (2004) *Social Backgrounds of Children Referred to the Reporter: A Pilot Study*. Stirling: Scottish Children's Reported Administration.

Scottish Office (1992a) *The Report of the Inquiry into the Removal of Children from Orkney in February 1991*. Edinburgh: HMSO.

Scottish Office (1992b) *Inquiry into Child Care Policies in Fife*. Edinburgh: HMSO.

Walgrave, L. (1996) 'Restorative juvenile justice: a way to restore justice in western European systems.' In S. Asquith (ed) *Children and Young People in Conflict with the Law. Research Highlights in Social Work 30*. London: Jessica Kingsley Publishers.

Waterhouse, L., McGhee, J., Whyte, W., Loucks, N., Kay, H. and Stewart, R. (2000) *The Evaluation of Children's Hearings in Scotland. Vol. 3 Children in Focus*. Edinburgh: Scottish Executive Central Research Unit.

4

Decision-making and Rights

11

The Place of Lay Participation in Decision-making

Barbara Reid and Ian Gillan

In this chapter we examine the role of lay people in judicial decision-making about children and young people. Our focus in the first section is on the justification of lay decision-making in general and the forms it takes. In the second section we consider the example of lay participation in the Scottish Children's Hearings System, outlining its functions, characteristics and rationale. We evaluate how well the Scottish system meets the requirements of legitimacy established in the first part of the chapter.

Lay participation and decision-making

Making decisions on behalf of the state in relation to children involves the exercise of authority, which needs to be justified in any account of community justice. The forms of authority contained within a judicial system must be held and exercised legitimately. By this, we mean that the legal and quasi-legal mechanisms within a justice system must reflect the moral principles appropriate to such a sphere.

It may be observed in general terms that all justice and welfare systems must give due consideration to the interests of legitimate parties. There is, however, room for diverse views as to who actually are legitimate parties. Whether, for instance, private victims of public offences are parties with an interest in the dispositions (retributive or restorative) is currently subject to review in different jurisdictions. Parents or guardians are a class of authorised actors when they have a legally recognised interest in proceedings. Whether parents and other family members are parties when their children offend is also subject to variation between jurisdictions.

What is clear is that when there has been a breach of public law, the public (or community) must be represented as a party with a legitimate interest in the response to it. Since youth offending and care and protection decision-making must both operate in ways acceptable to the community, to incorporate a lay element into their procedures is one means of achieving this. Detailed analysis of different models of decision-making will enable us to discern in what spheres it is deemed appropriate to include the lay element.

Commonly the state is represented in judicial proceedings through appointed personnel, usually legally trained (e.g. judges, prosecutors, attorneys), sometimes having particular knowledge of children, sometimes not. However, the public interest might equally be represented by members of the general public themselves, or by elected officials or lay appointees. Thus public or community involvement in decisions may be based on the appointment of professionals with appropriate expertise, or on the 'qualification' of representing fellow citizens, whether through democratic election or simply as a result of being an ordinary, 'typical' person. The mode of selection varies and has included elite networking, political appointment and administrative recruitment. In the UK, Justices of the Peace were traditionally appointed on the basis of their social status; while in Scandinavia the inclusion of local politicians has been long established in relation to children (Abraham 1993, p.112).

Lay people, however chosen, can legitimately participate in judicial decision-making, but this may occur at various stages in the process. It is helpful to distinguish roles related to youth offending and care and protection by means of the following fourfold classification.

First, there is a gatekeeper who decides which cases enter the system and which are diverted or not pursued. This role may, for example, be carried out by a public prosecutor (USA), the police, Juvenile Liaison Officers (as in Ireland) or by the Children's Reporter (Scotland) (Bala *et al.* 2002). Second, decisions about the facts of a case, and hence guilt or innocence, are often made by a judge, but in some circumstances a lay jury may decide this, albeit with guidance on the law. Third, dispositional or sentencing decisions are usually made by a judge, either by application of formulaic mandatory sentences or through the exercise of discretion within certain parameters. Such a role is carried out by the German Juvenile Court where a professional judge sits with two lay magistrates (confusingly known as 'jurors') (Cavadino 1996, p.127). In Scotland, Children's Hearings make disposal decisions after a judge (sheriff) decides on the facts if they are disputed. Finally, it is usual to have individuals who advise and assist the court or tribunal, possibly also recording and administering cases. Clerks fulfil such a role in England, as do Children's Reporters in Scotland.

We may ask why judges, juries or panels are authorised to decide at certain stages of the decision-making process as opposed to other possible decision-makers. Indeed, we may further enquire why one 'type' of person does not then decide at all stages of the process. The justification for granting authority to a decision-maker will differ between 'types'. Magistrates, judges and sheriffs are qualified to judge law (and more contentiously to judge the facts) by virtue of their legal expertise. Professional expertise in the law and/or in societal needs may justify empowering Reporters, police officers or prosecutors to refer children into the System. As for lay decision-makers, their authority is justified by virtue of being in one way or another 'representative' of the community. Therefore, lay representatives will be legitimate participants in those aspects of the decision-making process in which we would wish to see the moral priorities of the community reflected. As we will argue, this generates a strong measure of legitimacy for lay decision-making in the disposal of cases.

Drawing on the above observations the next section provides a more detailed analysis of two of the most significant lay decision-makers for our purpose, namely jury members and lay magistrates. This review is guided by three conceptual issues. First, how is the decision-maker selected or 'generated'? The main options are (i) random selection, (ii) popular election, and (iii) political appointment. A further option (iv) is to mix the above – the Scottish Hearings System, for instance, combines open application with executive selection. Second, from what moral perspective is the decision being made? Finally, what is the nature of the judgment required? By scrutinising the different responses to these three questions by particular types of decision-maker we may construct a picture of the decisional model most suitable to judgments concerning offending and care and protection disposals on behalf of children and young people.

The jury

The jury constitutes a common example of members of the public representing the community in a legal context. The concept of the jury is a complex and multifaceted one, however. The understanding of the jury that prevails in one jurisdiction is not necessarily the same as that to which other jurisdictions hold. In addition to their great symbolic significance, different forms of juries have roles founded on a variety of justificatory principles.

The types of judgment made by a jury vary. A distinction is often drawn between the finding of fact by the jury and the finding of law by the judge, but this may be blurred in certain circumstances. It has been suggested that since the eighteenth century enclosures juries have been required to disentangle legal guilt from motive (Cairns and McLeod 2002, p.103). In terms of a strict finding of fact juries would be required to judge that a crime was 'done' or 'not done', rather than find the accused 'guilty' or 'not guilty' (or the case 'not proven' in Scottish law).

In practice, juries have often been required to decide between murder and manslaughter charges, a blurring of the fact/law distinction. Law enters into the equation with the assessment of *mens rea* or 'guilty mind'. This represents the principle whereby people may be found guilty only if it can be demonstrated that they performed an illegal act, which they know or could have known to be wrong. Both technical guilt – you did it – and moral guilt – you knew it was wrong – must be satisfied for the accused to be legally guilty (except in cases of 'strict liability'). This is not a technical judgment but rather a moral and non-expert judgment made within a cultural context or lifeworld. Children below the age of criminal responsibility are assumed to lack the moral capacity to be guilty of crime. Also, juries in England and Wales may be required to assess the level of damages appropriate in libel cases. This is a matter of civil rather than criminal wrong, but does represent another example of a jury being required to exercise discretion in relation to the seriousness of a harmful act. This may bear comparison to role of Scottish panel members making disposals (see below).

With regard to decision-maker selection, random selection is the generative procedure most commonly identified with the citizen jury. In the USA, federal grand and petit juries are selected by lot from a list of registered voters or even the actual voters in the relevant political district (Abraham 1993, p.111); in England and Wales, the juries are initially cited from a list of house-holders supplied by the Local Authority, and appointed to the case by legal officers (Abraham 1993, p.112). There are often additional qualifications that jurors must fulfil, which vary between jurisdictions. The lists exclude certain people (e.g. non-householders) resulting in an element of unrepresenta-tiveness. Further exclusions result from entry criteria (adults only), category exemptions (prisoners, British peers) and individual exemptions (by application in the UK and legal scrutiny in the USA – the 'struck' jury). We may therefore class this process as quasi-random selection, subject to exemption criteria. It could be argued that this is legitimate since what is left is the ethical community whose moral sense we wish to be reflected in the procedures and outcomes of our judicial system. One may, of course, reasonably disagree with the grounds upon which exclusion from juries is justified.

In some other jurisdictions juries are not selected from citizen lists, but are generated through various forms of election or appointment. In Switzerland, juries sitting with the Criminal Chamber of the Federal Tribunal are elected by popular vote for six-year terms, on the basis of one juror per 3000 of the population (Abraham 1993, p.112). By contrast, Swedish juries are appointed for four-year periods by county councils (Abraham 1993, p.112). The justifi-catory basis for an elected or appointed juror as long-term decision-maker is different compared with a lay juror selected at random to make decisions for a temporary period. The moral perspective is not the same either.

The decisions reached by randomly selected juries cannot easily be viewed as making technical or professional judgments; rather they constitute non-expert judgments, arguably reflecting the moral standpoint of the community from which the jurors are chosen. Decisions thus viewed should be based on reasonableness and reflect common-sense community values. Thus the decision is socially embedded. The deliberation required of such juries also lends the decision a dialogical character.

It may be argued that the juror selected at random represents the value-community by being an instance of that community. By definition you can never predict the make-up of a jury chosen by lot. Nevertheless, one may be of the view that 12 (or however many) jurors chosen 'off the street' will more often than not comprise a satisfactory microcosm of the ethical community whose values we wish to see projected in jury decisions. Of course, the jurors may not reason from their own moral perspectives in the collegiate jury context anyway, instead choosing to adopt the moral outlook of the community at large.

Elected jurors, by contrast, have the advantage of an extended period in post during which they become more familiar with the processes involved and more confident in their decision-making. The predisposition to make politically popular judgments, reflecting the priorities of the majority or plurality of a community, may or may not be considered a legitimate aspect of this mode of selection. Juries subject to influences beyond the proceedings, once they are in train, are usually regarded as acting contrary to natural justice.

A similar issue of political partisanship arises for politically appointed jurors. This type is perhaps more problematic from the point of view of community values informing the jury decisions. One may, for example, question the independence of such a jury from the policy objectives of the government that appointed them. A similar concern arises from the political appointment of high or supreme court judges; the antidote to executive interference in judicial decisions is seen to lie in security of tenure. Who does the selection and appointment, and what is the tenure of appointments, are equally issues of importance for the independence of lay decision-makers. Voluntary appointments (in the sense of non-payment for service) may be regarded as a bulwark against untoward influence.

An element of meritocracy is present in appointment systems. This has great significance in terms of the nature of the decision-maker's judgment. The appointing body may wish to populate its juries with individuals notable for some measure of academic ability or knowledge of the judicial process, or who possess a relevant specialism such as training in social work, psychology or criminology, for example. It may be argued that decisions about disposals in care and offending cases cannot reliably be made without some background in the relevant professions such as those suggested above. To make such an assessment it will be helpful to examine one important aspect of the justification of the jury, which is the question of competence.

Historically, juries were not so randomly chosen are they are in the UK and USA today. Some measure of meritocracy was built into the system at various times. In response to concerns that many jurors lacked the mental capacity for carrying out such a responsible role, one-quarter of US states have, at one time or another, used 'blue-ribbon' juries. These required prospective jurors to pass a test to demonstrate their capacity to understand legal concepts and terminology with which they would find themselves presented in the course of a case. Such juries still have not been formally abolished in the United States. The British equivalent, 'struck juries', were abolished in 1971, having been introduced at the King's Bench in 1730 for 'trials of great consequence' (Abraham 1993, p.119). An echo of this is found in present-day debates about abandoning trial by jury for serious fraud trials and other cases involving complicated financial malpractice.[1] It is argued that the average juror would lack the wherewithal to come to an informed judgment, and would merely find him or herself at the mercy of bamboozling advocates.

Following this logic it may be concluded that the very delicate and complicated judgments required in care and protection or even certain offence cases are too difficult to be left to lay volunteers (see Chapter 6). In their place we should install professionals with appropriate training, technical expertise and experience to make authoritative and reliable decisions about the care and treatment of children and young people. This is a critique that must be addressed in order to justify the extensive lay involvement in the Scottish Children's Hearings System. Before explaining how this objection may be met we turn to the other significant example of lay judicial decision-making: the lay magistracy.

Lay magistrates

In the British context, criteria for selecting lay magistrates originally took the form of a fusion of presumptions regarding class and, by extension, competence. The tradition of lay magistrates in England and Wales, and Justices of the Peace in Scotland, descended from the practice of appointing members of the gentry to judicial and quasi-judicial roles on the basis of their hierarchical social privilege and thus their better education. It has been persuasively argued (Jones and Adler 1990, pp.41–52) that the elite social backgrounds from which Scottish Justices of the Peace continue to emerge (essentially thought to be the 'old boys' network'), as well as their extensive legal training and contact with the judiciary, cumulatively serve to render them 'lay' magistrates in name alone.

In the German Juvenile Court, as we have already noted, a professional judge sits with two lay magistrates (or 'jurors'). The role of these lay magistrates is controversial, however, with many German analysts arguing that the decisions of the Juvenile Court should be a matter for professionals alone (Cavadino 1996, p.127).

So what is the justification for the endurance of the lay magistrate's role? We shall scrutinise the concept of the lay magistrate in the light of our three-fold analytical model. In England and Wales, to give one example of the means of selection undergone by lay magistrates, they are 'are appointed by the Secretary of State for Constitutional Affairs and Lord Chancellor on behalf and in the name of the Sovereign'[2] following a written application. Furthermore:

> newly appointed magistrates are required to undergo a programme of training, prescribed by the Lord Chancellor, to help them to understand their duties, to obtain a sufficient knowledge of law and procedure, to acquire a working knowledge of the rules of evidence and to appreciate the nature and purpose of sentencing.

Scottish Justices of the Peace and German lay magistrates undergo very similar processes of selection and training.

The moral perspective and form of decision-making required of lay magistrates in England and Wales are largely indistinguishable from those of 'normal' professional judges and magistrates. The criteria called for by the Department for Constitutional Affairs include the 'ability to think logically, weigh arguments and reach a balanced decision', 'objectivity' and 'the recognition and setting aside of prejudices'. Essentially the lay magistrate is required to mirror the analytic, objective and rational form of decision-making adopted by professional judges. This appears to differ significantly from the communally reasonable form of decision made by a children's panel member in Scotland, for example.

It may be argued, following from these observations, that a lay magistrate's role in any child offending and/or care and protection system must be limited to those areas suited to a professional (or legally trained amateur) adopting a rational impartial perspective applying a universal legal norm. This fits with a conception of the lay element augmenting the professional without embodying a distinctively different perspective. It appears that the lay magistrate may be viewed as someone with a sufficient grounding in the law to judge both questions of fact and disposition in cases of lesser seriousness than those falling to professional judges. At most the lay magistrate might embody an enhanced element of objective disinterestedness, arising from the fact of their giving unpaid public service.

When we consider the nature of care and protection or young offender cases, we might think that satisfactory decisions must pay some regard to popular morality and communal understandings upon issues such as: the extent of culpability associated with age and maturity; the degree of parental responsibility for children's conduct; and what might be deemed an acceptable standard of care, or tolerable household environment. These are judgments with an irreducibly moral element that must be made within the horizon of the value community. Therefore the moral perspective they demand is not simply that of judicial rationality but instead must reflect the common-sense standard of popular reasonableness that lay people bring.

Having delineated the various justifications for lay participation in legal decision-making we will now look in closer detail at the operation of the Scottish Children's Hearings System, representing as it does a decision-making process founded heavily on lay involvement.

Lay decision-making in the Scottish Children's Hearings System

This brief analysis of the Scottish Children's Hearings System will examine how the characteristics of panel member participation within it fits with our general observations about the legitimate role of lay decision-makers. In order to adjudge the appropriateness of the 'division of labour' within the Scottish system we must first describe briefly the roles played by different the decision-makers.

Separation of function

The decision process for a child in need of compulsory supervision begins with referral to the Children's Reporter, who has the 'gatekeeper' function. She or he is a professional with legal training and often a background in other children's services, who judges, first, whether there is prima facie evidence to substantiate one of the legal grounds for referral and, second, whether there is need for compulsory intervention. When the Children's Reporter refers to a Children's Hearing, the case proceeds if the child and parent accept the grounds for referral. However, if the grounds are denied the case is either referred to the sheriff (a Scottish 'judge') for 'proof', or discharged. The proceeding before the sheriff considers only the facts as to whether the grounds are established. If they are, the case is returned to a Children's Hearing for disposal. The sheriff also has a role in considering appeals against Hearings decisions and granting initial warrants to investigate.

When grounds are either accepted or proved, the child and parents are required to participate in a Children's Hearing. The Hearing consists of child, parents (or person in parenting role), three panel members and such others as are deemed 'necessary to the disposal of the case' (this includes a Children's Reporter, who clerks the hearing – normally a social worker – and, less often, family representatives and other relevant parties).

As Lord Hope famously argued 'the genius of the (system) which has earned it so much praise'[3] resides in the separation of the adjudication of facts from the determination of disposition, the former being the proper provenance of a sheriff in the setting of a court and the latter being a matter to be decided at a Children's Hearing by lay people. The original justification of this fundamental separation of function is found in the Kilbrandon Committee Report, which provided the 'philosophy' of the system. It argued that while the formal adversarial process of a court was necessary for the finding of fact, or what it called 'the adjudication of the allegation' (Kilbrandon 1964, para. 52), it was an unnecessary and inappropriate procedure by which 'to consider the measures to be applied'. The latter essentially involved a judgement of what 'measures of education and training were most appropriate to the child's needs', which could best be decided outside 'the rigid framework' of a court, with the participation of parents and children, in 'an atmosphere of full, free and unhurried discussion' (Kilbrandon 1964, paras 73, 109).

The chief virtue of separating proof from disposal is that the latter decision process can be conducted in a relatively informal setting, which facilitates an open discussion between family members, panel members and professionals about what measures are needed. At best the decision will be consensual; at worst, differences will at least have been aired and the views of children and parents listened to.

We should notice in passing that the much vaunted separation is now less clear-cut than Kilbrandon envisaged, as a result of the changes made in the 1995 Children Scotland Act (Section 51), which allow sheriffs on appeal to alter Hearings' disposals. It is widely agreed that this is an unprincipled departure from a proper separation of functions, and that sheriffs should make scant use of this power (Lockyer and Stone 1998).

Selection and representativeness

The Kilbrandon Committee itself did not spell out the case for lay people having the decisive voice in disposal decisions, though it made clear that welfare judgments were not essentially matters of legal expertise. Persons appointed to panels should be those 'with knowledge or experience to consider children's problems' (Kilbrandon 1964, para. 92(a)). However, the White Paper *Social Work and the Community* (HMSO 1966) added to this by viewing panel members as 'representatives of the community'. These slightly different specifications were combined and amplified in the Scottish Office Guidance (Social Work Service Group 1969), which proposed those appointed should 'have knowledge and experience in dealing with children and families and be drawn from a wide range of neighbourhoods, age groups and income groups'. The document also made it clear that the success of the system depended upon finding 'suitable members of the community willing and able to serve on panels in adequate numbers' (para. 76) and this would require reaching people 'who might not have previously thought of themselves as candidates for public service' (Appendix A, para. 1).

Early fears about the lack of possible volunteers proved to be unfounded even though there was an initial underestimate of the numbers required (Cowperthwaite 1988). Recruitment is by open application, which has always produced a surfeit of volunteers, so the composition of authority panels is largely a result of selection carried out by the Children's Panel Advisory Committees (CPACs) or their subcommittees. Each committee sets the criteria needed to meet the needs of its particular panel, but a nationally consistent approach to recruitment and selection is in train. The issue of representation, and how this is to be balanced against the attributes and skills of individuals remains salient both for CPACs and for the Scottish Executive (Scottish Executive 2004).

The composition of panels was linked from the start with the capacity of members to empathise and communicate with families. There was a view, justified or not, that the quality of 'engagement' at Hearings might be impeded if there was too much social distance between panel members and families (Mapstone 1973; May and Smith 1971). Although it was never suggested that the relevant 'community' should be the section of Scottish society from which the preponderance of referrals came, CPACs did accept that the credibility of the System depended upon panels being broadly representative of the communities they served. CPACs have generally followed the policy of appointing the best applicants, while targeting recruitment campaigns on under-represented groups. The concept of panels being 'representative' and panel members expressing the voice of 'the community' on Hearings, remains very much part of government thinking.

The social composition of panels, and the age and gender distribution of panel members, have each been subject to scrutiny and are now, together with other characteristics, nationally recorded. Each has been subject to some significant change. Assessing changes in social composition comparisons is difficult for a number of reasons. The definitions and methods of recording social class have changed, which makes direct comparison of current with previous figures difficult. Changes will also reflect different patterns of employment and income in Scottish society and economy as a whole. Another factor is the increasing number of panel members not in full-time paid employment. Latest figures, which use the National Statistics Socio-Economic Classification (NS-NSEC), indicate that in 2004 almost 11 per cent of panel members defined themselves as being in the professional/ managerial category, with 25 per cent in intermediate occupations, and those in skilled and semi-skilled work comprising 37 per cent of current membership. Those who define themselves as carer/at home/ spouse, and those who are retired, amount to 17 per cent. This represents a shift away from early evidence of panels being dominated nationally by the professional/managerial class (Lockyer 1992; Reid 1998).

It was a feature of the system in the early 1970s that the age range of panel members was wider than that of judicial bodies in other systems. Panel membership included a class of 'new volunteers', which augmented the older age range of those who typically engaged in traditional volunteering (Gerard 1983; Lockyer 1992, Chapter 5). Those under 30 made up 11 per cent of members in 1971, 6 per cent in 1992, and up again to 8 per cent in 2004. The evidence is that despite lowering the minimum age to 18 and CPACs being willing to appoint young people, few of this age group regard panel membership as an appropriate form of voluntary service.

The upper age limit, originally 60, was increased to 65, but CPACs have been reluctant to appoint members over 60 (Lockyer 1992). Their numbers increased from 2 per cent in 1996 to 8 per cent in 2004. The 2004 national recruitment campaign removed the age barrier; it remains to be seen how this will affect recruitment. The greater availability for service of retired people may well make them especially welcome.

The predominant age group of panel members continues to be in the 40 to 59 age range – 58 per cent in 1971, 60 per cent in 1996 and remaining at that figure in May 2004. While the age distribution of panels cannot be expected to correspond to the population at large, CPACs have had an implicit policy to include members at different life-stages, some at least being in the same age range as the parents who come to the Hearings.

In the early years of the system there was little evidence of a difference in the proportion of men and women serving on panels. However, today there is a widening gap between the number of serving panel members, male and female, which reflects a greater difference in the proportions of each applying. During the 2003 recruitment campaign the number of applications from men accounted for only 30 per cent (National Representatives Group 2004). There is some concern that able women applicants are being turned away in favour of men in order to meet the legal requirement of mixed-gender hearings.

This invites reconsideration of the mixed-gender requirement. That said, at a time when there is a very strong case being made by 'Fathers for Justice' – particularly in relation to contact and care issues – keeping the gender mix on Hearings gives a strong message to all that child care is a matter for both sexes.

One of the continual concerns of CPACs has been the collective lack of experience among panel members due to a high resignation rate in the early years of service. Over recent years the numbers recruited have increased and most panels have a high percentage of inexperienced members (i.e. with fewer than two years' service). Panel service includes a substantial commitment to pre-service and in-service training, which for the individual is a significant burden (though an acknowledged personal benefit in terms of acquisition of transferable skills). From a budgetary point of view early resignations may be viewed as a waste of investment, as well as a loss of acquired knowledge and experience. Both the issue of retention and the concern to maintain broad community representation has led to payment for panel service being placed on the agenda for review. This, of course, has implications for 'layness'.

Panel member training

The Consumer Council research that compared children's panel membership with other voluntary tribunals found that appointments to panels were more 'open and representative' than those to other tribunals, but concluded that they might be able to secure an even wider cross-section of the community if CPACs did not 'look for the right people' but were 'prepared to train from scratch' anyone 'genuinely interested in children' (Jones and Adler 1990, p.114). The authors of the report were aware that there might be a conflict between the ideas of layness and of being thoroughly trained for the job, though they made no attempt to reconcile the conflict.

The statutory duty to train panel members lies with individual Local Authorities but the Scottish Ministers exercise their discretionary powers in supporting the training of panel members through four Children's Hearings Training Units located in four Scottish universities. Panel members are recruited subject to satisfactory completion of training, which in effect means that all new recruits undertake an Induction Training Course (minimum 40 hours) following a nationally agreed standard framework (Children's Panel Training 1999) and only after satisfactory completion are permitted to sit on Hearings. There are further stages of mandatory training for new members and those coming up for reappointment, in addition to training arranged at area level.

The standard training given to panel members is nationally consistent in terms of outcomes, content, amount of training offered, and in the forms of assessment and evaluation employed. These developments have also contributed to a more structured process at reappointment, where CPACs monitor performance, provide feedback to panel members and invite them to identify areas of weakness and training needs. The quality of the training now provided by training officers has been highly applauded by the Scottish Council of Tribunals (SCOTCOT 2001, 2002). It was suggested that it might provide a model for other national tribunals to follow.

However, the importance attached to training and monitoring raises the question as to whether lay members (presently unpaid) are in fact expected to perform as professionals, whose decisions are informed by an acquired expertise rather than reflecting their identity with the community at large. Some explanation is needed.

As we have noted, the Kilbrandon Committee saw the virtue of the lay tribunal to consist in its relative informality and discursive character. But the decisions of Hearings have statutory force and the framework of the procedure at Hearings is specified in law to ensure that the rights of children and families are observed. Both anecdotal evidence and research findings in the first decade indicated that informality led to procedural laxity (akin to the Gault experience in the US; see Chapter 12), as well as wide variations in practice between hearings (Martin, Fox and Murray 1981).

There was also a disposition for the Hearing chairs to be too dependent upon the advice of the Reporter in procedural matters. This risked at the very least a perception that the officer bringing the case exerted a strong influence on its disposals. The solution to these deficiencies was seen to lie in ensuring that lay members were thoroughly versed in the due process of Hearings, with an emphasis on providing training for members with some experience in chairmanship skills. As the system has developed there has been increasing attention to formal rights, and there have been changes in the law relating to Hearings that have required additional training. Lay members are therefore increasingly trained to a national standard of competence in the powers and procedures pertaining to Hearings (Competence Framework 2003).

Another aspect of training has focused on developing skills to communicate with families, while at the same time making best use of professionals and having knowledge of available resources. Panel members are not trained to be experts in child development, child psychiatry or juvenile delinquency, but their training seeks to engender a capacity to critically examine reports and care plans presented to them, and to know when to seek further professional or community involvement. What training does not attempt to do is teach lay members what to decide. This it could not do in principle.

Conclusions

Lay people have contributed to quasi-judicial decision-making with respect to children for centuries, notably through their roles as magistrates or jurors. Sometimes their involvement has been on the basis of elite membership, but more commonly they have been chosen on the basis of representing the whole local community, whether through election, qualified random selection or open application. This chapter has argued that in relation to both criminal behaviour by young people and concerns about parenting and care, the appointment of lay decision-makers is legitimised by the fact that decisions have a moral component, though not a moralistic one, and lay people reflect the range of moral opinion in the community. In particular the determination of a sentence or disposal is not reducible to any body of technical knowledge or professional expertise, but also requires ethical judgement. Decisions weighing a loss of liberty against the needs of the offender/victim and the community as a whole are arguably 'lay' assessments made within any given cultural context by people who inhabit that same moral space.

Different contexts and roles have different criteria and means of preparation. For instance in the Anglo-American jury system the purpose is to decide on facts, not the outcome. Hence the juror is expected to be impartial. Preparation is minimal and jury members hear only what is presented in court without bringing extraneous sources of knowledge or specialist insight with them.

By contrast, in the Scottish Children's Hearings System, three lay panel members make the disposal in nearly all cases, whether referred on the basis of an offence or on care and protection grounds. Panel members are recruited by open application with the aim of achieving a broad cross-section of the local community. Panel members bring their own value judgements to Hearings but these are affected by their training and by their experience of the Hearing process, including engagement with families and professionals. Much of what is misleadingly called 'training' is the discursive reflection on cases that takes place among the members of area panels themselves. It is in this context of shared experience that all the panel members serving an area provide a community of discourse that influences the moral perspective adopted in Hearings. In this way, it may be said that the training does not undermine 'layness' as it is not equivalent in scale or coverage to professional training. Instead it enhances the lay perspective for making complex judgements.

Notes

1. See, for example, http://news.bbc.co.uk/1/hi/uk_politics/4113296.stm for discussion of the present UK government's intentions in this area.
2. Details from the website of the Department for Constitutional Affairs, at www.dca.gov.uk/magistrates/index.htm.
3. In a much quoted legal judgment of 1991, found for example on the Scottish Executive's website, at www.scotland.gov.uk/library5/education/krcy-02.asp.

References

Abraham, H.J. (1993) *The Judicial Process* (6th edn) Oxford: Oxford University Press.

Bala, N., Hornick, J.P., Snyder, H.N. and Paetsch, J.J. (2002) *Juvenile Justice Systems*. Toronto: Thompson Education Publishing.

Cairns, J.W. and McLeod, G. (eds) (2002) *The Dearest Birthright of the People of England: The Jury in the History of the Common Law*. Oxford: Oxford University Press.

Cavadino, P. (ed) (1996) *Children Who Kill*. Winchester: Waterside, in association with the British Juvenile and Family Courts Society.

Children's Panel Training (1999) *Design, Content and Evaluation*. Edinburgh: Scottish Executive.

Competence Framework (2003) For Chairmen and Members of Children's Hearings. Edinburgh: Scottish Executive.

Cowperthwaite, D.J. (1988) *The Emergence of the Scottish Children's Hearings System*. Southampton: Institute of Criminal Justice, University of Southampton.

Gerard, D. (1983) *Charities in Britain: Conservatism or Change?* London: Bedford Square Press.

HMSO (1966) *Social Work and the Community*. Cmnd 3065. Edinburgh: HMSO.

Jones, C. and Adler, M. (1990) *Can Anyone Get On These?* Edinburgh: Scottish Consumer Council Report, March.

Kilbrandon, Lord (1964) *Report of the Committee on Children and Young Persons Scotland, Cmnd 2306*. Edinburgh: HMSO.

Lockyer, A. (1992) *Citizen's Service and Children's Panel Members*. Edinburgh: Scottish Office SWSG.

Lockyer, A. and Stone, F.H. (eds) (1998) *Juvenile Justice in Scotland: Twenty-five Years of the Welfare Approach*. Edinburgh: T&T Clark.

Mapstone, E. (1973) 'The Selection of Children's Panel Members for the County of Fife.' *British Journal of Social Work 3*, 4, 445–469.

Martin, F., Fox, S. and Murray, K. (1981) *Children out of Court*. Edinburgh: Scottish Academic Press.

May, D. and Smith, G. (1971) 'The Appointment of Aberdeen Children's City Panel.' *British Journal of Social Work 1*, 1, 5–27.

National Representatives Group (2004) *Recruitment Report*. Edinburgh: Scottish Executive.

Reid, B. (1998) 'Panels and Hearings.' In A. Lockyer and F. Stone (eds) *Juvenile Justice in Scotland: Twenty-five Years of the Welfare Approach*. Edinburgh: T&T Clark.

SCOTCOT (2001) *Special Report into the Children's Hearings*. Edinburgh: Scottish Committee of the Council on Tribunals.

SCOTCOT (2002) *Annual Report*. Edinburgh: Scottish Committee of the Council on Tribunals.

Scottish Executive (2004) 'Getting it Right for Every Child.' Online at www.scotland.gov.uk/Publications/2005/06/ 20135608/56098

Social Work Service Group (1969) *Guidance to Children's Panel Advisory Groups SW7/69*.

'Getting it Right for Every Child' (2004) at: www.scotland.gov.uk/Publications/2005/06/20135608/56098

12

Children's Justice: A View from America

Donald N. Duquette

Introduction

The children's justice systems of the United Kingdom and the United States of America evolved from common legal traditions and similar social philosophies. The first US juvenile court in 1899 rested upon a philosophy very familiar to the British: the US juvenile court was intended to address the needs of the whole child, the welfare of the child, and not just focus on the particular offences of a child (Watkins 1998). The early US juvenile court included both delinquent and 'dependent' children in its jurisdictional mandate (Act of 21 April 1899, Ill. Laws 131). 'Dependent' means a child who is offended against, such as abused or neglected children. 'Dependency' therefore refers to that portion of the juvenile court's business that handles the victimisation of children through child abuse and neglect or what is referred to as child welfare law[1] (Ventrell 2005). The focus of the early US juvenile court was 'saving' potentially criminal children from becoming criminal, irrespective of whether the condition that brought them to the court was delinquent conduct or dependent status (Ventrell 2005). There was no separate set of dependency proceedings.

The parallels between the early US juvenile court philosophy and the Kilbrandon philosophy of the Scottish Children's Hearings System are striking. Professor Sir Neil MacCormick captured the essential Kilbrandon philosophy in his 2001 lecture:

> We look at children in trouble, whether they are in trouble on the basis of their own actions or the actions of others, 'needs and deeds' as the saying has it, and we seek such remedial action as will improve the situation in the child's interests. (MacCormick 2001, p.11)

The later US path has hardly been a smooth one, however. After 70 years of pursuing the goal of the welfare of the child, the US Supreme Court concluded that the rehabilitative welfare ideal of the juvenile court, as implemented to that point, was a failure. In the landmark case of *in re Gault* (387 US 1 (1967)), the US Supreme Court determined that Gerry Gault and young people like him suffered from the worst of both worlds – getting neither the benevolent guidance and assistance promised by the juvenile court founders nor the procedural protections guaranteed to persons by the US Constitution.

As the international community struggles with developing jurisprudence and social welfare systems to achieve justice for children and youth, what lessons may Britain and other countries learn from the evolution of the US juvenile justice system? One key question explored in this book is 'whether the ends of justice and effective intervention are better served by treating young people according to the grounds upon which they come to public attention or on the basis of their individual needs in the context of family support'. In response, the thesis of this chapter, drawing from some of the US experience, is that it is not an either/or choice. Some level of procedural due process, particularly in finding grounds for coercive state intervention, seems required as a basic element of individual liberty. Yet there is a valid concern, voiced by Bill Whyte among others (see Chapter 8), that procedural correctness will divert both scarce funds and our attention from the needs of the whole child (and her/his family). This chapter suggests a broader view of 'justice for children', in the sense of 'social justice for children', which opens up the possibility that the hard edges of formal legal process can be softened, through restorative justice, mediation and family conferencing, as well as similar conflict-resolving and problem-solving devices, without losing the essential protections of personal liberty. If, whenever possible, social supports for children and youth and their families are extended generally, voluntarily and without coercion, the social supports may reduce the need for coercive intervention to assist the child and family and, because they raise no question of limitation of personal liberty, may be administered without the formal processes of the courts.

Procedural fairness and *in re Gault*

On 9 June 1964 in Gila County, Arizona, Deputy Probation Officer Flagg picked up Gerry Gault, aged 15, and took him to a detention home for the crime of making an obscene phone call 'of the irritatingly offensive, adolescent sex variety' to one Mrs Cook. Gerry's parents were not told of his arrest but found out where he was and appeared for an informal hearing in juvenile court the next day. Gerry remained in state custody. The informal hearing before Judge McGhee was held in chambers with no notice of charges against Gerry, no witnesses except for Officer Flagg's hearsay statements, no record and no lawyer representing Gerry. A propos of the discussion later in this chapter, there was no community involvement in the episode in the form of youth services, prevention, mediation or diversion services. Gerry was held in detention from June 8–11 and then sent home.

Following a second informal hearing, on 15 June 1964, Judge McGhee committed Gerry to the State Industrial School until he was 21 – a period of some six years. An adult convicted of a similar offence would be subject to a fine of from $5 to $50, and imprisonment for no longer than two months. Commitment of young offenders to the state reform school for the duration of their minority was a common disposition at the time. A young person might be released earlier at the discretion of the state authorities if he (or, rarely, she) was evaluated by the staff as reformed and ready for release back to the community. Such was the operation of a juvenile system intended to be an informal but benevolent intervention for the welfare of the youngster.

Gerry Gault's case eventually reached the US Supreme Court as a result of appeals from the Arizona courts. The US Supreme Court carefully reviewed the history of the juvenile court and, in stirring and now classical language, extended constitutional due process rights to youth accused of crime.

'[N]either the Fourteenth Amendment nor the Bill of Rights is for adults alone,' said the Court.

Accordingly, the highest motives and most enlightened impulses led to a peculiar system for juveniles, unknown to our law in any comparable context. ... Juvenile Court history has again demonstrated that *unbridled discretion* [emphasis added], however benevolently motivated, is frequently a poor substitute for principle and procedure. In 1937, Dean Pound wrote, 'The powers of the Star Chamber were a trifle in comparison with those of the juvenile courts...' The absence of substantive standards has not necessarily meant that children receive careful, compassionate, individual- ized treatment. The absence of procedural rules based upon constitutional principle has not always produced fair, efficient, and effective procedures. Departures from established principles of due process have frequently resulted not in enlightened procedure, but in arbitrariness. (*Re Gault*)

The Court offered this memorable and oft-quoted line: 'Under our Constitu- tion, the condition of being a boy does not justify a kangaroo court.'

The *Gault* court then required certain procedural protections in de- linquency cases, including notice of charges, right to counsel, confrontation of witnesses, right against self-incrimination, and right to call and cross- examine witnesses. Although the court did not require it, subsequent reforms also generally include additional due process requirements of a record of proceedings, stated grounds for judicial conclusions and a right of appeal.

Gault has been called the 'Magna Carta for juveniles' (Kalman 1990) and, like the original Magna Carta, has lessons for citizens of many countries. The most relevant lesson in this discussion of whether intervention on behalf of youngsters should be on the basis of the grounds on which they come to public attention or their needs is that, under US law, where state coercion or abrogation of personal liberty is at stake, a disciplined, predictable process of finding grounds for intervention is absolutely required. Benevolent and good intentions alone do not justify encroachment on personal liberty. Let me quote yet another US Supreme Court opinion, this time a dissent by Mr Justice Louis Brandeis:

> Experience should teach us to be most on our guard to protect liberty when the Government's purposes are beneficent. Men born to freedom are natu- rally alert to repel invasion of their liberty by evil-minded rulers. The greatest dangers to liberty lurk in insidious encroachment by men of zeal, well-meaning but without understanding. (*Olmstead v. United States*, 277 US 438, 479 (1928) (Mr Justice Brandeis dissenting))

Gault formally and technically addressed delinquency[2] cases only – and not dependency cases, i.e. child protection cases. Nonetheless *Gault* had a profound effect on the development of the law and procedure in relation to dependency. Although the procedures and purposes for dealing with dependency differ somewhat from those concerned with delinquency, both types of cases involve the needs of children and youth, and they continue to be handled by the same court, the family or juvenile court. Much of the constitutional analysis of *Gault* applies to children and parents in dependency cases, and subsequent decisions of the US Supreme Court and the various state supreme courts have recognised the fundamental and constitutionally protected rights and interests at stake in dependency (child protection) cases. These rights, for parents and children, include the right to be let alone, to personal privacy, to autonomy and to family relationships. The principal and most generalisable lesson of *Gault* and subsequent cases is that these rights and interests cannot be limited without 'due process'.

What process is due and is due process necessarily incompatible with a focus on the welfare of the child? The English and Scottish courts, like their American counterparts, require a finding of grounds or the establishing of legal 'guilt' before the questions of proper disposal are considered. That is as it should be and the implementation of the procedure for this should be monitored and subject to court or administrative review, as discussed later in this chapter.

Who should decide a child case? Diverse legal systems identify quite different persons to sit as fact-finders or judges. The US uses primarily full-time professional judges who are legally trained judicial officers of fairly high standing. Some American states provide for juries in child protection or delinquency cases in order that lay people determine 'guilt'. England and Scotland both use lay persons in the judicial role as magistrates in England and members of the Children's Hearings System in Scotland (although they enter into the judicial process at slightly different stages). Each of these approaches is compatible with basic due process provided that certain safeguards are in place. They are good examples of similar legal systems coming to somewhat different approaches to implement the central due process concept.

Legal representation of the child

In the United States and United Kingdom the importance of the child's interests and right to be heard has a long history in law. In the American case of *Harvey v. Harvey* (22 D 1198, 1860) the court said: 'the wishes and feelings of the child are entitled to a degree of weight corresponding to the amount of intelligence and right feeling which he may exhibit'.

In the Scottish context Sheriff Kearney writes:

> The concept of the importance, if not paramouncy, of the interests of the child and the right of the mature child to express a view have long been recognised as principles which the courts would uphold, at least for those who could afford to go to law. (Kearney 1999)

In contemporary times the UN Convention on the Rights of the Child (UNCRC) provides for legal and other assistance for the child when liberty is threatened:

> Every child deprived of his liberty shall have the right to legal and other assistance, as well as the right to challenge the legality of the deprivation of his or her liberty before a court or other competent, independent and impartial authority, and to a prompt decision on any such action. (UN Convention on the Rights of the Child (37(d))

Though the USA is not a signatory to the UNCRC, the US experience reflects this international attitude about a child's right to be heard and represented. The right to counsel in delinquency cases, based in the US Constitution since *Gault*, is now codified and implemented in all state laws. The role of counsel for the young person accused of a criminal offence is nearly always that of a traditional attorney, with the same duties of aggressive advocacy on behalf of the youth's stated position, arrived at after counselling with the lawyer, as the lawyer would for an adult in similar circumstances. Where a lawyer is concerned that the young client may lack capacity to make important decisions related to the legal process, this should be handled in the same way as for an adult client with diminished capacity. Thus, the lawyer's duties on behalf of a young person accused of an offence are not affected, modified or in any way diminished by the mere fact of the child's minority, no matter the child's age.

In delinquency cases, where the young person is accused of a crime, there is no distinction between the child's right to be heard and the right to be legally represented. They are essentially part of the same concept and blend in American legal practice. The lawyer is directed by the wishes and goals of the young person and is obliged to try whatever means seem likely to achieve the client's goals. That could mean calling the youngster to formally testify or not, as the circumstances and the judgement of client and lawyer dictate.

This clarity of the role of the child's lawyer in delinquency cases, as champion, is not present in the child protection proceedings, however, where it is alleged that the child is a victim rather than an offender. The US Child Abuse Prevention and Treatment Act (CAPTA) (Public Law 93-273; 42 USC 5101, 1974; reauthorised in 2004) requires representation of children in child protection court proceedings as a condition of states receiving federal money for child protection services. CAPTA provides that each state require the appointment of a guardian *ad litem* for a child in every child abuse and neglect court case (42 USC 5106a(b)(A)(ix)). CAPTA permits the guardian *ad litem* representative of the child to be a legally qualified representative or a lay advocate, or both. It also requires the guardian *ad litem* to obtain, first hand, a clear understanding of the situation and needs of the child, and make recommendations to the court concerning the interests of the child. CAPTA requires that states make training available to guardians *ad litem*.

The role of the child's legal representative, in other than delinquency cases, is unique in American jurisprudence and not well defined in law or tradition, and this is the situation in many other legal systems as well. A lawyer representing a child has a client who may or may not be competent and who may be competent for some decisions but not for others. There is little guidance for the lawyer as to how he or she should fulfil the role compared to the better-developed legal and ethical obligations governing lawyers as representatives of competent adults or corporations.

For over two decades the major dilemma in the development of the child advocate's role in America has been the extent to which the lawyer represents the child's wishes or the child's best interests as determined by the lawyer. The debate is still not resolved. A 1998 survey by the National Council of Juvenile and Family Court Judges found that 40 of the 50 US states appoint counsel for children in child abuse and neglect cases. In 30 of these, an 'attorney-guardian-ad-litem' is typically appointed who serves a dual function of representing both the best interests and the wishes of the child. The actual name of this legal representative may vary from state to state and guidance to the lawyer as to how to identify the 'best interests of the child' is generally lacking. The result is often that the individual attorney decides when and to what extent he or she defers to the wishes of the child when determining the goals of the case. In the ten other states that appoint counsel for a child, a guardian *ad litem* is appointed in addition to an attorney so that the attorneys perform the single role of representing the child's wishes. In the remaining ten states where an attorney is usually not appointed for the child, in all but one a non-attorney guardian *ad litem* is appointed for the child (National Council of Juvenile and Family Court Judges 1998a).

Both the pure best interests model and the pure wishes/client-directed model are criticised. The common objection to a pure best interests model is that the older child, faced with the loss of the fundamental interests at stake in child protection proceedings, deserves to have his or her voice heard and advocated. The older, mature child should have a right to counsel in such cases. But where should the line be drawn? Arguments have been made for this to be anywhere between age 7 and 18. One commentator advocates not for a specific age, but that there be an age specified, for example 10, 12, or 14, above which the young person is entitled to a traditional attorney (Duquette 2000). Another major objection to the best interests model is that it may inappropriately substitute the values and judgement of a lawyer for the older competent child so that the 'wrong person' ends up deciding the goals and objectives of the advocacy. With an infant or young child, the pure best interests approach fails to set out principles to guide the advocate's discretion in identifying the child's best interests (Duquette 2000).

Similarly, the pure wishes, or client-directed, model is criticised where a child of limited capacity and poor judgement sets immature and even harmful goals for the outcome of the case. For example, many younger abused children commonly want to return to the custody of the parent – even if it was that parent who caused the injuries. Child advocate lawyers say they do not wish to use their advocacy skills when they think this will put a child in continued danger.

There is more agreement about the child advocate's role in US child protection cases than the above discussion would lead the reader to think. Whether the goals are determined by the child-client or by the 'best interest of the child' judgement of the lawyer, there is widespread agreement that the lawyer for the child should be an active and aggressive advocate. While recognising the difficulty of determining the goals of the litigation in the face of a client of limited capacity, every major authority speaking on this subject has nonetheless endorsed the portions of the American Bar Association

Standards that address the basic obligations and required actions of the lawyer for the child (American Bar Association 1996; US Children's Bureau 1999). Whether or not a child is competent to direct the attorney and even if the role of the attorney is defined as other than purely client directed, the wishes and preferences of the child are always relevant and should be communicated to the court in the US proceedings. There is strong support in America that no matter what weight is given to the child's preferences in determining the goals of advocacy, the attorney should elicit the child's preferences in a developmentally appropriate manner and communicate those preferences to the court (American Bar Association 1996; Fordham Conference 1995; US Children's Bureau 1999).

Thus the child's voice should be heard and should be independently represented by an advocate, preferably a lawyer knowledgeable in the child law field. Where does the court find the experienced child law expert? Recently the American Bar Association accredited the National Association of Counsel for Children (NACC) to certify lawyers as experts in child welfare law, representing the child, parent or state. The US Children's Bureau has funded the NACC programme to pilot certification of child welfare lawyers in three states (Duquette and Ventrell 2003).

What legal assistance is required for the parents potentially deprived of custody in a child protection case? In the USA parents are entitled to counsel in child protection cases and most states provide parents on low income with representation at state expense, but the practice is not universal. If the case is complex, the US Supreme Court has held that a parent has a right to counsel in a termination of parental rights proceeding (*Lassiter v. Dept of Social Services,* 452 US 18 (1981)).Useful publications have begun to appear that guide lawyers in the role of representing parents in child welfare cases (see Rauber and Granik 2000).

One of the most problematic elements of the Scottish Children's Hearings System is that parents often do not understand their rights and are unable to obtain counsel to act for them when disposals are being made (Lockyer and Stone 1998). Commentators and panel members are often concerned about lawyers negatively impacting on the System with irrelevant technicalities. But one person's technicality is another person's ticket to liberty. More importantly, the negative effects of adversarial process (to which US and UK lawyers are accustomed) can be mitigated by training and selection of lawyers.

The most effective advocacy for parents and young people is often done in a problem-solving style, which can be promoted by training and selection of the lawyers. Even though a collaborative family law style, in contrast to a criminal defence style, is likely to be more effective for most parents, children and the System, a resort to the traditional adversarial process is an important guarantee in those cases where irresolvable issues of fact or law persist.

Lockyer (1994) is rightly concerned about the danger of over-proceduralising society's intervention on behalf of children. With respect to the Children's Hearings System, Lockyer asks whether Scotland has moved beyond the traditional due process model. With the Scottish Children's Hearings System now required by the Human Rights Act 1998 to apply the rights embedded in the European Convention on Human Rights (adopted in 1949), he asks the provocative question of whether, in effect, the welfare philosophy of the (Scottish Children's) Hearings System is being sacrificed to the standards of criminal and civil justice of 50 years ago. This concern can be finessed in various ways, rather than faced head on, including exploring non-adversarial means of conflict resolution, building up the social network of family and child supports, and offering those services voluntarily or under court order. We turn to non-adversarial means of conflict resolution next.

Alternatives to legal formality and the adversarial approach

Mere procedural formality does not achieve justice for children. A predictable and fair process is an essential – but not sufficient – component of a justice system for children. Procedural formality fails without caring, competent, individualised, professional, helpful intervention wrapped in a philosophy of rehabilitation and hope. The first step in implementing a model of justice that treats children appropriately is the manner and tone in which the grounds are established, and the clinical judgement of what intervention is appropriate. The hard edges of the adversarial process can be softened without losing their basic integrity. (I have seen this done in Scottish Children's Hearings with considerable sensitivity and skill.) The USA is learning that non-adversarial case resolution provides a process of decision-making and problem-solving that can divert large numbers of cases from formal processes and set an important rehabilitative tone going forward.[3]

Professionals in the USA who work with children and parents have become increasingly dissatisfied with the customary reliance on the traditional adversarial system in resolving family-related disputes, including cases involving children's protection, placement and permanent care. The power struggle in contested child welfare-related cases and hearings may foster hostility among the parties and dissipate money, energy and attention that could otherwise be used to solve problems co-operatively. Parties may become polarised, open communication may be discouraged, and there may be little investment in information-sharing and joint problem-solving. Children may suffer when adversarial tensions escalate and ameliorative services are delayed.

The formal system is, however, essential and well suited to resolving conflicts when differences are irreconcilable regarding the true facts of a case, or the proper response to a young person's offence or family's child protection-related problems. Nonetheless, most cases in the USA – delinquency and child protection – are resolved through informal settlement negotiations. Unfortunately, these settlements are often made quickly, in courthouse hallways, and the interests of all parties may not be carefully or fully considered. Hastily made agreements, or stipulations made immediately prior to a hearing, can do a disservice to both children and their families.

Non-Adversarial Case Resolution (NACR) has become an accepted and increasingly popular alternative to the traditional adversarial processes of the courts (National Council of Juvenile and Family Court Judges 1998b). The NACR approaches in child welfare and juvenile justice typically expect that a resolution agreeable to all disputants will be achieved. If no voluntary resolution is achieved, the parties are left to the formal court processes to resolve the questions. Some level of informal pressure is involved, but if parties are legally represented there is protection from resolutions that are not within the range of what a court would order, given the facts and circumstances. Thus due process rights are preserved and respected.

NACR approaches used in youth crime/delinquency cases take the form of restorative justice programmes such as victim–offender mediation, parent–child mediation, apology and reparation. These innovative conflict resolution mechanisms offer considerable promise in trying to achieve justice and rehabilitation for young persons accused of crime (US Office of Juvenile Justice and Delinquency Prevention 2003).

Two forms of NACR are in common use among the states and are particularly promising in improving decision-making in the courts: mediation and Family Group Conferencing.

Mediation in the child welfare context is well established in many jurisdictions. It is commonly defined as an intervention into a dispute or negotiation by an acceptable, impartial and neutral third party who has no authoritative decision-making power but who assists the disputing parties in voluntarily reaching their own mutually acceptable settlement of disputed issues in a non-adversarial setting. Mediation is widely used today to resolve conflicts among substitute care providers, foster care caseworkers and case reviewers, and children's court-appointed advocates about the needs of children during periods of substitute care. Furthermore, this approach may be adopted in order to resolve matters more promptly as part of the court process among the various attorneys and other advocates, caseworkers, therapists, other involved professionals, and the parents and other family members in child protection judicial proceedings.

Mandatory mediation facilitated by a trained independent mediator can help focus attention on collaborative problem-solving on behalf of the child (US Children's Bureau 1999). Family and juvenile courts recognise that the adversarial process in child abuse and neglect cases can sometimes exacerbate hostility, divisiveness, and rigid position-taking between participants, most notably between the parents and the child protective agency and/or the child's attorney. Mediation, on the other hand, brings all significant case participants together in a non-adversarial and problem-solving setting (Edwards and Baron 1995).

Family Group Conferencing is a fairly new and promising form of NACR that focuses on engaging the extended family in planning for a child, and does not necessarily involve the mediating of disputes. Recently imported to the USA from New Zealand, the Family Group Conference (FGC) may take the form of Family Group Decision-making or a Family Unity Meeting. These are characterised as a family-focused, strengths-orientated and community-based process where parents, extended family members and others come together to collectively make key decisions for children involved in the child welfare system (Merkel-Holguin 1996). Family Group Conferences are often administered by the child welfare agency, as in Oregon. An FGC can also be a form of court-approved NACR (Lowry 1997).

NACR techniques can be used in various ways and at various times in a child welfare case. Mediation and Family Group Conferences can both be used in a number of situations and to a variety of ends. Both approaches may be pursued in order to resolve conflicts between child welfare agencies and parents, concerning proposed case plans and final case resolutions, to help divert cases from the court system, and to work out disputes over a child's supervision, placement, visitation, family reunification, and permanent plans for the child (e.g. mediated relinquishment of parental rights or guardianship, as well as facilitation of co-operative adoption agreements where appropriate and permitted by law). Furthermore, such approaches contribute to an increased intra-familial involvement among parents, relatives and other extended (kinship) family members in fashioning case resolutions and improving co-operation and co-ordination with government child protection and child welfare authorities.

Voluntary settlements arrived at through restorative justice methods, mediation, or Family Group Conferencing may be the basis for a finding of grounds if required in the court process, or may divert the matter entirely from legal process into the realm of social agency services. These are procedural devices that could help bridge the gap inherent in the tension between a youth's deeds or needs.

Procedural correctness alone does not meet the needs of youth

The requirements of social justice cannot be met through the courts alone. Procedural correctness, while fundamental, is not the sole object of justice for children, and courts are not the exclusive means of delivering social justice. A responsive support system for children and youth and their families is an essential component. That is, although procedural correctness on the question of grounds is essential, a children's justice system is not complete without follow-through services that reflect a rehabilitation philosophy.

It is not an either/or choice between achieving justice or achieving the welfare of the child. MacCormick (2001) is right to condemn a 'welfare versus justice' fallacy in the debate about the Scottish Children's Hearings:

> Our system is not a welfare system that works better than a justice system. It is a better system because it matches a better conception of justice than in this context the so-called 'justice model' would do. …My final homily

would be, never accept that our system, whatever its merits, diverges from what could properly be called a justice model. That is to sell a conceptual pass that should be defended in the last ditch. Say rather, that we have here a model of justice that tells us why to treat children differently from adults. (MacCormick 2001)

The primary responsibility for children and youth in trouble or at risk must not be vested in a judicial body but rather with a range of social groups that co-ordinate with one another (Howell, Pallmer and Mangum 2004). Court is required only if the services offered are not voluntarily acceptable to the child and family. Then there is a question of coercion and abrogation of liberty so that an adjudication by a court is required. The USA has moved to a system of strict judicial review of social services delivery in cases of child welfare and juvenile offenders. The principal theoretical justification for this judicial involvement is that the abrogation of personal liberty, which the court authorises through its orders, is justified in part by provision of effective rehabilitative services. The view has been codified extensively in the federal Adoption and Safe Families Act of 1997 (Public Law 105-89, Section 302 amending 42 USC Section 675(5)(C)), which requires state procedures whereby case plans are reviewed and ordered by the court and the parents, child and agency are held accountable for complying with those case plans. In the USA the orders of family or juvenile court implement the case plan, and the court can enforce the plan, and its orders, through contempt power. The US Adoption and Safe Families Act requires a judicial finding that the agency has provided 'reasonable efforts to prevent or eliminate the need for removal'. It also requires a judicial finding within 12 months of a child's being in placement, that the agency has provided 'reasonable efforts to achieve permanency for the child'.

This extensive involvement of the judiciary in child welfare service delivery is problematic and should not necessarily be copied by other legal systems. For most of its history, the juvenile court in America has been a hybrid mix of a judicial body and a social services delivery system with its own staff of probation officers, caseworkers and psychologists. These individuals work for the court directly, with the judge or court administrator as their ultimate superior. This mix of judicial and executive functions creates a conflict in many situations, including when a party might ask a judge to hold a caseworker in contempt of court for failing to provide a service ordered by the judge. Is the judge to hold his employee in contempt of court?

A more appropriate allocation of responsibility is to divide the judicial responsibilities for adjudication and determining the appropriate services (disposal) from the executive (service delivery) responsibilities. This distinction is useful both conceptually, in terms of understanding which due process requirements are appropriate at which stages, and functionally, as it clearly separates the procedural aspects of justice from the sentencing and service aspects.

The administration of youth services, separate from the judicial system, could be engaged on behalf of youth either as ordered by a court or on a voluntary basis without involvement of the court. The court need not, and should not, be the only or even the principal body involved in providing services to children and families. 'Justice for children' includes social pro-grammes meant to assure an equal opportunity for success in life, including antipoverty programmes, early child enrichment, basic family supports, equal and adequate access to education, and early and preventive responses to antisocial youth behaviour. There is a considerable body of literature on delivery and co-ordination of services for youth. The provision of social justice for children is too important to leave to a single branch of society, the courts. The courts have a fairly narrow duty to determine when compulsory measures are justified, determine extent of deprivation of liberty, or what measures are justified. A separation of judicial powers from social service delivery is a key development.

The argument for separation of the powers of the court to adjudicate from the responsibility of organising and delivering services gets some support from an unlikely source – the American movement to abolish the juvenile court. Some commentators praise the American juvenile court movement as combining benign coercion and effective treatment. The Juvenile court was described, for example, as 'one of the most important and enduring contributions the US has made to the world' (Drizen 1999). However, others say that the US juvenile court has changed from a rehabilitative institution to a second-class criminal court. One of the leaders of this school of thought writes:

> If we were to develop a child welfare policy ab initio would we choose a juvenile court as the most effective agency through which to deliver social services? And make criminality a condition precedent to the receipt of

services? ...States should abolish juvenile court's delinquency jurisdiction and formally recognize youthfulness as a mitigating factor in sentencing... (Feld 1997, p.91)

Feld argues that children get the worst of both worlds. The idea that 'judicial-clinicians' can combine social welfare and penal social control in one agency represents an inherent conceptual flaw and an innate contradiction (Feld 1997).

The criticism of Feld and others can be addressed in part by cleanly separating the adjudicative from the service delivery aspects of the court. Increased involvement of the broader community also goes a long way towards helping achieve the rehabilitative ideals of a children's justice system. The United Kingdom certainly has a long tradition of community involvement and building upon that strength holds much promise.

Conclusions

Drawing on the American experience of youth justice it has been argued that a rigid distinction between treating young people according to the grounds on which they come to public attention and treating them on the basis of their individual social needs is unnecessary. The importance of due process in finding grounds for coercive intervention has been demonstrated, while at the same time the benefits of NACR methods have been clearly shown. They permit a softening of the hard edges of the judicial process without compromising the liberty of the subject. This reflects a core concern of this chapter, which is the fact that procedural correctness alone will not assure 'justice for children' as more broadly understood. Instead, a broader view of 'social justice for children' has been advocated. Central to this is the question of what society is to do to help a child in trouble and his or her family. The interrelationship of the court process, when it is engaged, and the social welfare services of the community could be carefully defined. Co-ordination of community services, whether engaged voluntarily or by court order, is essential to address both the needs and deeds of youth.

Notes

1.   'Dependency' cases or proceedings correspond approximately to that which we have elsewhere elected to call 'care and protection' cases or proceedings. We have left the

author's American term in place except where care and protection is the more appropriate term.

2. Another note on terminology: while the word 'delinquent' has largely passed from use in many jurisdictions it remains popular in the USA. This is synonymous with use elsewhere of phrases such as 'youth crime' or 'young offending', for example.

3. Non-adversarial case resolution (NACR) is a term coined by Howard Davidson, Director of the ABA Center on Children and the Law (see US Children's Bureau 1999).

References

American Bar Association (1996) *ABA Standards of Practice for Lawyers Who Represent Children in Abuse and Neglect Cases.*

Drizen, S.A (1999) 'The Juvenile Court at 100.' *Judicature 83*, 9, 14–15, July/August.

Duquette, D. (2000) 'Legal Representation for Children in Protection Proceedings: Two Distinct Lawyer Roles are Required.' *Family Law Quarterly 34*, 441, Fall.

Duquette, D. and Ventrell, M. (2003) 'Certification of child welfare attorneys: the next step in building a profession dedicated to justice for children.' *Children's Legal Rights Journal 23*, 53.

Edwards, L.P. and Baron, S. (1995) 'Alternatives to Contested Litigation in Child Abuse and Neglect Cases.' *Family and Conciliation Courts Review 33*, 275–285.

Feld, B.C. (1997) 'Abolish the Juvenile Court: Youthfulness, Criminal Responsibility, and Sentencing Policy.' *Journal of Criminal Law and Criminology 88*, 68, 91–97.

Fordham Conference (1995) 'Fordham Conference on Ethical Issues in the Legal Representation of Children.' Reported in *Fordham Law Review LXIV*, 4, March 1996.

Howell, Kelly, Pallmer and Mangum (2004) 'Integrating Child Welfare, Juvenile Justice and Other Agencies in a Continuum of Services.' *Child Welfare 83*,143; special issue, *Child Welfare and Juvenile Justice: Improved Coordination and Integration.* March/April.

Jonson-Reid, M. (2004) 'Child Welfare Services and Delinquency: The Need to Know More.' *Child Welfare 83*, 157; special issue, *Child Welfare and Juvenile Justice: Improved Coordination and Integration*, March/April.

Kalman, L. (1990) *Abe Fortas: A Biography.* New Haven: Yale University Press. (Chief Justice Earl Warren, quoted at 254).

Kearney, B. (1999) *Children's Rights and Children's Welfare in Scotland.* London: UK Family Law Conference, 25–26 June.

Lockyer, A. (1994) 'The Scottish Children's Hearings System: Internal Developments and the UN Convention.' In S. Asquith and M. Hill (eds) *Justice for Children.* Dordrecht: Martinus Nijhoff.

Lockyer, A. (1999) 'The impact of the European Convention on Human Rights on the Children's Hearings System.' In B. Reid (ed) *Facing the Future: Challenges of the 21st Century.* Glasgow: Glasgow University, Children's Panel Training Publication.

Lockyer, A. and Stone, F.H. (1998) *Juvenile Justice in Scotland: Twenty-Five Years of the Welfare Approach.* Edinburgh: T&T Clark.

Lowry, J.M. (1997) 'Family Group Conferences as a Form of Court-Approved Alternative Dispute Resolution in Child Abuse and Neglect Cases.' *University of Michigan Journal of Law Reform 31*, 57, Fall.

MacCormick, Professor Sir Neil, MEP (2001) *The Fifth Annual Kilbrandon Child Care Lecture.* Glasgow University, 1 November.

Merkel-Holguin, L. (1996) 'Putting Families Back into the Child Protection Partnership: Family Group Decision-Making.' *Protecting Children 12*, 3, American Humane Association, Summer.

National Council of Juvenile and Family Court Judges (1998a) *Child Abuse and Neglect Cases: Representation as a Critical Component of Effective Practice.* Report by Dobbin, Gatowski and Johns.

National Council of Juvenile and Family Court Judges (1998b) *Summaries of Twenty-five State Court Improvement Assessment Reports.* National Council of Juvenile and Family Court Judges, March.

Rauber, D.B. with Granik, L.A. (2000) *Representing Parents in Child Welfare Cases.* American Bar Association, Center on Children and the Law.

Re Gault 387 US 1, 87 S.Ct. 1428 (1967).

UN Convention on the Rights of the Child (UNCRC) (1990). Available at www.unicef.org.uk.

US Children's Bureau (1999) US Dept of HHS ACF ACYF *Adoption 2002: The President's Initiative on Adoption and Foster Care. Guidelines for Public Policy and State Legislation Governing Permanence for Children,* 1999, page VII-11. Also available online at: www.acf.dhhs.gov/programs/ cb/publications/adopt02/index.htm

US Office of Juvenile Justice and Delinquency Prevention (2003) 'Guide for Implementing the Balanced and Restorative Justice Model'; http://www.ojjdp.ncjrs.org/pubs/ implementing/accountability.html

Ventrell, M. (2005) 'Legal history of child welfare law.' In D. Duquette and M. Ventrell (eds) *Child Welfare Law and Practice.* Denver, CO: Bradford Legal Publishers.

Watkins, J. Jr (1998) *The Juvenile Justice Century: A Socio-Legal Commentary On American Juvenile Courts.* Durham, NC: Caroline Academic Press.

13

Children's Rights and Juvenile Justice

David Archard

Introduction

What does fairness require of a juvenile justice system?[1] And how are the requirements of justice to be squared with the according to children of rights? We can start to answer to these questions by acknowledging that children have, under the United Nations Convention on the Rights of the Child (UNCRC),[2] a wide range of rights. As a ratifying state the United Kingdom must seek to ensure that its statutory and case law conforms to the provisions of the UNCRC. This requirement, in turn, means that any juvenile justice system has to respect the according to children of a very range wide of rights.

Yet one model for dealing with children in trouble or at risk – one that the Children's Hearings System in Scotland arguably instantiates – attends not so much to the rights of children as to their needs (Kilbrandon 1964; Lockyer and Stone 1998). The assumptions underpinning a 'welfare' model of juvenile justice seem on the face of it to be in tension with the idea of young people as possessed of rights. How, it will be asked, can we think of children both as vulnerable young persons whose needs must be met and as agents capable of exercising fundamental rights? Hence I want to take up the questions of how a rights discourse affects the way we conceive a juvenile justice system. In doing so I want also to address a question the legal theorist Neil MacCormick posed about how a 'welfare' approach to children in trouble with the law can be made consistent with the requirements of justice (MacCormick 2001).

Children and rights

Children are accorded rights under the United Nations Convention on the Rights of the Child. These rights need not be enshrined in, nor even protected by, the domestic law of those states that have ratified the Convention. Indeed these rights are extensively violated throughout the world. It is important to recognise that moral rights need not be legal rights, just as legal rights need not be viewed as moral rights. Moreover, even if we think of the Convention rights as purporting to be moral rights, that does not settle the question of whether or not children ought to have these rights.

Because someone has a moral right to something does not mean that she[3] will have this same right legally recognised, although of course the case that supports a moral right lends powerful backing to the claim that it should be a law. There is a basic distinction between the rights that persons have under law – sometimes called their 'positive' rights or legal rights – and rights that they have morally. This is not a distinction between two very different sets of rights. One and the same right can be both a moral and a legal right. The distinction concerns the status of the rights. A black slave in antebellum America had a moral right to his freedom that the southern states' laws denied him.

Throughout history demands for legal rights have been driven by the view that whatever persons are morally entitled to they should also be legally entitled to. Rights campaigns are motivated by the claim that the law should catch up with, and recognise, what is universally acknowledged as a moral truth. Nevertheless not all moral rights should be legal rights. There are many things to which I am morally entitled – to the showing to me of basic respect, to the expression of gratitude for services rendered, and to being cared for in my dotage by my adult children – which are, properly, not a legal entitlement. From the other side, what is recognised as a right by the law need not be a moral right. It is perfectly coherent to argue that the law has been mistaken in giving rights to individuals who are not morally entitled to have them. A significant number of philosophers and theorists have indeed maintained that children should not be conceived as the possessors of rights (O'Neill 1988; Purdy 1992). This has been done for a variety of reasons: for instance, that children are not qualified, as adults are, to possess rights; that it is not in the interests of children to accord them a liberty to lead their own lives; that it subverts the valued institution of the family to regard its members as being able to exercise claims against one another. It is important to add that the denial that children should have rights does not amount to the view that adults are under no obligation to care for or to promote the interests of children. We may be duty bound to behave in certain ways towards others who nevertheless cannot claim such behaviour from us as their right.

However, giving children legal rights or according them a certain status at law will make a huge difference to how we then think about them. If the law represents children in a certain light – as entitled, for instance, to make claims against adults – then it is correspondingly harder to continue seeing them as helpless dependants. At the same time children may make good use of the status they have been accorded legally to show that they do indeed merit that standing. Or they may simply employ the opportunities provided to acquire the requisite abilities. Children may be able practically to prove that it was right to give them rights.

The UNCRC is not a legal instrument and is not incorporated into the UK's domestic law in the way that the European Convention on Human Rights is now incorporated as the Human Rights Act 1998.[4] Yet the UNCRC has considerable influence on our understanding of the legal status of children. It remains the single most important contemporary formulation of what by general agreement children are entitled to. Yet, just as according a right in law does not settle the matter of whether such a right is properly possessed, so the UNCRC's list of children's rights does not close discussion of what rights children should have. There are, and have been, other charters of children's rights, and some of these give children rights that are not included in the UNCRC.

Nevertheless the UNCRC is an inescapable starting point and context for thinking about the status of children. Over 190 countries have ratified the Convention, which codifies a recognisable body of generally shared thinking about the rights of children. It gives children those rights we – and the 'we' here is the unavoidably parochial subject of modern western, liberal democratic thought – agree they should have wherever they might live in the world today. The fact that the systematic and prevalent abuse of children's rights continues should not blind us to the UNCRC's acknowledged significance.

One feature of the UNCRC deserves special mention: it explicitly recognises, and affirms, that children are different from adults. Existing international charters and covenants on human rights, such as the European

Convention on Human Rights (1950)[5] or the International Covenant on Economic, Social and Cultural Rights (adopted by the United Nations in 1966 and came into force in 1976), give all human beings fundamental rights. As small and young human beings, children might be thought to have at least and perhaps only all those rights accorded their adult counterparts. Yet the UNCRC gives rights to children because and to the extent that they are children. Indeed the Preamble to the UNCRC quotes from the previous Declaration of the Rights of the Child, which states that 'the child, by reason of his physical and mental immaturity, needs special safeguards and care, including appropriate legal protection, before as well as after birth'. In very similar terms the Preamble of the African Charter of the Rights and Welfare of the Child (1990) recognises that 'the child, due to the needs of his physical and mental development requires particular care with regard to health, physical, mental, moral and social development'. In other words it is because a child is not an adult, and in respect of the differences between child and adult, that the UNCRC gives the rights it does to children. In sum, the UNCRC gives to children some of the rights that adults have, such as the right to life. It does not give to children some of the rights that adults are given, such as the right to vote or to work. It gives to children rights that adults are not given, such as the right not to suffer abuse or neglect.

Types of children's rights

It is conventional to offer the following typology of children's rights. On the one hand are participation rights. These, to simplify, represent children as subjects or agents, capable of exercising for themselves certain fundamental powers. Examples from the UNCRC are the rights of children under Article 13 to freedom of expression or that under Article 15 to freedom of association and to freedom of peaceful assembly. On the other hand, there are protection rights. These – again to simplify – represent children as patients or 'objects of concern' (Butler-Sloss 1988, p.245), potential victims of forms of harmful treatment. Key examples from the UNCRC are the right of the child under Article 19 to be protected from all forms of physical or mental violence, injury or abuse, neglect or negligent treatment, maltreatment or exploitation; or Article 32, which accords the child the right to be protected from economic exploitation and from performing hazardous work.

This distinction between protection and participation rights is often invoked in the service of an argument that children are, simultaneously and contradictorily, viewed as both capable and incapable of looking after their own interests. They are seen as needing to be protected and yet as entitled to make their own life choices. Yet we should proceed cautiously. For their part adults are given both liberty and welfare rights. The latter – such as rights to health care, to adequate housing and to gainful employment – are rights to be treated in certain ways or to receive certain goods. By contrast, liberty rights are rights that empower their possessors to act in ways that they choose.

Think of protection rights as a subset of welfare rights. It is true that adults have protection rights – not to be assaulted, for instance. However, the kinds of protection rights accorded to children are not normally those given to adults. Children merit protection against forms of ill-treatment they can suffer only inasmuch as they are not adults capable in principle of caring for themselves. There is thus in law no equivalent of an Article 19 to protect adults from abuse or neglect. This state of affairs derives from a strong antipaternalist assumption that adults should, in general, be at liberty to suffer the risks of their own actions so long as they are choosing voluntarily and are adequately forewarned of the dangers. We do not extend this antipaternalist assumption to children who are thought of as in need of forms of protection it would be utterly inappropriate to accord to adults. John Stuart Mill's celebrated antipaternalist liberty principle is qualified in the following manner:

> It is, perhaps, hardly necessary to say that this doctrine is meant to apply only to human beings in the maturity of their faculties. We are not speaking of children or of young persons below the age which the law may fix as that of manhood or womanhood. Those who are still in a state to require being taken care of by others must be protected against their own actions as well as against external injury. (Mill 1859, p.69)

It is worth adding that Mill himself clearly distinguished between a doctrine of social and political liberty, and the rules appropriate to the regulation of economic activity. Mill was disposed, as many libertarians are not, to safeguard the interests of labourers and to protect them from exploitation or from subjecting themselves, even voluntarily, to injurious or disadvantageous working conditions (Mill 1848, Book IV).

Protection and participation rights

The tension, or perhaps contradiction, between participation and protection rights finds its most dramatic expression in the two rights that are at the heart of the UNCRC, and indeed of all legislative instruments that deal with children. Article 3.1 of the UNCRC states that:

> In all actions concerning children, whether undertaken by public or private social welfare institutions, courts of law, administrative authorities or legislative bodies, the best interests of the child shall be a primary consideration.

The key legislative instruments of the United Kingdom in respect of children state that the child's welfare shall be the paramount consideration in determining key questions in respect of a child (Children Act 1989; Children (Scotland) Act 1995).

Article 12.1 of the UNCRC, on the other hand, affirms that

> State parties shall assure to the child who is capable of forming his or her own views the right to express those views freely in all matters affecting the child, the view of the child being given due weight in accordance with the age and maturity of the child.

Once again, legislation in England and Wales requires a court to have regard to the 'ascertainable wishes and feelings of the child concerned (considered in the light of his age and understanding)' (Children Act (1(3) (a))), with a similar provision in Scotland (Children (Scotland) Act 1995, para. 16(2)). Whereas Article 3.1 requires that the interests of any child, whatever her age and maturity, be promoted, Article 12.1 relativises the entitlement of a child to have her views taken account of to her capacities: her capacity to 'form' a view and her 'maturity'. Thus the Article stipulates, first, a threshold requirement upon the possession of the right to express one's views, namely that the child should be 'capable of forming' views, and, second, accords a weight to any such views proportionate to the child's maturity (for criticisms of these separate tests see Lockyer and Stone 1998, p.106).

In essence Article 3.1 is paternalist as are those other UNCRC Articles that can be described as 'protectionist'. For Article 3.1 requires that those entrusted with or in a position to provide for the care of children do what they, but not necessarily the child herself, judge is best for the child. By contrast the tenor of Article 12.1 is antipaternalist, as are those other UNCRC Articles that may be described as 'participatory'. Article 12.1 requires those who can care for or protect children to take seriously (the more seriously the more mature the child) what the child wants to happen. In the final analysis what a carer judges best for the child may diverge from what the child herself views as being for the best. Yet the UNCRC does not specify any more of a hierarchy of rights or principles than UK legislation. Article 4 of the UNCRC simply asks signatory states to take 'all appropriate measures' to implement the rights of the UNCRC. 'The rights' may reasonably be read as 'all the rights equally'.

Much then may depend on the precise formulation of the 'best interests principle'. It is thus worth noting that whereas the UNCRC speaks only of the child's best interest as a primary consideration, the UK legislation says that the child's welfare shall be the court's 'paramount' – that is, most important – consideration. On the stronger formulation a child's interests or welfare, as determined by those best placed to determine it, shall trump her own expressed views as to what shall happen.

Yet there is surely more to say about the relationship between Articles 3.1 and 12.1. First, showing that a child has got it wrong about her own best interests does not of itself show that she lacks the maturity to decide for herself. There is a general point of importance at stake here that is relevant even to the decisions of adults and to the proper scope of any paternalistic intervention into these decisions. A paternalist is warranted in usurping a person's choices only if the person is not competent to make her own choices and not just because the person chooses foolishly. It is the incapacity to choose that uncontroversially justifies paternalism. The folly of the choice counts in favour of that putative incompetence; it does not directly justify the paternalism.

Imagine a child who disputes what an official agency thinks should happen to her: an award of parental custody, a determination of where she shall live, a programme of social or educational work. The fact that the agency disagrees with the child does not of itself prove that the child lacks the maturity to decide for herself. It may think that she would be making a bad choice if allowed to do so, but this does not of itself warrant the judgement that she is incapable of making her own choices. After all adults are allowed to make – and very frequently do make – stupid decisions. Hence the views of a child as to what shall happen must still be given a weight proportionate to her maturity even when those views are judged to be contrary to her own best interests or welfare.

A further point to make about the relationship between Articles 3.1 and 12.1 is as follows. What a child confidently says she thinks is in her best interests need not be in her best interests. Indeed it will very often not be. Moreover those entrusted or empowered to act in her interests would be failing in their obligations under Article 3.1 if they did not accord a significant weight to what they so judged to be in the child's best interests. However two further comments are in order. First, what a child views as being in her best interests can provide us with an invaluable insight into what in fact is in her best interests. When a child tells us what she wants to happen she gives us important, and probably irreplaceable, information about her desires, beliefs, hopes, anxieties, fears, attachments and commitments.

Second, it surely cannot always be in a child's best interests to be compelled to do what she does not think is in her best interests. An influential claim in contemporary political philosophy is expressed under the title of the 'endorsement constraint' (Kymlicka 2002, p.216). This is held to apply to any sane adult and maintains that her life only goes well, and can only go well, if it is led from the inside according to values that she herself endorses. Many believe that the endorsement constraint is sufficient to show that paternalism, in respect of adults at least, is self-defeating. For you cannot force a person to lead the life that you think is better for him, since if he does not share your judgement and himself think it better, then he will not find it worth leading and it won't be better for him.

Something similar if not, strictly, exactly the same may be the case with children. We may not think that children are capable, as adults are, of choosing how to lead their lives, of having well-formed views about the best thing to do. Nevertheless, forcing them to do what you, but not they, think is for the best need not in fact be for their best. Children, like adults, do have beliefs and preferences. Enforcing courses of action that go against the grain of these beliefs and preferences can simply be counterproductive.

Justice and welfare

The distinction between participation and protection rights might be thought to bear some relation to an influential distinction between 'justice' and 'welfare' models of dealing with young offenders (see the Introduction to this book). The distinction can broadly be drawn as follows. A welfare model addresses the needs of the child, viewing these as the source of her misdeeds.

It seeks to rehabilitate or to treat the child, but not to punish her for her errors. By contrast the justice model focuses on the deeds of the child, viewing those that are misdeeds as meriting appropriate penalties. The child is to be punished, not helped or treated. In arguably similar terms protection rights are given to a child in respect of her needs, whereas participation rights are given to the child as an agent with her own wishes and views. The Scottish Children's Hearings System is often cited as a classic welfare model that speaks to the 'needs not deeds' of the child, although supporters of the system increasingly emphasise the importance of focusing on both. This prompts the question of whether or not such a 'welfare' system for dealing with young offenders answers to the requirements of justice. A further question is how it is possible to reconcile the welfarist approach to young offenders with an ascription to them of rights.

An approach that attends to 'needs not deeds' is not disposed to see any fundamental difference between the child who offends and the child who is in need of protection against abuse, neglect and other harms. Such indeed was the case with the Kilbrandon Report, which gave birth to the Scottish Children's Hearings System (Kilbrandon 1964). Hence any talk about how a juvenile justice system addresses the welfare of the child offender cannot be separated from broader questions of how the interests of *all* children are protected and promoted. That this is a proper matter of justice, more broadly understood, will be defended in the following section of this chapter.

But can we protect a child's interests or welfare and at the same time see the child as having participatory rights? Protecting someone against certain harms is not inconsistent with attributing to that person the capacity to exercise agency and rights. Some adults are vulnerable to forms of harm and ill-treatment that cannot be, or are unlikely to be, suffered by other adults: the disabled, members of ethnic minorities and the elderly, for example. We do not conclude that a vulnerability to suffer a harm that another will not suffer makes for an inability to secure adequate protection against that harm, or to act to demand protection. Protection rights protect children against harms that they suffer only or principally inasmuch as they are children. For instance, we believe, rightly, that a greater wrong is done to a child who suffers sexual abuse at the hands of an adult than is done to an adult who suffers non-consensual sex. But if we are to see children as the holders of protection *rights* we must guard against seeing them as passive, defenceless patients, or 'objects of concern', incapable of recognising their own interests. Protection rights are there to protect children against abuse by adults; they are not rights that of their nature cannot be exercised by children against adults. In short, the granting of protection rights to children does not, of itself, construe them as only the loci of needs.

Within western jurisdictions there has been a perceptible shift away from welfare towards criminal justice models (Muncie 2002, pp.27–35). Some of this may be due to a popular perception of the wickedness of contemporary youth – doubtless reinforced by the reporting of youth crime in the popular press – and a demand that the misdeeds of the young not be condoned but be appropriately punished. A common misperception of welfare-orientated systems of juvenile justice, such as the Scottish Hearings System, is that they simply spoil and indulge young offenders who know only too well how to exploit a non-punitive system (Morris *et al.* 1980).

However, the shift to a criminal justice model may also be attributable to a changing perception of children as agents, a change that can be explained in part by the increasing use of a participatory rights discourse in respect of children. If children do have and do exercise rights, especially liberty rights, then surely, the reasoning runs, they are properly thought of as responsible for their own actions? And if they are responsible in this manner then their misdeeds should be punished accordingly. The American Supreme Court determined in the landmark case *In re Gault* (1967) that the Fourteenth Amendment, which affords all citizens of the United States the equal protection of its laws, is not for adults alone. Thus children are entitled to the very same fundamental legal protection as adults.

The Supreme Court in the Gault case did not suggest that a 15-year-old should have appeared in an adult rather than a juvenile court. However, when children are conceived of as having the same due process rights as adults rather than simply being in need of protection by adults, it is natural to see them as more accountable to society for their actions. Hence the greater appropriateness of a criminal justice model for dealing with their offences. However, it is a gross oversimplification to think that the welfare model represents the child as not responsible for her actions, whereas the criminal justice model presupposes a capacity for wrongdoing on the part of the punished person. Certainly it is unfair to punish someone whom we view as not responsible for their actions. That is why we do not normally punish those persons whose 'crimes' can be explained by, and hence excused in virtue of, their insanity or ignorance.

Yet though this may be true, the converse does not hold. Even when we can reasonably hold a child to be responsible for her actions it does not follow that it is proper to try her in a court. The Scottish Law Commission's *Report on the Age of Criminal Responsibility* (Scottish Law Commission 2002) made the entirely correct distinction between two senses of an age of criminal responsibility. In one sense this age marks the point at which someone may be held responsible for their actions – that is, be properly viewed as capable of appreciating the difference between right and wrong and of acting voluntarily in the light of this difference. In another sense the age marks the point at which it is appropriate to subject someone to the processes of a criminal trial. The two ages need not correspond.

In the UK, in 1993 two 11-year-old boys were convicted of the murder of a toddler, James Bulger. There is little doubt that they acted maliciously, knowing and understanding the wrongfulness of their actions. They were morally responsible for the murder. In 1999 the European Court of Human Rights ruled that the proceedings at the original trial had violated their rights to a fair trial.[6] The original proceedings were unfair in that the defendants were compelled to sit in a large court, packed with people, whose conduct had all the formality of an adult trial – the judge and counsel, for instance, wearing wigs and gowns. The European Court ruled that the defendants were simply unable to follow the proceedings and hence to act in their own best interests.

We should thus remember that a criminal court does at least two things. First, it adjudicates on the truth of the matter, and determines whether or not the person committed the offence and displayed the required *mens rea* – that is, was guilty as charged. Second, it apportions an appropriate penalty in the light of this determination. Thus a court serves the ends of truth and those of the good of the offender and of others (the victim, society as a whole). It is not at all evident that a child's participation in a court of law will serve the ends of truth. We need only to remind ourselves of how distressing and intimidating it can be for a child to stand before adults and give testimony, how inappropriate the manner of eliciting information by the means of antagonistic cross-examination is for a child, and how very difficult it can be for a child to recall the past in a consistent and convincing manner.

Even if the child's appearance in court, appropriately modified in its proceedings, did serve the end of determining the truth there would still be the further question of whether it was appropriate, having made an adjudication of the facts, to punish the child for what it was found she had done.

In fact we need carefully to distinguish three matters. The first is that of guilt and responsibility. The second matter is the disposal of the case: what is a justifiable form or degree of punishment or compulsion in the light of what the child has done? Third, what is a fair procedure for determining guilt and an appropriate disposition?

Procedural fairness in the conduct of any trial or hearing is a prerequisite of a just decision. It must not only be fair to the child (which it was palpably not in the Bulger trial),[7] but to all affected parties. The procedures of a juvenile justice system must be regulated by rules that ensure there are proper opportunities for evaluating all the evidence and hearing from all parties (or their representatives) with a legitimate interest in the disposal. The silencing of anyone or failure to acknowledge some salient fact is unfair to the child.

In all three respects – attribution of responsibility, the determination of the disposal, and the decision procedures – we can talk about what is and what is not fair or just to the child and to other relevant parties. It is not thus that in adopting a 'welfare' model of juvenile justice fairness is set aside in the service of the child's needs or well-being. Such a model can be appraised for its fairness or unfairness. Justice is not sacrificed to welfare. Rather attending to the needs of the child may be what justice requires. It is entirely consistent with the approach that recognises the child's right to protection, her right to participation in matters that affect her, her welfare and the rights of other parties.

Social justice

There is one last but extremely important respect in which justice features. It is conventional to distinguish between justice within the sphere of the criminal and civil law and distributive or social justice. In the first sphere, as we have seen, principles of fairness regulate the procedures for fixing guilt or innocence and the proportionate determination of penalties or disposals. In the latter, principles of fairness regulate the distribution of social goods such as freedom, wealth and power, and burdens such as taxes. Now although the two sets of principles are often considered separately there are important relations between the two spheres of justice. To take the most obvious: if there is a strong correlation between socio-economic status and criminality, then the worse off may be argued to suffer an unreasonable, and unfair, burden in being legally punished for crimes whose commission is explicable by their poverty. Hence attending to the needs of those children who offend is demanded by justice if their offending is indeed attributable, in some significant measure, to their familial and social problems.

When we turn to child protection we can also see the relevance of considerations of social justice. The emerging approach to child protection – that, for instance, adopted in the recent report, *Every Child Matters* (Department for Education and Skills 2003) – can be termed 'holistic'. This means a number of things, including a requirement that the law in respect of the care and upbringing of children is unified and that there be integrated governance in respect of children – that is, the systematic co-ordination of health, educational and child care provision. Of direct relevance to the present discussion, holism means two things. The first, and most important, element of holism is a commitment to the view that child protection must be seen in the context of efforts to promote the general well-being of all children, an acknowledgement that child protection cannot be separated from policies to improve children's lives as a whole.

The second key element of a holistic approach to child protection is to be found in its characterisation of and response to child abuse and neglect. There is always a danger in this context of speaking in terms of mutually exclusive options when one should instead talk of ideal types. So with this caveat in mind, here are the features of very different approaches to child abuse. One sees abuse in episodic terms, as taking the form of occasional dramatic outbursts of harm or neglect. The opposite approach sees abuse as enduring, sustained, and exemplified in the form of a stable but dysfunctional relationship between a child and her guardian(s). The latter approach is arguably more disposed to see abuse as symptomatic of deeper problems that are not restricted to, though they may obviously include, the psychological characteristics of the child's guardians.

In terms of how abuse and neglect are treated, one approach seeks to be preventive rather than purely reactive. In other words it tries to identify those circumstances in which abuse is likely to occur and takes steps to forestall the need for intervention after the event. In related terms one approach to child abuse strives to work with the family as a whole, putting in place measures that allow the child to continue living with her guardians free from abuse or neglect. It provides the family with positive support and resources to facilitate this end. By contrast the other approach to abuse intervenes within the family, removing the child or the abusing guardian from the home. It prevents future abuse not so much by addressing its underlying causes as by making it impossible through the physical separation of abuser and abused child.

To repeat, the 'two' approaches thus characterised are more properly viewed as ideal types than as mutually exclusive options. In all likelihood child protection practices will be a mixture of both. Furthermore, to avoid gross oversimplification the following should be added. A holistic understanding of what abuse is does not automatically imply a holistic approach to its proper treatment. A child protection system could see a child's abuse as symptomatic of deeper underlying problems and yet regard the enforced separation of a child from its abuser as the appropriate response of the relevant agencies. Nevertheless the disposition to see abuse as part of a pattern of dysfunctional parenting, which may have broader causes, may well incline child protection organisations to respond with measures that go beyond the simple identification and judicial punishment of the perpetrator. The broader understanding of abuse can recognise that the child's interests are not best served by viewing her as a victim whose abuser should be locked up.

It should also be evident why a holistic approach to child protection broaches questions of justice. This is because both the protection of children against abuse and the broader promotion of every child's welfare must necessarily involve general social, economic and political measures that are egalitarian in import. Here too we rejoin the discussion of children's rights and reacquaint ourselves with the central significance of the CRC. Ensuring that every child enjoys a minimally decent life – which follows from the holistic commitment to improve children's lives as a whole – is best understood as making certain that every child enjoys the majority of those rights accorded to children in the UNCRC.

If any child is entitled to the enjoyment of some right then all are, equally. Moreover, the UNCRC accords every child a range of fundamental rights. These comprise liberty and welfare rights, the latter including protection rights. The UNCRC does not just accord children some liberty rights but, for instance and crucially, a right 'to the enjoyment of the highest attainable standard of health' (Article 24) and 'to a standard of living adequate for the child's physical, mental, spiritual, moral and social development' (Article 27).

The guaranteeing of these kinds of rights does have substantial and sub-stantive egalitarian implications. It is clear that very many children do not currently enjoy the second of these welfare rights, and that they fail to do so because of deep, structured inequalities. It needs to be added, not least because it is often forgotten, that many of the children in question live not in the developing world but in developed western societies. They are brought up below the poverty line. A commitment to end child poverty is also a commitment to eradicate the poor circumstances of those adults who rear such children. In sum, a holistic approach to child protection that sets it within the context of a commitment to promote equally the welfare of all children has substantial and substantive egalitarian implications.

In the previous section it was argued that fairness in a juvenile justice system requires us to address the needs of the offending child. We can now recognise that there is a broader requirement of justice that the needs of any child be addressed. The offending child is treated unfairly by a juvenile justice system that does not recognise what it is to be a child offender, and any child is unfairly treated if their needs, as a child, are not recognised.

Conclusions

Two overall conclusions can be drawn. First, the operation of a 'welfare model' of juvenile justice within the context of the UNCRC, which ascribes to children a wide range of legally protected rights, does not make the system any less a 'welfare' one. Indeed giving children rights is fully consistent with recognition of their special needs and the requirement to promote their best interests. Nevertheless, the tension between the demands of participation and of protection needs to be fully acknowledged.

Second, a welfare model of juvenile justice is not somehow beyond or outside the demands of fairness. On the contrary, such a system's treatment of young offenders can be fair and proportionate. Moreover, whether it is a child offender or a child in need of protection from abuse or neglect that is in question, it is imperative that their circumstances be examined, and ameliorated, in the light of a broader view of what social justice demands.

Notes

1. The term, 'juvenile justice system' here refers to institutional arrangements embodied in public law by which the state authorises compulsory intervention either in response to

offences committed by minors, or to protect young people from harm or risk of harm, or to meet their welfare needs.

2. For more on the UN Convention on the Rights of the Child (UNCRC) (1990), see www.unicef.org/crc/crc.htm.

3. Throughout this chapter I deliberately employ both male and female pronouns and possessive terms when denoting unidentified individuals. This is true of both adults and children.

4. Human Rights Act 1998, see www.hmso.gov.uk/acts/acts1998/19980042.htm.

5. European Convention on Human Rights (1950), see www.hri.org/docs/ ECHR50.html.

6. The Court also ruled that the British Home Secretary, in raising the original tariff, had violated the right for sentencing to be determined by a court independently of the executive.

7. For more on the Bulger case (1999), see http://cmiskp.echr.coe.int/tkp197/ portal.asp?sessionId=517772&skin=hudoc-en&action=request.

References

African Charter on the Rights and Welfare of the Child (1990), at www1.umn.edu/ humanrts/ africa/afchild.htm.

Butler-Sloss, E. (1988) *Report of the Enquiry into Child Abuse in Cleveland 1987*. London: HMSO.

Department for Education and Skills (2003) *Every Child Matters*. London: HMSO.

International Covenant on Economic, Social and Cultural Rights (CESCR) (adopted by the United Nations in 1966 and came into force in 1976), see www.unhchr.ch/html/menu3/ b/ a_cescr.htm.

Kilbrandon, Lord (1964) *Report of the Committee on Children and Young Persons, Scotland* (Kilbrandon Report), Cmnd 2306. HMSO; republished 1995 with F. Stone, 'Introduction', Children in Society Series, Edinburgh: HMSO.

Kymlicka, W. (2002) *Contemporary Political Philosophy: An Introduction (2nd edn)*. Oxford: Oxford University Press.

Lockyer, A. and Stone, F.H. (eds) (1998) *Juvenile Justice in Scotland: Twenty-Five Years of the Welfare Approach*. London: Butterworths.

MacCormick, N. (2001) 'A Special Conception of Juvenile Justice: Kilbrandon's Legacy.' Fifth Kilbrandon Child Care Lecture, see www.scotland.gov.uk/library5/education/ ch30-00.asp.

Mill, J.S. (1848) *Principles of Political Economy* (Book IV), edited with an Introduction by D. Winch. Harmondsworth: Penguin, 1985.

Mill, J.S. (1859) *On Liberty*, edited with an Introduction by G. Himmelfarb, Harmondsworth: Penguin, 1974.

Morris, A., Giller, H., Szwed, E. and Geach, H. (1980) *Justice for Children*. London: Macmillan.

Muncie, J. (2002) 'Policy Transfers and "What Works": Some Reflections on Comparative Youth Justice.' *Youth Justice 1*, 3.

O'Neill, O. (1988) 'Children's Rights and Children's Lives.' *Ethics 98*, 445–463.

Purdy, L.M. (1992) *In Their Best Interest? The Case Against Equal Rights for Children*. Ithaca, NY and London: Cornell University Press.

Scottish Law Commission (2002) *Report on the Age of Criminal Responsibility*. Edinburgh: The Stationery Office.

14

Human Rights and Children's Rights in the Scottish Children's Hearings System

Kathleen Marshall

Introduction

This chapter discusses the challenges that one institution, the Scottish Children's Hearings System, has faced and may face in the future as a result of the incorporation of the European Convention on Human Rights (ECHR) into UK law by the passage of the Human Rights Act 1998. This is viewed in the context of the additional commitment to the UN Convention on Rights of the Child (UNCRC), to which the UK has subscribed since November 1989. The narrative reveals that the Scottish system that has developed over 35 years has had to accommodate changed thinking about children's rights in relation to other family rights, which are given different prominence under the two conventions. Some issues and tensions remain as Children's Hearings seek to do justice to children and parents, substantially within a less formal setting than that of a court. The requirement to achieve a balance between the human rights of children and other parties has salience beyond the Scottish case.

The European Convention on Human Rights (ECHR)

The UK Human Rights Act 1998 applies the provisions of the ECHR 1950 to domestic law. The ECHR is part of the extensive progeny of the Universal Declaration of Human Rights, passed in 1948, in the aftermath of the Second World War as a response to the abuses perpetrated by totalitarian governments and to secure the individual freedoms that had been fought for. While children are equally entitled to benefit from almost all of the rights set out in the Declaration and the ECHR, few children and young people have (understandably) taken advantage of the rights and related processes, with the consequence that emphasis has, in practical terms, been placed on the *parents'* rights to due process and to protection from interference in family life, rather than the child's. In many cases the rights of parents and children will converge; parents might well be viewed as the defenders of the child and family against the forms of totalitarianism that these documents were designed to address. Today, while the role of parental rights in defending family life is not to be trivialised, they must in appropriate situations be balanced against the rights of the child. There is now greater recognition that it cannot always be taken on trust that parents will unerringly protect and care for their children. Increasing evidence of parental abuse and neglect in recent years has required some rethinking of the sanctity of the private sphere.

The rights of the child and the need of the child for protection, sometimes from parents, are a central focus of the UNCRC. While this does not have the same status in UK law as the ECHR, the European Court of Human Rights has come to regard it as a common standard to guide the interpretation of child-related law, since all European governments subscribe to the principles of the UNCRC. This mitigates what has been perceived as the parental focus of the ECHR (Lockyer 1999). So, how do these concerns fit in with the principles and philosophy of the Children's Hearings System?

The Kilbrandon principles

The Kilbrandon Commission, whose report led to the establishment of the Children's Hearings System, reported in 1964, chronologically between the adoption of the two conventions. The remit of the Committee was:

> To consider the provisions of the law of Scotland relating to the treatment of juvenile delinquents and juveniles in need of care or protection or beyond parental control and, in particular, the constitution, powers and procedure of the courts dealing with such juveniles, and to report. (Kilbrandon 1964)

A primary aim was to reduce, and ideally eliminate, juvenile delinquency (para. 12). The Committee considered that, if prevention was to be effective, it must focus on the ongoing needs of the individual child, rather than on a one-off punishment (Lockyer and Stone 1998). This approach created a bridge between the treatment of those who had offended and those requiring care and protection for other reasons. This common approach to both sets of initiating concerns was further supported by an examination of the personal and family situations out of which the concerns arose. The report identified the following as the 'basic problem':

> In terms of the treatment measures to be applied, the children appearing before the courts, whatever the precise circumstances in which they do so, show a basic similarity of underlying situation. The distinguishing factor is their common need for special measures of education and training, the normal upbringing processes for whatever reason having failed or fallen short. (Kilbrandon 1964, para. 15)

Thus, while there were at that time two court-based *processes*, focusing separately on offending and welfare issues, Kilbrandon was arguing that the *treatment* required for both classes of subject was the same. Young offenders and children presenting as in need of care and protection both needed 'educational' measures that would require the co-operation of parents, whose own behaviour might well have fallen short of what was expected. Kilbrandon therefore proposed to replace the two court-based processes that dealt separately with cases arising out of offending by the child, and the need for care and protection, with a unified system embracing both sources of concern as grounds for appropriate and similar 'treatment'.

The Children's Hearings System that was proposed would require the co-operation of parents to further its 'educational' approach. It was recognised that the element of compulsion could involve great inroads into family life and the liberty of the individual, and potential charges of 'unjustified interference' in the relationship between parent and child (paras 76, 111). The 'compulsion' was, however, focused on the child. Kilbrandon considered, and concluded against, imposition of compulsion or punitive measures on *parents*, on the basis that these would be both inappropriate and ineffective.

While conjoining the types of proceedings, Kilbrandon introduces the major innovation of institutionally separating the adjudication of proof from the disposal decision. The former was to be decided by the sheriff (a Scottish judge) and the latter – the 'measures to be applied' – by a lay panel. Proceedings before the panel would 'rarely raise legal issues' (para. 98). Thus the panel did not need to have the formal character or procedure of a court.

Questions of justice that did arise could be addressed by an appeal to the sheriff. Parents should have the right to be legally represented before the sheriff (children's rights are not mentioned) and legal aid should be available for that purpose (para. 116).

The independence of panel members would be secured through their appointment by a sheriff from a list submitted by the education authority. The independence of the 'Reporter' to the panel would be safeguarded by allocating to the sheriff authority to appoint and remove. It was recognised that this Reporter should also be demonstrably 'impartial', on the model of the public prosecutor (who is independent of the police). It should be noted here that the focus was on the Reporter's independence and impartiality in relation to the referring authorities (generally, police and social education), rather than the panel. It was envisaged that the Reporter would advise on such few legal issues as arose at the Hearing and would present the panel's case before the sheriff where there were disputed issues of fact, or appeals (para. 100). So a close association between Reporter and panel was in mind.

The Kilbrandon Committee recognised the need to keep attendance at Children's Hearings to the minimum required for effective functioning, in order to facilitate a 'full, free and unhurried discussion'. The three panel members, the Reporter and a clerical assistant would be present, as well as the child and his or her parents and the director of social education or one of his staff (para. 109). Emphasis was placed upon the involvement of both parents and child; although the report says that it might be appropriate in some cases for the child and parents to be seen independently of each other (para. 108). The emphasis throughout was that Hearings should be relatively informal and aim at seeking the co-operation of all parties.

Kilbrandon implementation and the ECHR

The recommendations of the Kilbrandon Committee, with a few exceptions, were largely those given effect by the Social Work Scotland Act 1968, which still forms the basis of the system in place today under the Children (Scotland) Act 1995.

It could be said that Kilbrandon was already taking account of some of the concerns of the ECHR, certainly with regard to parents' rights, even though the convention was not specifically referred to. The Kilbrandon Report acknowledges that there are justice implications in a potentially open-ended 'educative' process, involving some compulsory intervention in family life. These were more complex than affixing a punishment to crime, which could more easily be assessed on some objective scale of proportionality and have a definite point of termination. The report rejects the suggestion of fining parents for children's offences or requiring them to make compulsory restitution (paras 30–33) since this is not likely to enjoin their co-operation. However, attendance of parents at their child's Hearing is to be expected and required. There was to be a presumption that in 'the great majority of cases' children should 'remain within the home' where 'the most powerful and direct influences lie' (para. 17).

The ECHR's perceived focus on parents and family is consistent with the philosophy of the Kilbrandon Report, which speaks of the rights of *parents* rather than children to appeal decisions (para. 116), identifies the antagonists in any debate about unjustified interference in family life as the *parents* and the state (para. 111), and refers to the virtually complete lack of rights and responsibilities adhering to children under the age of puberty (para. 67). (Apart from *criminal* responsibility, of course. A paradox that remains.)

Nevertheless, Kilbrandon inches towards the protective function of the rights of the child in its recognition of the desirability in some cases of the Hearing seeing children and parents apart from each other, despite its perception that the numbers of children in need of care and protection from their parents would not be numerous.

With respect to children's rights it could be said that the Social Work (Scotland) Act 1968 took them a stage further. It did not unambiguously explicitly state the right of the child to attend the Hearing, although some consider this was implied (Kearney 2000). However, the right of appeal was afforded to both parent *and* child; and, importantly, the criterion for referral to the panel was not the 'public interest' but the child's need for compulsory measures of care.

In 1975, the potential for a conflict of interest between child and parent was explicitly recognised by insertion into the Act of a power of the Hearing to appoint a person to safeguard the interests of the child in the proceedings, where these might conflict with those of the parent. However, this was not implemented until 1985 and there was no presumption that the provision ought always to be used when such a conflict was identified (Lockyer 1994).

It seems that the interests and rights of children as individuals were gaining a higher profile with the march of time and experience. There was also increasing recourse to the language of rights and the prospect of rights-based challenges. Thus it is interesting to note that Kilbrandon referred to the possibility of seeing the child and parents separately, almost as a practical matter, without any indication that this might raise questions of human rights for either of them. There is a case to be made that the Hearings System at its inception was some way ahead of the ECHR with respect to children's rights, even though it reflected the parental focus of family rights in common with the European convention.

Human rights challenges to the Children's Hearings System

The following paragraphs set out some of the human rights challenges that have arisen since the introduction of the Children's Hearings System, arranged thematically, together with some relevant current debates and lingering questions.

To begin with it should be acknowledged that many of the pressures and trends that have affected the Scottish system during its 35 years have been driven by social changes and political responses more than provoked by issues of rights. Both the increasing number of care and protection referrals and concerns that these have taken precedence over dealing with persistent offending have led to demands for change. The growing complexity of cases and the requirement to measure effectiveness have developed alongside worry about the impact of crime, family breakdown and the proportionality of inter-ventionist measures. There is currently an impetus towards a greater separa-tion of care and protection from dealing with offenders that is linked with these concerns.

What is evident is that there remains an important human rights dimension to how Children's Hearings go about their business. As we have already seen, Kilbrandon identified and tried to address issues of justice and welfare, many of which had implications for the rights of family members. The challenges to the system that have emerged are in many of the areas that Kilbrandon anticipated.

The following discussion examines more closely some questions that have arisen under these headings, upon which the ECHR has a direct bearing. The most relevant articles of the ECHR are: Article 5, concerned with the right to liberty and security; Article 6, concerned with the right to a fair trial; and Article 8, concerned with the right to respect for family and private life. Some questions have actually given rise to legal challenges and some represent potential challenges that might in future require adjudication.

The adequacy of judicial scrutiny

Article 5 requires that the lawfulness of proceedings for any detention be decided speedily by a 'court'.

Kilbrandon considered that recourse to the sheriff would satisfy the requirement for judicial scrutiny. Some of the questions that subsequently arose on this issue were taken into account in the provisions of the Children (Scotland) Act 1995, in line with the government's stated intention to base that law on the two pillars of the ECHR and the UNCRC (Scotland's Children 1993).

European cases dealing with mental health patients and with the parole of discretionary life prisoners had given rise to questions about whether the place of safety order procedure under the 1968 Act satisfied the requirements of Article 5. In terms of that Act, a Children's Hearing would meet on the 'first lawful day' after the child's detention in a place of safety to 'consider the case' and decide whether further detention was necessary. But the Hearing was not a 'court' in respect that: (a) the Hearing had no power to hear evidence or adjudicate on disputed facts or law; and (b) its procedures did not meet the requirement of 'equality of arms', in that there is no guarantee of legal representation or entitlement to access reports.

In the run-up to the Children (Scotland) Act 1995, various suggestions were put forward to address this concern (Scottish Office 1993). One option was to make the Children's Hearing more like a 'court'. This was rejected as inconsistent with the fundamental character of the Hearing. Instead, Section 60(7) of the 1995 Act was introduced to allow child, parents and identified others to apply to the sheriff to have the new child protection order set aside or varied; thus providing a real and quick recourse to a proper 'court'.

There remains a question about the relevance of Article 5 to secure accommodation authorisations attached to supervision requirements. The condition may be appealed to the sheriff in terms of Section 51 of the 1995 Act, but it does not benefit from a 'fast track' procedure in the same way as an appeal against a warrant does; Section 51(8) says appeals against warrants must be disposed of within three days. Should there be a speedy procedure for appeals against secure authorisations too?

Procedures for more general appeals from the Hearing to the sheriff were also considered vulnerable. First, this was because sheriffs had interpreted their appellate function narrowly, as a mechanism for reviewing the legality of the Hearing's decision-making process, rather than as a rehearing of the merits with the possibility of a substitution of their decision (Kearney 2000). The second reason was that appeals before the sheriff also suffered from the lack of 'equality of arms' because of the inability of parents and child to have access to reports before the court.

The question of the restricted appellate function of the sheriff was addressed by Section 51(c)(iii) of the Children (Scotland) Act 1995, which permitted the sheriff allowing an appeal to 'substitute for the disposal by the children's Hearing any requirement which could be imposed by them' under Section 70 of this Act. This had the potential for blurring Kilbrandon's distinction between the legal forum that adjudicated on facts and the Hearing that decided on treatment; but it does not appear to have made a great impact in practice (Norrie 1995).

Access to reports

The question of the availability of reports is relevant primarily to Article 6 of the ECHR, which guarantees the entitlement to a fair trial (which may be civil or criminal in character). The question was brought to a head by the case of *McMichael v. UK*, which came to judgment in 1995. The European Court of Human Rights concluded that the parents' lack of access to reports within the Children's Hearing and associated processes undermined the fairness of that civil 'trial' (*McMichael v. UK* 1995).

The subsequent amendment of the Children's Hearing (Scotland) Rules to make reports available to parents or 'relevant persons' concluded the matter as regards parents arguably too generously, but left it dangling as regards the children who were the focus of the proceedings. This lack was the subject of debate in the more recent case of *S v. Principal Reporter and the Lord Advocate* (para. 38), during which an assurance was given that the deficit would be remedied by introduction of procedures to make reports available to children and young people, subject to some kind of 'sifting' to ensure that no inappropriate information was given to them. This procedure has now been put in place.

Legal representation

Article 6 is also relevant to legal representation. The question of the availability of free legal representation was central to *S v. Principal Reporter and the Lord Advocate*, a case involving an alleged offence by a 15-year-old. Article 6 was invoked because, as indicated above, the right to a fair 'trial' includes the determination of civil rights and obligations, such as those relating to interference in family life. However, there was a debate about whether Article 6 applied to this case in its civil or criminal aspect. If the procedure whereby the grounds of referral to the Hearing were put to the child and family, and accepted or denied at the Hearing, was classified as the determination of a *criminal* charge, this would bring in those parts of Article 6 that were *specific* to criminal charges – in particular Article 6(3), requiring the availability of legal assistance and the opportunity to examine witnesses, and so on. Further, these standards would have to be met within the Hearing itself. It would not be sufficient to rely upon the possibility of recourse to the sheriff. However, the court decided that, while consideration of a criminal offence was clearly involved, S was not 'charged' with it at the Hearing, and it was not a criminal process because there was no penal element in the disposals available to the Hearing. Nevertheless, other provisions of Article 6 applied.

It was accepted that the fairness of the proceedings in terms of Article 6.1 could be determined with reference not only to what went on at the Children's Hearing, but to the court processes to which the participants had access, as Kilbrandon had envisaged (*S v. Principal Reporter and the Lord Advocate* para. 38). However, the court concluded that the lack of legal representation at the Children's Hearing adversely affected the ability of the child to influence the outcome of the Hearing and therefore breached Article 6.1. This did not mean that legal representation had to be available in all cases, but it should at least be possible in those cases where it was in the interests of justice to do so. This matter was remedied by the Children's Hearings (Legal Representation) (Scotland) Rules (dated 2002).

The issues of access to reports and the availability of legal representation were linked in respect that supplying information to children would often be an 'empty gesture' if they did not have help to interpret and use it (*S v. Principal Reporter and the Lord Advocate*, paras 37, 66, 74).

The whole debate about Article 6 is relevant in terms of the development of the Children's Hearings System and indeed any alternatives to traditional criminal procedures. Article 40.3 of the UNCRC encourages states to develop laws and procedures specific to child offenders, including 'whenever appropriate and desirable, measures for dealing with such children without resorting to judicial proceedings, providing that human rights and legal safeguards are fully respected'.

Taken together with Article 6.3 of the ECHR, this means that extra-judicial procedures must always respect Article 6.1 of the ECHR, even if they focus on welfare rather than punishment. If penal measures are included, then the more formal and stringent requirements of Article 6.3 must also be factored in.

Impartiality of the Reporter

The impartiality of the Reporter has also been called into question. It has been suggested that the Reporter's dual role in bringing the case to the Hearing and advising the panel is analogous to what would happen if the Procurator Fiscal, having brought the case to a district court, then advised the magistrate what to do. The problem here is that, viewed in the context of the model of 'equality of arms', it is not always clear who is fighting whom. The answer seems to depend upon the stage of the process under consideration. Kilbrandon had considered the impartiality question at the stage of the presentation of the case to the panel. Here the battle may be seen to be between the referring authorities (police and 'social education') and the family. On this view, the Reporter is an independent presenter of the case and also able to give impartial advice to the Hearing on any legal issues that arise.

However, let us look more closely at the different stages. First, at the stage when the Hearing puts the grounds of referral to the family, the Reporter's impartiality might be questioned. It is the Reporter who brings the case to the Hearing, since social workers or police have a duty only to investigate and report; it is the Reporter's judgement that there is a sufficiency of evidence to prove the grounds and also that the child might require compulsory measures of supervision. Norrie (2000) has rightly pointed out that this role of adviser is not conferred by law, but in practice advice is sought and given. It is also exactly what Kilbrandon envisaged (Kilbrandon 1964, para. 100).

Second, at the stage of proof of the grounds before the sheriff, as Norrie agrees, 'the reporter is certainly the opponent' (Norrie 2000, p.21). This does not, it seems, disqualify the Reporter from advising the sheriff on whether the child would benefit from having independent representation, or that a safeguarder might be needed to act in the child's interests, advice that sheriffs apparently recognise as disinterested (Hill *et al.* 2002, Chapter 6).

At the third stage of Hearing's disposal decision, Norrie argues that:

> the reporter has an entirely disinterested position so far as the outcome is concerned. It is the local authority (through the social work department) who is trying to persuade the hearing to adopt the recommendation that they make and if the child has an 'opponent' it is this body. (Norrie 2000, p.21)

It seems doubtful that the professional independence of the Children's Reporter is sufficient to guarantee his or her impartiality at all stages of the Hearings process. Suffice to say that it is especially important for the lay Hearing chair to be competent in matters of procedure, especially at the stage prior to proof (Lockyer 1999).

Delay

Anyone reading the law reports will notice the extent to which allegations of delay have been used in support of claims of breach of convention rights in criminal cases. With regard to children, there has been judicial acknowledgement of the particular need to bring offenders under 16 to trial swiftly (*Craig Garry Cook v. HMA* 2000). In child welfare cases too there has for some time been recognition of the adverse impact of delay; a principle built in to the Children Act 1989 for England and Wales, but not as explicit in the Scottish legislation. The Children's Hearings System has acknowledged the need to deal with cases expeditiously through the Blueprint for the Processing of Children's Hearing Cases. The question of whether other parties are adversely affected was discussed in an Inner House Court of Session case on 26 June 2003 (*EC and Mrs MC v. Alan D. Miller, Principal Reporter*). This was concerned with serious offences alleged to have been committed against children by their father. For various reasons, the establishment of grounds was subject to considerable delay. The court was subsequently asked to find that the applicant's human rights under Article 6 had been breached, and that the sheriff's establishment of the grounds should be rescinded. There were many complex issues raised in this case; as regards delay, Lord Osborne observed:

> Having regard to the purpose of such proceedings as these...we have the greatest difficulty in accepting that a reduction of the sheriff's decision, at the instance of a party who is not the child whose welfare is sought to be promoted in the proceedings, could ever be appropriate where the nature of the complaint was unreasonable delay. If indeed in such proceedings, the human rights of some other individual or individuals, such as the appellants, had been shown to have been breached, it appears to us that any remedy to be granted would require to avoid undermining the primary purpose of the proceedings themselves. (*EC and Mrs MC v. Alan D. Miller, Principal Reporter.* Opinion of the court delivered by Lord Osborne, para. 97)

He concluded that, while an award of damages might appropriately be pursued in other proceedings, the interests of children would not be served by reduction of the finding.

Human rights and parties to proceedings

One of the major areas of dubiety and possible contention for the Children's Hearings System relates most closely to Article 8 of the ECHR, which is concerned with respect for family and private life.

Kilbrandon had envisaged the attendance at Hearings of parents (or guardians) and children. But family structures have become much more complex since the 1960s, with a large increase in non-marital relationships, which comes together with the increase in child protection cases. This raises a range of issues that relate both to who should be entitled to be considered parties to the Children's Hearing proceeding and what rights this entails.

Before addressing the question of whether Article 8 has been breached, courts have to consider whether the question of 'family life' is relevant. The European Court of Human Rights has dealt extensively with this issue, and approaches it on the basis of whether de facto family ties exist. In some cases they might exist even where there is no legal relationship between the parties. Thus the Court held that family life *might* exist in a case involving an uncle and his nephew, who had been taken into care, on the basis of their close ties. It did not come to a conclusion because the case moved to a 'friendly settlement' (*Boyle v. the UK* 1994). On the other hand, it has spoken about the potential for the bond of family life between child and parent to be broken, even where the child was the product of a marital union and parental responsibility existed. However, this would be the case only in exceptional circumstances (*Gul v. Switzerland* 1996, paras 32–43).

In the Children's Hearings System, the right of attendance of family members other than the child since the 1995 Act has related to the definition of 'relevant persons'. The definition in the Act is slippery (Norrie 1995, 36.5); it includes those having parental responsibilities or rights, and anyone who, it appears, 'ordinarily' has charge of or control over the child, other than by reason only of his employment. Other persons with something to contribute may be invited to attend at the chairman's discretion, but this is far short of the standing of a 'relevant person', which is a powerful status. 'Relevant persons' have a right to attend Hearings, to accept or reject the grounds, to appeal, to call for reviews, and to receive all the information that is presented to the panel members. So let us look at how that applies to some people who may, or may not, be regarded as 'relevant' in the more colloquial sense of the word.

Unmarried fathers

European jurisprudence does not insist on the recognition of unmarried fathers, on the basis that no common standard yet exists between member states. The issue was raised in the *McMichael* case, where the Court recognised legal arrangements seeking to allow identification of 'meritorious' fathers from among the spectrum of possible relationships involved. However, given the shifting pattern of family relationships, this is something that may change, as the Court operates on a principle of 'evolutive interpretation' in which it allows itself the latitude to develop its interpretations in line with changing circumstances. Many unmarried fathers in Scotland will sometimes of course fall within that part of the definition of 'relevant persons' relating to 'ordinary' charge or control over the child. As for others, under the 1998 Act the rights and responsibilities of unmarried fathers are largely at the discretion of mothers (4.1). This has been viewed as contrary to UNCRC Article 18, placing common responsibilities on both parents, and ECHR Article 14 against sexual discrimination (Norrie 1997). The Scottish Parliament recently amended the law to extend parental rights and responsibilities to those unmarried fathers who, after 4 May, 2006, register the birth of their child jointly with the mother (Family Law (Scotland) Act 2006). This will go some way towards addressing these concerns.

Abusive parents

A few years ago, the *Herald* contained an article by Ruth Wishart headed, 'When Two Human Rights Make an Inhuman Wrong' (Wishart 2001). She described a Children's Hearing case in which an abusive father insisted on his human right to attend and to deny the ground of referral. Even though the Hearing saw the parties separately, as far as the child victim was concerned, 'the thought of her father's proximity was so devastating she threatened suicide'. She was also disturbed at the thought that all the papers relating to the case were sent to Peterhead Prison where her father was now residing. The article refers to the father's 'inalienable right' to be consulted and involved in decisions about his child's future, and asks where that leaves the rights of the child.

Of course, parental rights are not truly 'inalienable'. The courts are well accustomed to removing or restricting parental rights. One might argue that, just as the courts are now prepared to award parental responsibilities and rights to allow an unmarried father to attend a Hearing, so they should be willing to entertain applications to restrict them in order to keep an abusive 'relevant person' away.

On the other hand, those alleged to have committed offences against children, including allegedly abusive fathers where there has been no conviction, might have a real interest in the proceedings without any right to be involved. If they are not 'relevant persons', and the grounds are accepted by the child and mother, there appears to be no forum in which to challenge it. That does not seem right and could constitute a breach of Article 6.

Other 'relevant persons'

A 'relevant' person might be the temporary partner of the principal carer who for a time has the 'ordinary' charge or control of the child. This raises the question of what length of contact and degree of attachment is required to obtain this legal standing in relation to a child's affairs. The Children (Scotland) Act 1995 does provide a mechanism whereby, in cases of doubt, the 'relevance' of a person can be discussed at a 'business meeting' of panel members prior to a Hearing. It is important to note that 'relevant person' is so powerful a position that it should not be conferred lightly.

A particular instance of this is the relatively recent extension of the status of 'relevant person' to some foster carers; a determination facilitated by the case of *JS and TK v. MN and Ewan Cameron* in February 2002, in which foster carers were successful in claiming that status. I understand that, on the back of that decision, informal guidance has advised on the length of time before foster carers might generally be considered as 'relevant persons'.

It may seem fair to regard long-term foster carers as 'relevant persons', even though the Fostering of Children (Scotland) Regulations 1996 define 'fostering' as the placement of a child with someone who is not a 'relevant person'. However, if this category is extended too far, it may breach the rights to privacy of the child and natural parents by allowing someone with a relatively short involvement to have access to all the information about the family, and a very strong status in the proceedings. It may well be helpful to invite such people to attend, and perhaps the intimation provision relating to appeals (the issue at stake in this case) could be extended, but to call them 'relevant persons' – a dangerously innocuous phrase – runs the risk of breaching Article 8.

The child

There has been a growing recognition of the participatory rights of children within the Scottish system. From the outset it could be argued that Children's Hearings were ahead of their time in enjoining the participation of children in advance of adopting the UNCRC (Lockyer and Stone 1998). The formal entitlements of children have continued to expand. As already referred to, children now have a right to attend most decision-making fora and a carefully circumscribed right to receive information. They also have a right to have a legal representative present when critical matters, such as their liberty, are at stake. There may still be questions about how we make their participation real and effective.

An issue that relates to the opportunity that children have to express their views is the extent to which these may be given in confidence. There is something of a paradox, in terms of the current rules, that the child's views cannot be kept confidentially from relevant persons at a Children's Hearing, but can if the case reaches the sheriff. The Children (Scotland) Act 1995 permits the exclusion of relevant persons and their representatives from parts of the Hearing to allow the child to speak more freely. However, the excluded persons must, on their return, be told the substance of what the child has said (Section 46). Further, all reports to the Hearing, including any written by the child, must be passed on to the 'relevant persons'. On the other hand, the rules of court allow the child's confidential views to be put in a sealed envelope, available only to the sheriff (Sheriff Court Child Care and Maintenance Rules 3.5(4) 1997). Sheriff Kearney (2000) points out the problems this can raise in the context of the law of evidence.

This is a classic instance of a clash between the right of children to privacy, and perhaps protection, and the rights of parents that were upheld (without reference it should be said to children's rights) in the *McMichael* case. Whether a challenge along the lines of *McMichael* would be successful depends upon the extent to which the court would be willing to balance the human rights of the parents in terms of Articles 6 and 8 with those of the child.

Conclusions

With respect to the general question of the relationship between the Children's Hearings System and the ECHR it can be concluded that the interpretation of the Convention and the development of the System have converged. Both were creatures of their time, each started out with greater explicit focus on the rights of parents rather than those of children. The implicit recognition of the rights of children was present to a greater extent from the inception of the Hearings System in the 1960s than was evident in the 1950 Convention, in immediate post-war Europe. These rights have become more explicit as the System has embraced the UNCRC, which has also influenced the application of the ECHR. The Human Rights Act has required UK jurisdictions to give greater formal recognition to human rights, and this has led to changes to the Children's Hearings System.

This has not, however, been matched by an updating of the actual content of the ECHR alongside the revision of Scottish law, which has gradually given more explicit recognition to the rights of the child. Therefore the capacity of the ECHR to embrace the rights of the child fully is dependent upon the extent to which those interpreting and applying it are willing to promote the 'evolutive interpretation' of the Convention in that direction.

Even if this process were proceeding in an acceptable way, there would be considerable merit in revising the ECHR in the light of the UNCRC. The basic concepts about justice, fairness and equality of arms embedded in the ECHR envisage equal entitlements, which overlook the relative disadvantage and the particular needs of children. This is because the extension of human rights to children requires recognition of their special status – some rights are peculiar to children.

As for the actual or threatened changes to the purpose of the Children's Hearings, these seem to have come about as a reaction to pragmatic considerations and political imperatives. Recalling the debates about whether Article 6 applied to the Hearing in its civil or criminal aspect, one must remember that the decisive factor in saying it was not criminal was the lack of a punitive element. If a punitive element is integrated into the Hearings System, then it must become more like a real court.

One of the most difficult issues identified above is the question of the entitlement of parties to participate in Hearings. This is much more than a matter of procedure: it goes to the heart of who are to be considered 'family members' with rights and duties relating to children, and what impact this has on children and their rights to privacy. The status of 'relevant persons' is the Scottish form of a universal issue, which goes far beyond the entitlement to participate in judicial or quasi-judicial proceedings. Even though other jurisdictions can avoid the problem of relevant parties by treating young offenders as individuals outwith the context of their families, it re-emerges not only in care and protection proceedings, but in all those contexts where families have to be conceptualised, or 'constructed', to determine who may enjoy family rights. As adults appear to exercise greater freedom of choice in constructing familial relations it seems reasonable to give children a greater say as to who are persons 'relevant' to them.

This chapter has not sought to differentiate between Hearings by grounds for referral. The finding in the important case of *S v. Principal Reporter and the Lord Advocate* means that the human rights of parties in the proceedings are essentially the same (even though the standard of proof differs between offences and care and protection grounds).

The relevance of human rights to the issue of separate or conjoined systems seems to be this: human rights are basically about human dignity, which requires that a person be regarded as whole and not as a package of separable 'issues'. This was a central insight of Kilbrandon, and one that we are today in danger of losing. It seems nonsensical to divide children and young people up into their offending parts and their developmental parts.

There is a lot of talk today about the need for 'joined-up government', but there is little point if governments are not directed towards the 'joined-up child'. All we will have done is to shift the locus of fragmentation. We have come to adopt the saying that the child is not merely an 'object of concern' – neither is he or she a separable bundle of concerns. It is all one, and so it should remain.

References

Boyle v. The UK (1994) A 282-B, Application 16580/90.

Craig Garry Cook v. HMA Sheriff Court, 21 August 2000.

EC and Mrs MC v. Alan D. Miller, Principal Reporter. Inner House, Court of Session, 26 June 2003 (Scottish Courts Website). Opinion of the Court delivered by Lord Osborne.

Gul v. Switzerland. 1996-I, 159.

Hill, M., Lockyer, A., Batchelor, S., Morton, P. and Scott, J. (2002) *Safeguarding Children's Interests in Welfare Proceedings.* Scottish Executive CRU and EYPRU Publications, www.scotland.gov.uk/cru and www.scotland.gov.uk/edru.

JS and TK v. MN and Ewan Cameron. Inner House, Court of Session, 8 February 2002 (Scottish Courts website).

Kearney, B. (2000) *Children's Hearings and the Sheriff Court* (2nd edn) Edinburgh: Butterworths.

Kilbrandon, Lord (1964) *Children and Young Persons.* Edinburgh: Scottish Office.

Lockyer, A. (1994) 'Interests and Advocacy: Identifying the role of Safeguarders in the Scottish Children's Hearings System.' *Children and Society 8,* 1, 55–68.

Lockyer, A. (1999) 'The impact of the European Convention on Human Rights on the Children's Hearings System.' In B. Reid (ed) *Facing the Future: Challenges of the 21st Century.* Glasgow: Glasgow University, CPT publication.

Lockyer, A. and Stone, F.H. (1998) *Juvenile Justice in Scotland: Twenty-five Years of the Welfare Approach.* Edinburgh: T & T Clark.

McMichael v. United Kingdom. 24 February 1995, A 307-B; 20 EHRR 20.

Norrie, K. (1995) *Children (Scotland) Act 1995.* Edinburgh: W. Green/Sweet & Maxwell.

Norrie , K. (1997) *Children's Hearings in Scotland.* Edinburgh: W. Green/Sweet & Maxwell.

Norrie, K. (2000) 'Human Rights Challenges to the Children's Hearings System.' *Journal of the Law Society of Scotland (LSJ) 45,* 4, April.

S v. the Principal Reporter and the Lord Advocate. Scottish Courts website. (Also reported as *S v. Miller* 2001 SLT 531.

Scotland's Children: Proposals for Child Care Policy and Law (1993) (White Paper) Cmnd 2286. Edinburgh: HMSO.

Scottish Office (1993) Consultative Proposal on *Emergency Protection of Children in Scotland.*

Wishart, R. (2001) 'When Two Human Rights make an Inhuman Wrong.' *Herald,* 1 November.

15

Conclusions

Andrew Lockyer, Malcolm Hill and Fred Stone

The broader context to youth crime and children's well-being

In conclusion, we draw together the main themes that have emerged throughout this book. In this chapter, references to authors that are not followed by a date refer to earlier chapters. This book has been concerned with state intervention in relation to threats to children's well-being and 'threats' that children are seen to pose to the well-being of society when they commit crimes. The particular focus has been on the implications of treating these two different kinds of concern about children in similar ways within the same system or through separate mechanisms with different principles and procedures. In particular, a Scottish system that emphasises an integrated approach has been considered alongside and compared with other countries where, to differing extents, youth justice and child care and protection are dealt with separately. Our focus has deliberately been circumscribed to allow for in-depth consideration of vital issues involving vulnerable young people, but it is essential to acknowledge the broader context.

It was not intended, or indeed possible, to cover all aspects of this issue. Consideration has been confined to countries in western Europe and North America. The book has concentrated on responses to problems affecting or involving children. Consequently it has not attended to questions about what actions by governments or other social institutions within civil society might stop those problems arising in the first place – or reduce their incidence. This would include measures to tackle poverty and social inequalities (Korpinen and Pösö), as well as more immediate causes of family problems. Archard and others have observed that this is a matter of social justice as much as a function of children's welfare. The well-known association between poverty and referrals concerning many kinds of child care and family problems reflects the impact of material disadvantage on family life (Ennis; Korpinen and Pösö). In addition, the attention of law-enforcement and helping professionals tends to concentrate on the less well-off, while the affluent are better able to defend themselves from the gaze of public authorities (Waterhouse).

Ideas about prevention and early intervention have been prominent in policy, theory and practice for some time with respect to both child care and protection and youth justice. There have been different emphases and there may be scope for mutual learning across the boundaries. In the UK, prevention in relation to child care and protection has often been conceptualised using stage or level models derived from public health and social policy frameworks (Canavan, Dolan and Pinkerton 2000; Hardiker, Exton and Barker 1991). The emphasis has often been on support to parents and/or strategies for changing parental attitudes and behaviour (Quinton 2004). Less commonly, it has been recognised that broader social inequalities, attitudes and practices require tackling (e.g. as regards poverty, the status of children and women, and ideas about punishment) (Boushel 1994; Dominelli 1999). Account also needs to be taken of wide-ranging demographic, social and technological changes that are impinging on family life and young people's behaviour. For instance, trends such as individualisation and detraditionalisation (Beck and Beck-Gernsheim 2002) heighten opportunities for greater freedom and diversity, but also increase the scope for challenging consensual expectations about children's care and behaviour.

There is clearly overlap here with the long-standing idea that one of the root causes of much youth crime lies in defective parental upbringing. Hence a prominent strand in early intervention strategies with respect to youth crime is policies and programmes that offer support to parents, often explicitly or implicitly linked to training parents and older children to adopt ideas and actions that promote pro-social behaviour (Korpinen and Pösö). Indeed some of the main types of programmes advocated for crime prevention were set up primarily to overcome child care problems among poor households in disadvantaged communities (Schweinhart and Weikart 1997). However, a distinctive element in crime prevention has been directed at reducing the opportunities to commit crime, in contrast to affecting individuals' criminal propensity. This has been associated with a range of situational and neighbourhood responses, ranging from the use of CCTV to Neighbourhood Watch schemes and comprehensive risk-resilience area-based initiatives (Jonkman, Junger-Tas and van Dijk 2005; Whyte). With some exceptions (Gilligan 1999), similar whole-community and situational initiatives have not been developed in relation to child care and protection, but there is scope for exploring further how lessons could be applied.

Within youth justice thinking in the 1980s, opposition was strong towards certain kinds of preventive action, because it was feared that engaging young people at an early stage of their criminal career in formal preventive programmes might reinforce their criminal identity and lay them open to more intrusive sanctions if they did not co-operate. Hence influential academics favoured diversion or minimal intervention to prevention, and this approach influenced many practitioners as well as government policies in the UK (Burnett and Appleton 2004; Whyte). While this view still holds considerable sway in England and Scotland, recent policies have encouraged a return to preventive action at an early stage, though targeted at young people assessed as having a high risk of reoffending (Bottoms and Kemp). As Whyte notes, the minimal intervention approach may be appropriate for some who will simply grow out of crime, but may be a missed opportunity for others, whose earlier behaviour problems will escalate into persistent offending unless early service input is provided.

The links between decision-making and service delivery

While several chapters have referred to prevention, this book has largely focused on situations when prevention has failed, so that judicial or quasi-judicial decisions have to be made about whether compulsory state intervention is warranted to modify the care environment or criminal behaviour of children. National patterns for separating or integrating these decisions are diverse. In Finland and Sweden, offending is subsumed by courts within holistic appraisals of children up to 15, as in Scotland's Children's Hearings up to 16 (Hollander and Tärnfalk; Korpinen and Pösö; Whyte). In England and many US states, the courts differentiate offending cases from a younger age (Bottoms and Kemp; Creekmore). Irish policy has recently aimed to maintain within the care and protection system very troubled young people who commit crimes (Buckley and O'Sullivan).

Whatever the legal institutional context, decision-making is inextricably bound up with the actions of varied service agencies that carry out assessments and, most importantly, implement the decisions (Hollander and Tärnfalk; Kuenssberg). In most countries the service agencies and professionals are separate from the courts, but in some jurisdictions certain service providers or probation officers may be court based, while in the USA courts quite commonly provide a wide range of services themselves. Duquette believes it is not appropriate to combine judicial and executive functions and powers in a single institution and recommends that social services be separate from courts.

Just because the law or a judicial decision requires a service to be offered, this does not necessarily mean that the service will be provided to the extent or in the manner expected. While high priority is usually given to statutory obligations, there are other influences on practice (Creekmore), including the impact of resources, and differing values and interpretations at policy-making managerial and front-line levels. In a Scottish context, Waterhouse pointed to evidence about deficiencies in social work operationalisation of Children's Hearings disposals – for example, vague plans and goals, inadequate staff resources to offer a sufficiently intensive service. Ennis described acute staff shortages in several areas. By contrast, in Ireland there has been a rapid expansion of public provision over the last 15 years (admittedly from a low base), due in part to a loss of confidence in religious institutions as a result of specific child abuse scandals and a more general trend towards secularisation (Buckley and O'Sullivan). The latter echoes earlier trends in other countries such as the USA (Creekmore). It has been noted in many countries that service effort has been focused on 'high risk' cases, whether these be of child abuse or youth crime, with intensive preventive and family support services relatively underdeveloped (e.g. Buckley and O'Sullivan; Kuenssberg).

In the USA a prominent recent development has involved steps to oblige welfare agencies to comply with judicial orders. Courts can review case progress, and if agencies have not provided the services stipulated they can be held in contempt (Duquette; Ennis). Similarly collective actions can be brought to court on behalf of children to compel provision of services they are thought to be entitled to (Robinson Lowry, Freundlich and Gerstenzang 2002). Such measures are not without problems, especially when sometimes the persons responsible for the services are employed by the courts (Duquette).

The nature and extent of separation in judicial or quasi-judicial management of decisions about offending and non-offending referrals may not have close correspondence in the service sector. In Sweden, youth offending from age 15 is dealt with by separate courts, but the sentences are carried out by the same service agencies as handle care and protection cases (Hollander and Tärnfalk). In recent years, the decision-making system in England has remained separate, with different kinds of courts (family proceedings and youth courts) dealing with care and protection and youth crime, and making distinct orders. However, there has been more 'convergence' within the associated services that implement orders, particularly as a result of government policies encouraging multidisciplinary approaches in recognition of the importance of 'welfare' issues as criminogenic factors (e.g. family matters, education and employment) (Bottoms and Kemp). At the front line, a shift in professional practice has occurred. The 1990s were characterised by sharp boundaries between remits and expertise in youth justice and child care, whereas in the early years of the new millennium, practitioners increasingly value co-operation (Bottoms and Kemp). The inter-agency partnership approach favoured by central government has helped create more comprehensive assessments and interventions, although with a risk that young people lack a single key person they can relate to (Burnett and Appleton 2004). Also problems about structures, roles and communication have arisen that echo those long experienced in child protection (Buckley 2003; Hallett 1995). By contrast, Scotland has retained its integrated decision-making system with the same forum and range of disposals for all kinds of referrals, but the service sector has become more specialist, especially with regard to young people over 15 (Whyte). Following the English pattern, Local Authorities now usually have distinct youth justice teams and children and families teams. These may provide helpful divisions of responsibility between different workers, but uncertainty and discontinuity can also result, as in the American experience (Creekmore). In the UK, child care and protection services have typically focused on family support or remedial care and assistance to the child. The links between deficient care and behaviour problems have been widely recognised (e.g. Cairns 2002; Taylor 2004), but interventions have paid little attention to the strong likelihood of future offending and methods for avoiding this.

It seems that in all countries, regardless of the approach, inter-agency co-operation is underdeveloped (Ennis; Jonson-Reid 2004). This can mean poor co-ordination between child care and youth justice agencies, as in the USA, but also involves other relations, as between children's and health services (Buckley and O'Sullivan; Creekmore). A particular concern is that agencies that focus on helping adults (e.g. in relation to parental drug misuse) may neglect the needs of children (Ennis).

Most countries in western Europe have witnessed a shift away from residential provision as a way of responding to both children's care needs and youth crime, except for the most extreme circumstances (Buckley and O'Sullivan; Hill 2000; Korpinen and Pösö). In Sweden, though, there was a growth in custodial sentences for young people in the 1990s, while there were also surges in the use of custody in the USA and UK during the later part of the twentieth century (Haines and Drakeford 1998; Hollander and Tärnfalk; Whyte). England and Scotland have far higher proportions of young people in custody and secure accommodation than most countries in western Europe, despite evidence of high rates of recidivism (Goldson; Whyte). This has paradoxically been accompanied by values that support social inclusion as far as possible, and also place faith in dialogue and activity-based measures in the community.

In many countries, including Sweden, England and Scotland, quite commonly the same residential establishments are used both for young people who offend and those with major care needs, even though this mix can be problematic for staff and residents alike. This applies to those placed in locked provision, whether to protect others or themselves (Berridge and Brodie 1998; Hollander and Tärnfalk; Rose 2002). Goldson argues that such confinement is often detrimental to young people's welfare and unjustified as regards both rights and outcomes.

Monitoring and assessing whole systems

It was noted in the Introduction that national and local policies are increasingly judged on evidence about their effectiveness, though establishing 'what works' is not straightforward (Creekmore; Trinder and Reynolds 2000). The impact of specific interventions can be assessed in various ways, but making judgements about the effects of whole systems, especially across jurisdictions, is very difficult because of the complex interplay of many factors, processes and institutions (Waterhouse). It may be possible to identify whether or not desired changes have occurred, but not necessarily to attribute with confidence the 'cause' of the change to particular decisions, service interventions or any of a wide range of environmental factors. Clearly, though, if the desired changes are not happening (e.g. youth crime is rising), then in a simple sense the system is not achieving its desired end. Even then, if progress is better than elsewhere (youth crime is rising more slowly than in other countries), this may still be seen as a form of success. Kuenssberg argues that, although there are many difficulties involved in judging the success of decision-making and the associated service interventions, it is nevertheless a vital task to assemble a wide range of evidence in order to see what aspects are satisfactory and what needs to improve. Waterhouse stresses that any system should be careful to ensure that children are not harmed by the processes of decision-making or the subsequent interventions. Avoidance of such 'collateral damage' has been a key consideration in arguments for separating youth justice, in order to lessen the chances of net-widening and disproportionate responses by adults acting on the basis of what they regard is best for children.

Integrated systems require to be judged on a wide range of dimensions concerning children's safety, welfare and behaviour, which makes judgements about outcomes complicated (Waterhouse). Kuenssberg describes how the Scottish system has been subject at different times to criticisms that it is not meeting either its offending-reduction or its welfare-promotion goals well, but concrete evidence about actual effectiveness has been sparse. Waterhouse notes that crime rates for 12–15-year-olds in Scotland increased at a considerably slower rate than in England during the 1990s, but this cannot conclusively be attributed to differences in the systems (such as the higher proportion of cases formally processed in Scotland). Separate systems are judged on more specific criteria, but youth justice policies have implications for children's welfare, while care and protection measures will affect children's behaviour in the community and at school (Goldson; Waterhouse).

The paucity of research evidence has reinforced a reliance on inquiries and audits (Buckley and O'Sullivan; Ennis; Waterhouse). These can certainly provide helpful pointers to problems and potential solutions (Munro 2002), but are often prompted by extreme cases or particular concerns that may not represent typical practices.

A key feature of governance in the late twentieth and early twenty-first centuries has been the emphasis on seeking to control and improve organisational performance by means of setting targets and standards, combined with the production of agency statistics to judge the actual performance in relation to these goals (Kuenssberg; Lawrence 2004). A crucial consideration is thus how appropriate are the targets. Also, critical awareness is necessary about the construction and meaning of numerical indicators and the sometimes unintended or even perverse consequences these may have, alongside the benefits of knowing how well organisations are meeting their goals. Kuenssberg observes that it is essential to understand the outcomes of intervention at the level of both the individual child and aggregate populations. Hence both case and statistical data are required. Decision-makers like members of Scottish children's panels and English Youth Offender Panels are involved in regular reviews of progress (Bottoms and Kemp; Reid and Gillan). Hence they are aware of individual outcomes at least in the sample of cases they are exposed to, whereas commonly judges do not know the effects of their sentences unless the same person reappears on a new charge. Kuenssberg also highlights the importance of feedback from service users (mainly children and parents) about the quality of communication and services.

Having considered the ways in which different systems may be organised, we now concentrate on the position of children and community members, with the notion of citizenship providing a connecting thread.

Citizenship: rights and responsibilities

Citizenship is a concept that illuminates both children's position when subject to state intervention and the role of those making decisions about when and how to intervene. At the centre of the debate on the proper treatment of young people are questions concerning what ought to be done for them (rights) and what can legitimately be expected of them (responsibilities). In pre-modern times there was a standing presumption that the nurture, care and education of children, together with their discipline and control, was almost entirely a matter for the family or household, while the public sphere was exclusively the domain of adult male citizens. Just as classical thought and democratic theory were slow to acknowledge the equality of women and the relevance of the private sphere to the business of the state, the legacy of which remains in many contemporary institutions, finding the proper place for the child in relation to the state has been equally testing. It is not an overstatement to say that the purportedly democratic states whose institutions this book discusses have been implicitly redefining the boundaries between private and public, thereby contributing and responding to changing conceptions of youth and childhood. The general shift has been increasingly to view children not merely as passive subjects, who deserve what others decree is for their good, but as potential or actual citizens.

The ambiguous status of children permeates current theory and policy on citizenship (Lister 2005; Lockyer 2003). There is considerable uncertainty as to whether those below the age of majority should be regarded as current citizens or what Marshall calls 'citizens in the making'. This depends partly on whether a legal entitlement to vote in state elections is deemed a necessary condition for being a citizen or whether it is sufficient to have the social rights and responsibilities associated with state membership. These include rights to safety and protection, as well as responsibilities to behave lawfully. The expansion of the rights and duties of young people that has taken place in the last three decades supports the case for conceptualising them as active citizens, before they are invested with all the political rights of adults.

Viewing children as citizens involves acknowledging both their rights and their responsibilities. Evidence suggests that children themselves see citizenship to be closely tied to accepting responsibilities towards others beyond the family and not harming them (Graham *et al.* 2005; Lister *et al.* 2003). Observing the law is an important aspect of respecting the rights of others. The reciprocity between rights and duties is more than a logical relationship; that involves an ethical connection immature citizens must learn about (Lockyer 2003).

The UN Convention on the Rights of the Child (1989) in its Preamble acknowledges that many of the rights declared to be universal in other charters of rights apply to children just as to adults, but that children have a special class of rights in virtue of their particular vulnerability. Archard reminds us that the UNCRC does not settle the question of what legal rights children ought to have, but does provide 'the single most important contemporary formulation of what by general agreement children are entitled to' (p.254). It is often noted that the UNCRC contains a dichotomy between participation and protection rights, and that a balance must be struck between them that reflects a particular child's age and maturity. Rights to receive the necessities of life, care, protection and education (welfare rights of recipience) are unconditional, since they are not dependent on the developed capacity of rational choice, unlike rights of action, to exercise liberties and participate in life-affecting decisions, which are. Archard and others detect an element of tension between protective rights and participatory rights in the Convention, but this reflects the reality that 'children' include both the very young with little or no rational capacity and those whose competences are at least the equal of many adults.

It is a long-standing and widespread criticism of the 'welfare approach' to dealing with young offenders that well-meaning adults, whether parents, community representatives or agents of the court, have too much discretion to determine what children need. Making children's interests paramount, or 'a primary consideration' (as required by Article 3), is no safeguard against indeterminate loss of liberty and a harmful outcome (Bottoms and Kemp). The experience of juvenile justice in America exemplified by the Gault case and the judgment delivered by the US Supreme Court, carries a universally valid warning about the dangers of unrestrained paternalism (Duquette). However, it is not so clear whether or not salvation lies in using the standards of due process that apply to adults, and replacing indeterminate compulsory welfare by determinate and proportionate sentences (Goldson; Korpinen and Pösö). Seeking to reconcile proportionality and suitability in relation to an offence with appropriateness for the child's welfare needs is a complex matter (Hollander and Tärnfalk). In child protection proceedings, increasing formality runs the risk of losing the participation of parents (Duquette).

A potentially powerful check on the excesses of paternalism is provided by the principle of Article 12 of the UNCRC to take account of children's views and give them 'due weight in all matters that affect them', and ensure children's views are represented in any judicial proceeding. But adopting the formal principle of listening to children and making provision for child advocacy carries no guarantees of 'due weight' or 'equality', which Marshall observes is required by the European Convention on Human Rights. It is necessary to strike a balance between the rights of children and of parents, including their respective rights to privacy, while also taking account of the legitimate interests of the state in preserving peace and order (Marshall).

The growing recognition of the capacity for young people to make competent choices and be self-determining to a degree undermines the disposition to explain or excuse their shortcomings through lack of maturity, which underpins the differential treatment of crime by children and adults. Archard suggests that the attribution of participatory rights to children may reinforce the view that they should be treated more like adults with respect to the criminal law. Antipaternalism risks denying some of the legitimate protection that children deserve, including being treated as less culpable than adults.

Shifts in the US and Canadian systems for dealing with youth crime, away from consideration of children's welfare and towards approaches based on protecting communities from offenders and on targeted responses, have been associated with a growth in custodial responses (Creekmore; Waterhouse). Young people in their teens have increasingly been treated in just the same way as adults, which has often meant punitively. In England, too, there has been a sharp increase in the incarceration of young people and of tragic consequences of this following the transfer of youth offending to criminal justice legislation and organisations, away from child care legislation with its emphasis on minimum necessary intervention (Goldson). In contrast, Ireland has a clear statutory commitment to use of detention as a last resort, albeit accompanied by a growth in actual provision (Buckley and O'Sullivan).

One of the virtues of the UNCRC is that it acknowledges that children develop from dependency to relative autonomy within particular cultures, with states having universal obligations to observe human rights and respect cultural differences. All states recognise that children have rights to welfare and protection before they acquire duties to others. States must intervene with remedial measures if parents fail to meet fundamental welfare needs. Once children have developed the capacity to exercise liberties, or enjoy participatory rights, they must also be able to acknowledge their responsibilities, including respecting the rights of others. This does not mean that care and protection gives way abruptly or smoothly to the rights of competent agency and the exercise of civic duties. There is a developmental process that is cognitive, psychodynamic and social; it includes learning within families, from peers, at school and in the associations of civil society. Viewing childhood as the development of citizenship acknowledges an interdependence of the personal and the public interest.

The state's task may be conceived as that of the overseeing umpire or the gardener, both facilitating and nurturing (Oakeshott 1975). All states have mechanisms to assist in the process both by uniformly providing mandated education and selectively offering support, where necessary under compulsion. It is important that the community's interests in producing the citizens required for its future stability and prosperity do not override doing what is best for particular children now (Qvortrup *et al.* 1994).

Although development is varied and gradual, all jurisdictions operate with age thresholds, including an age of presumed incapacity below which young people cannot be held to have committed a criminal offence. In the Introduction we noted that these are widely variable. A common feature, though, is a mechanism for compulsory intervention below the age of criminal capacity to respond to serious harm caused by children, as well as when children are victims or at risk. There is no neat shift from child protection to child prosecution. The need for the former is not cancelled or negated by the occasion of the latter. The overlapping identity of offenders and those in need of care has been a recurring theme in this book (e.g. Buckley and O'Sullivan; Creekmore; Goldson; Waterhouse).

What has been relatively neglected in the preceding chapters is the ground for intervention that often correlates with both offending behaviour and inadequate parental support, namely failure to attend school. What Aristotle called 'right upbringing', at home and in the community, is education for citizenship as well as for individual self-realisation. It is certainly something in which the community at large must have an interest and is equally a duty that the citizen owes to be able to make his or her due contribution to state and society. Failure to attend school may be viewed as a comprehensive loss to individuals, families and communities alike, quite apart from associated dysfunction and trouble. Conversely, compulsory measures to improve children's care or behaviour are forms of remedial education. Uncertainty about how best to handle school non-attendance is shown by the fact that at different times and in different countries it has been dealt with, in court or elsewhere, as an offence by child and/or parent or an administrative matter, with the child's welfare or behaviour as the primary focus (Blyth and Milner 1999; Wardhaugh 1991).

Community involvement

Increased community involvement by adult citizens is a current trend in decision-making in both care and protection and youth justice proceedings.

Several chapters of this book have illustrated growing attention in several countries to the involvement of lay members of the community instead of, or more commonly alongside, the contribution of professionals and officials (Bottoms and Kemp; Hollander and Tärnfalk; Korpinen and Pösö). There are, of course, long-standing traditions of unpaid local community involvement in judicial decision-making, notably in the form of lay magistrates and juries. The former were recruited in the past mainly from the local elite and juries selected largely by a quasi-random process to achieve a cross-section of the eligible adult community (Reid and Gillan).

English youth courts have typically been presided over by lay magistrates (with advice from a legally qualified clerk), while Finnish juvenile courts normally comprise one legally trained and three lay judges (Korpinen and Pösö). In Scandinavia, it has been common for elected representatives to play a key part in major decisions about children, as with Swedish Social Welfare Boards, whose conclusions are normally accepted by the courts (Hollander and Tärnfalk). This democratic mode of community representation contrasts with selection elsewhere based on status, expertise, random choice or open application (Reid and Gillan).

Lay panel members have been central to the Scottish Children's Hearings System over the past 35 years and their role in making disposals has recently been paralleled by Youth Offender Panels in England, which deal with initial offending referrals, except that one of the three panel members is a youth offending professional (Bottoms and Kemp). In all these instances, the involvement of lay people is associated with greater informality compared with the courts. This is generally seen to provide greater opportunity for decision-makers to engage with young people and their families in the decision process.

Reid and Gillan describe how lay representation in decision-making must blend with legal and child-specific expertise. Community representatives may be involved in decisions about facts or outcomes relating to child welfare and safety, and in determining appropriate responses to offending. The legitimacy of involving non-expert citizens derives from their representation of the public interest and, more specifically, the interest of the communities to which young people and their families belong. This depends in turn on the claim that intervention decisions are moral judgements that cannot be the preserve of experts. Lay members bring to bear notions of acceptable child rearing and parenting, which reflect community norms. Crucially, the good that might be achieved by compulsory measures has to be balanced with the loss of liberty to children and their parents, and this, ultimately, is for fellow citizens not paid experts to judge.

The Scottish Children's Hearings System is presented by Reid and Gillan (and endorsed by Kuenssberg, Marshall and Whyte) as an appropriate model for lay decision-making. As both Marshall and Duquette observe, there are provisions within this system to protect the rights of parties, including importantly the right of appeal to a more formally constituted court. Nonetheless Ennis argues that subject-specific expertise concerning the nature and implications of child abuse is essential for appropriate decision-making. He questions whether it is right for lay people to make decisions about children's protection, given the complexity of the individual cases and the wide range of relevant knowledge required. While the history of child abuse inquiries is largely the story of professional failings, this cannot itself be the sole ground for greater reliance on community common sense.

Similarly, Finnish lay social welfare boards have been criticised for lacking the qualifications to make complex decisions about families (Korpinen and Pösö). While the knowledge and understanding thought necessary to make sound decisions can be provided by professional testimony and reports, lay people may be thought incapable of assessing risk and resisting the plausible assurances or emotional appeal of distraught family members.

According to Ennis and others, lay people lack the knowledge necessary for effective decision-making in child protection even though they do receive some training. An opposite criticism can be made that any significant training is undesirable as it will professionalise lay decision-makers, thereby distancing them from ordinary citizens and detracting from their community representation. Reid and Gillan suggest that this misrepresents the nature of appropriate training. Drawing on Scottish experience, they argue that its purpose is not to create experts. Training teaches how to conduct proceedings according to the rules and how to make use of specialists. At least as important, it promotes learning through peer discussion about the bases of decisions. Discursive reflection on common experience helps citizens think through the moral precepts held by themselves and members of the communities they represent.

Marshall makes the point that an independent tribunal is one of the prerequisites of a fair decision procedure. Citizen decision-makers begin with the advantage of having no professionally vested interest in the decision or the process. This might require that their appointment and tenure should not be at the discretion of any body with an involvement with the outcome of cases. There is an issue as to whether impartiality requires that prior knowledge of a case should disqualify lay decision-makers. In jury trials, unexamined knowledge of the case is grounds for a juror standing down, although after proof informal knowledge might be deemed valuable rather than prejudicial. This raises a bigger question about community-based justice.

Most western countries have now developed their own versions of the New Zealand Family Group Conference (Duquette; Korpinen and Pösö), itself modelled on traditional kin network ways of dealing with family problems and deviance from approved behaviour. These can apply with respect to concerns about child safety, youth offending or both. For instance, Irish law now requires a Family Welfare Conference to be held when admission of a child to secure accommodation is being considered (Buckley and O'Sullivan).

When we consider that for many the primary influences for good or ill are located within the familial community, its exclusion from decision-making forums is a major weakness of formal juvenile justice systems. However, there is an implicit trade-off between the virtues of due process and impartiality (also perhaps proportionality) and the partiality of family-based justice. For this reason state officials seldom hand complete control to the extended family and significant others. They normally retain a right to impose their disposals where necessary, but seek to facilitate and prioritise an agreed informal solution whenever possible.

Such measures are primarily aimed at eliciting family help to divert children from formal action (Duquette). At the same time, many countries have introduced measures to compel the family to control its members more effectively. In Ireland, as in England and Scotland, parenting orders are now available to oblige parents to attend treatment or training (Buckley and O'Sullivan) and in California parents can be required to attend drug treatment facilities (Ennis). There are obvious dangers in adopting what may be seen by parents as punitive measures, especially since the shortcomings of parents and their partners often include the disposition to blame the child. Measures to encourage and facilitate parental responsibility are normally best delivered outside the formal court setting.

Especially in relation to youth crime, the popularity of restorative justice principles has encouraged the development of a wide range of community-based problem-solving and mediation practices (Duquette; Korpinen and Pösö). These often involve members of civil society, including victims, being willing to engage with the response to criminal activity. Creekmore says that these indicate a convergence in approaches to social welfare and youth justice. In Duquette's view, they offer a means of reconciling the value of access to informal processes with the safeguards of procedural protections to personal liberty, softening the hard edges of the adversarial process.

While the research on the effectiveness and success of restorative justice projects is mixed (Haines 2000), the significance of confronting young offenders with the consequences of their actions and providing the opportunity for those directly harmed, or indirectly affected, to elect to contribute to rehabilitation should not be underestimated. The concept of listening to the young, seeking to understand them and allowing them to contribute to the resolution of problems, whether of their own creation, or those for which others bear more responsibility, is a way of investing them with the respect due to citizens. The degree to which state institutions permit or encourage community solutions to problems arising therein has important implications for the extent to which the citizens affected, child and adult, are included in their communities rather than separated from them.

Conclusions

The origins of this volume lay in widespread beliefs that integration of care and protection issues alongside offending, and indeed school non-attendance, in the Scottish Children's Hearings System formed a sharp contrast with most other countries in western Europe and North America, where many commentators indicated that youth justice systems were largely separate from care and protection (e.g van der Laan 2003; Muncie 2004). Closer review of the literature and contributions to the book have shown that the situation is much more nuanced. Quite often youth crime is dealt with by separate courts and on a different basis compared with care concerns, but in many countries this division operates only above the age of 15, so integration persists for younger children. The position of associated services, ranging from community-based initiatives to secure accommodation, are also complex, with much overlap in clientele and attention to both children's needs and deeds.

Similarly, both academic literature and policies have commonly presented the case for and against separation of youth offending in terms of a debate between so-called 'welfare' and 'justice' approaches. Both the terminology and polarisation are misleading. Integration does foreground the child's best interests whatever the grounds for considering state intervention, but is also based on age-old principles of justice. Conversely, arguments in favour of separation are based on support for formalised procedural rights partly because of beliefs that this results in better and fairer outcomes for children. The principles underpinning compulsory state intervention related to social justice, children's rights and notions of punishment, suggest the need for all systems to take account of children's welfare whatever the basis for action, as required by the UNCRC, but do not lead on to a presumption that either integration or separation is inherently right. Rather any system has to balance a complex set of principles as well as an array of empirical evidence about the origins of childhood problems, the effectiveness of different kinds of intervention and the importance of inter-agency collaboration.

What we learn most emphatically when examining child protection and youth offender systems in parallel is that the subjects of intervention are neither typically passive innocents nor demonic reprobates, but young citizens in trouble having both rights and duties. It is clear that the causes of risks to children and of risks posed by children to others have much in common, while often the same individuals will be involved with decision-making bodies and service agencies on the basis of both welfare needs and behaviour. Hence, whether or not systems are integrated, conjoined, separated or overlapping, our thinking about young people does need to be integrated and holistic.

References

Beck, U. and Beck-Gernsheim, E. (2002) *Individualization*. London: Sage.

Berridge, D. and Brodie, I. (1998) *Children's Homes Revisited*. London: Jessica Kingsley Publishers.

Blyth, E. and Milner, J. (1999) *Improving School Attendance*. London: Routledge.

Boushel, M. (1994) 'The Protective Environment of Children: Towards a Framework for Anti-oppressive, Cross-cultural and Cross-national Understanding.' *British Journal of Social Work 24*, 173–190.

Buckley, H. (2003) *Child Protection Work*. London: Jessica Kingsley Publishers.

Burnett, R. and Appleton, C. (2004) *Joined-up Youth Justice: Tackling Youth Crime in Partnership*. Lyme Regis: Russell House Publishing.

Cairns, K. (2002) *Attachment, Trauma and Resilience: Therapeutic Caring for Children*. London: BAAF.

Canavan, J., Dolan, P. and Pinkerton, J. (2000) *Family Support: Direction from Diversity*. London: Jessica Kingsley Publishers.

Dominelli, L. (1999) *Community Approaches to Child Welfare: International Perspectives.* Aldershot: Ashgate.

Filmer, R. (1949) *Patriarcha and other Political Works.* (ed P. Laslett). Oxford: Blackwell.

Gilligan, R. (1999) 'Enhancing the Resilience of Children and Young People in Public Care by Mentoring their Talents and Interests.' *Child and Family Social Work 4,* 3, 187–196.

Graham, A., Shipway, B., Fitzgerald, R. and Whelan, J. (2005) *Children and Young People's Perspectives on Rights, Responsibilities, and Citizenship in Australia.* Australia: Centre for Children and Young People, Southern Cross University.

Haines, K. and Drakeford, M. (1998) *Young People and Youth Justice.* Basingstoke: Macmillan.

Haines, K. (2000) 'Referral Orders and Youth Offender Panels: restorative approaches and the new youth justice.' In B. Goldson (ed) *The New Youth Justice.* Lyme Regis: Russell House Publishing.

Hallett, C. (1995) *Interagency Coordination in Child Protection.* London: HMSO.

Hardiker, P., Exton, K. and Barker, M. (1991) *Policies and Practices in Preventative Child Care.* Aldershot: Avebury.

Hill, M. (2000) 'The residential child care context.' In M. Chakrabarti and M. Hill (eds) *Residential Child Care: International Perspectives on Links with Families and Peers.* London: Jessica Kingsley Publishers.

Jonkman, H.B., Junger-Tas, J. and van Dijk, B. (2005) 'From Behind Dikes and Dunes: Communities that Care in the Netherlands.' *Children and Society 19,* 2, 105–116.

Jonson-Reid, M. (2004) 'Child Welfare Services and Delinquency: The Need to Know More.' *Child Welfare 83,* 2, 157–173.

Lawrence, A. (2004) *Principles of Child Protection: Management and Practice.* Maidenhead: Open University Press.

Lister, R. (2005) 'Investing in the citizen-workers of the future.' In H. Hendrick (ed) *Child Welfare and Social Policy: An Essential Reader.* Bristol: The Policy Press.

Lister, R., Smith, N., Middleton, S. and Cox, L. (2003) 'Young People Talk about Citizenship: Empirical Perspectives on Theoretical and Political Debates.' *Citizenship Studies 7,* 2, 235–253.

Lockyer, A. (2003) 'The political status of children and young people.' In A. Lockyer, B. Crick and J. Annette (eds) *Education for Democratic Citizenship: Issues of Theory and Practice.* Aldershot: Ashgate.

Marshall, K. (1997) *Children's Rights in the Balance: The Participation – Protection Debate.* Edinburgh: Stationery Office.

Muncie, J. (2004) 'Youth justice: globalisation and multi-modal governance.' In T. Newburn and E. Spark (eds) *Criminal Justice and Political Cultures.* Devon: Willan.

Munro, E. (2002) *Effective Child Protection.* London: Sage.

Oakeshott, M. (1975) *On Human Conduct.* Oxford: Clarendon Press.

Quinton, D. (2004) *Supporting Parents: Messages from Research.* London: Jessica Kingsley Publishers.

Qvortrup, J., Bardy, M., Sgritta, G. and Wintersberger, H. (1994) *Childhood Matters.* Aldershot: Avebury.

Robinson Lowry, M., Freundlich, M. and Gerstenzang, S. (2002) 'Class Action Litigation: Judicial Reform of Child Welfare Systems in the United States.' *Adoption and Fostering 26,* 3, 50–57.

Rose, J. (2002) *Working with Young People in Secure Accommodation.* Hove: Brunner-Routledge.

Schweinhart, L. and Weikart, D. (1997) *The High/Scope Preschool Curriculum Comparison Study Through Age 23: Executive Summary: OMEP Update Number 87.* London: OMEP.

Taylor, C. (2004) 'Underpinning Knowledge for Child Care Practice: Reconsidering Child Development Theory.' *Child and Family Social Work 9,* 3, 225–236.

Trinder, L. and Reynolds, S. (2000) *Evidence-based Practice: A Critical Appraisal.* Oxford: Blackwell Science.

van der Laan, P. (and Committee of Experts) (2003) *European Committee on Crime Problems: Final Activity Report.* Strasbourg: Council of Europe.

Wardhaugh, J. (1991) 'Criminalising truancy: legal and welfare responses to school non-attendance.' In T. Booth (ed) *Juvenile Justice in the New Europe.* Sheffield: Joint Unit for Social Services Research.

The Contributors

David Archard is Professor of Philosophy and Public Policy at Lancaster University. He was previously Reader in Moral Philosophy at the University of St Andrews. He has published extensively in social, political, legal and applied moral philosophy, especially on the topic of children, family and the state. Among his most recent publications is the second revised edition of *Children, Rights and Childhood* (London: Routledge, 2004). He is Chair of the Society for Applied Philosophy. For seven and a half years David was a member of the Dundee Children's Panel.

Anthony Bottoms is Wolfson Professor of Criminology at the University of Cambridge and Professorial Fellow in Criminology at the University of Sheffield. He is a Fellow of the British Academy. Recent writings in the field of youth justice include essays on 'The divergent development of juvenile justice policy and practice in England and Scotland' (in M.K. Rosenheim *et al.*, *A Century of Juvenile Justice* (Chicago University Press, 2002)) and, with James Dignan, 'Youth justice in Great Britain' (in M. Tonry and A.N. Doob, *Youth Crime and Youth Justice* (Chicago University Press, 2004)). His principal current research is focused on desistance from crime among young adult recidivist offenders.

Helen Buckley is a Senior Lecturer in the School of Social Work and Social Policy at the University of Dublin, Trinity College. She recently directed a research project on the development of an integrated service for children who have experienced domestic violence and was a co-author of the recently published Ferns Inquiry into clerical sexual abuse in Co. Wexford in Ireland. She is a qualified social worker, and practised for a number of years in the areas of intellectual disability, adult mental health, and child and family services. She is the author of *Child Protection: Innovations and Interventions* (Dublin: Institute of Public Administration, 2002) and *Child Protection Work: Beyond the Rhetoric* (London: Jessica Kingsley Publishers, 2003).

Mark Creekmore has taught social welfare policy and practice for the last 15 years at the University of Michigan School of Social Work and is currently teaching community-based research in the UM Department of Psychology. He is founder and Executive Director of Community Service Systems, Inc., a non-profit organisation that conducts evaluation research with arts and social service agencies, especially juvenile courts, and substance abuse, domestic violence and violence prevention programmes. His focus has been on quality improvement for service models. Recently, he has focused on community-based participatory action research involving campus–community collaborations that increase civic engagement among diverse individuals, organisations and communities. Before focusing on research and teaching, he worked for 15 years in administration and programme development in social service agencies. He participated in the deinstutitionalisation and the creation of community services for developmentally disabled and mentally ill adults and for delinquent and neglected youth.

Donald N. Duquette is Clinical Professor of Law and Director of the Child Advocacy Law Clinic at the University of Michigan Law School, where he has developed one of the most respected and influential child advocacy law programmes in the country. Most recently he has been co-director, with Marvin Ventrell of the National Association of Counsels for Children, a national effort to certify lawyers as specialists in child welfare law. The NACC National Certification Project has been accredited by the American Bar Association and supported by the US Children's Bureau. Duquette and Ventrell are the editors of a recent book that represents the body of knowledge that defines child welfare as a specialised field of law practice in the USA: *Child Welfare Law and Practice: Representing Children, Parents and State Agencies in Abuse, Neglect and Dependency Cases* (Bradford Legal Publishers, 2005). He has published over 40 articles and book chapters on the subjects of child protection, foster care and child advocacy. Professor Duquette has received a number of awards, including the NACC Outstanding Legal Advocacy Award, the North American Council on Adoptable Children Adoption Activist Award, and the Gerald G. Hicks Child Welfare Leadership Award from the Michigan Federation of Private Child and Family Agencies.

Jim Ennis is a social worker with 30 years' experience of work with vulnerable children in need of care and protection. He followed 15 years in practice agencies with a 15-year spell in the university sector and was Director of Studies for the National (Scotland) Child Care and Protection programme from the early 1990s until moving to be a Senior Consultant with Outcomes UK in 2003. The organisation operates in the broad social care field across the UK, specialising in change management and staff development work in child care and is part of the FCA group of companies. During his period at the University of Dundee, his work included faculty leadership to an annual international five-day Child Forensic Interview Training Clinic and he had a particular interest in examining practitioner learning and practice outcomes. Jim continues to provide consultations on complex individual child care and protection cases to practitioners and to staff groups, has provided expert witness reports on child protection issues to courts in England, Scotland and Ireland, and has lectured across Europe and in the United States. He recently completed a six-year appointment as an external examiner for the Open University's social work degree programme, currently chairs the Foster Care Associates (FCA) Fostering Panel for Scotland and writes a quarterly column for *FosterTalk*.

Ian Gillan is research assistant to Professor Andrew Lockyer in the Department of Politics, University of Glasgow. He recently completed a postgraduate degree in Human Rights and International Politics at the same institution, writing his thesis on theories of human nature and human rights.

Barry Goldson is Professor of Criminology and Social Policy in the School of Criminology and Social Policy at The University of Liverpool, where he is also Director of Research. His teaching and research interests include the sociology of childhood and youth, criminology and criminal justice (particularly youth crime and youth justice), and state welfare policy. He has published extensively in each of these areas and his books include: *Youth Justice: Contemporary Policy and Practice* (1999); *The New Youth Justice* (2000); *Children, Welfare and the State* (2002, with Lavalette and McKechnie); *Vulnerable Inside: Children in Secure and Penal Settings* (2002); *In the Care of the State? Child Deaths in Penal Custody in England and Wales* (2005, with Coles); *Youth Crime and Justice* (2006, with Muncie) and *Comparative Youth Justice* (2006, with Muncie). He has presented over 100 papers at conferences in the UK, Europe, Australia and the USA, and is the editor of *Youth Justice*, the leading peer-reviewed journal in the UK specialising in youth crime and youth justice.

Malcolm Hill is Research Professor at the University of Strathclyde. For ten years he was the Director of the Glasgow Centre for the Child & Society and previously a social worker and lecturer. He has written widely on issues to do with child care and protection – for example, about foster and residential care, with colleagues John Triseliotis and Moira Walker. In recent years he has led research on the Scottish Children's Hearings System in relation to Safeguarding and the Fast Track pilot. Among his publications are *Children and Society* (with Kay Tisdall, Longman), *Effective Ways of Working with Children and Families* (Jessica Kingsley Publishers) and *Shaping Child Care Practice in Scotland* (BAAF).

Anna Hollander has been a Professor of Legal Science and Social Work at the Department of Social Work, Stockholm University, Sweden since 2000. She finished her doctoral degree at the Department of Law in Umeå, Sweden, in 1985 and has held different university positions in other countries, for example, Sydney, Australia, and Toronto, Canada. Her main research areas are in child welfare and legal regulation for disabled people. She is presently a member of the faculty board at Stockholm University and a member of the Swedish Council for Working Life and Social

Research. Anna Hollander is also a member of the advisory board of three scientific journals. Recent publications include 'The Social Services Act on Contract – Legal Conditions for Private Investigators in Child Care Cases.' *Socialvetenskaplig Tidskrift* *2–3*, 208–225 (2005) and, with Nygren and Olsen Uppsala, *Children and Rights.* Uppsala, Sweden: Iustus förlag (2004).

Dr Vicky Kemp is a Principal Researcher at the Legal Services Research Centre, an independent research arm of the Legal Services Commission. She has specific responsibility for research into criminal legal aid and the wider criminal justice system. Vicky recently completed her doctorate into youth justice reforms at the Institute of Criminology, University of Cambridge. Recent publications regarding youth justice issues include 'Youth justice: discretion in pre-court decision-making' (co-authored with Loraine Gelsthorpe, in Gelsthorpe and Padfield (eds) *Exercising Discretion: Decision-making in the Criminal Justice System and Beyond* (Willan Publishing, 2003) and 'Comparative juvenile justice: England and Wales' (co-authored with Loraine Gelsthorpe) in J. Winterdyk (ed) *Comparative Juvenile Justice* (2nd edn) (Canadian Scholars' Press, 2002). She has also published, together with Sorsby, Liddle and Merrington, *Assessing Responses to Youth Offending in Northamptonshire* (NACRO Research Briefing No. 2, 2002).

Johanna Korpinen obtained an MA in social policy and, at the time of writing, is a doctoral student in social work at the Department of Social Policy and Social Work, University of Tampere, Finland. Her dissertation deals with the institutional practices and encounters that take place in oral hearings in the administrative courts concerned with taking children into care. The research project is funded by the SOSNET postgraduate school.

Sally Kuenssberg had a varied career in education and publishing, both in Scotland and abroad, then worked for 20 years in the Scottish juvenile justice system, as a volunteer children's panel member, a lecturer in Glasgow University responsible for the training of panel members in Strathclyde and Dumfries and Galloway, and from 1995–2002 as the first chair of the Scottish Children's Reporter Administration. She led the national group that produced a *Blueprint for the Processing of Children's Hearings Cases* (1999) including national standards and protocols for the referral of children to the Reporter by different agencies. From 1993–2004 she served on the Board of the Yorkhill NHS Trust, Glasgow, latterly as its chair, and remains a member of the NHS Greater Glasgow and Clyde Board. She has taken a particular interest in children's services and the rights of children and young people within health care. Among other voluntary activities, she has since 2003 been a Trustee of Save the Children and chairs its Scottish Council. She was awarded the CBE in the Millennium Honours for services to child welfare and justice.

Andrew Lockyer is Professor of Citizenship and Social Theory and is currently head of the Department of Politics at Glasgow University where he has taught since 1970. He has researched and published in the history of political thought and political, social and legal theory. He served for many years as a lay children's panel member in Scotland, and has published extensively on the Children's Hearings System. His publications include: *A Study of Children's Hearings in Relation to Resources (1989); Citizens Serving Children: A Study of Children's Panel Membership in Scotland* (1993); with F. Stone, *Juvenile Justice in Scotland: Twenty-five Years of the Welfare Approach* (1998). More recently he has written on citizenship education with Crick and Annette (eds) in *Education for Democratic Citizenship: Issues of Theory and Practice* (2003) and is involved in promoting children's rights and political literacy in schools.

Kathleen Marshall holds degrees in law, philosophy and theology, and qualified as a solicitor in 1975. Her early experience was in local government in Glasgow. She was Director of the Scottish Child Law Centre from 1989 to 1994. On leaving the Centre, she worked as a child law consultant, addressing many aspects of the lives of children and young people, including family matters, education, international child abduction, health, public care, criminal justice and participation in court processes. She is Visiting Professor at the Glasgow Centre for the Child & Society at the University of Glasgow. In April 2004, she took up post as Scotland's first Commissioner for Children and Young People, with a remit to promote and safeguard the rights of children and young people in Scotland. Publications include *Children's Rights in the Balance* (Edinburgh: The Stationery Office), and *Honouring Children: The Human Rights of the Child in Christian Perspectives,* with Paul Parvis (Edinburgh: Saint Andrew Press, 2004).

Eoin O'Sullivan lectures in Social Policy in the School of Social Work and Social Policy at the University of Dublin, Trinity College. His research interests include the history of child welfare and use of institutions to regulate populations. Recent collaborative publications include: *Crime, Punishment and the Search for Order in Ireland* (Dublin: Institute of Public Administration, 2004); *Crime Control in Ireland: The Politics of Intolerance* (Cork: Cork University Press, 2001); and *Suffer the Little Children: The Inside Story of Ireland's Industrial Schools* (Dublin and New York: Continuum Books, 1999, 2001).

Tarja Pösö is professor in Social Work at the Department of Social Policy and Social Work, University of Tampere, Finland. She has been studying families, social problems and social work, especially child protection, from different perspectives for several years. Her latest research deals with young people in residential care and focuses in particular on the methodological and ethical issues in that field of study.

Barbara Reid is Head of the Children's Hearings Training Unit, based in the Department of Adult and Continuing Education, Faculty of Education at Glasgow University. The Unit is responsible for training members of Children's Hearings, children's panel advisory committee members and safeguarders. She has been involved with the Children's Hearings System since 1974, first as a panel member. In 1996 she received an OBE for her services to the system. During her involvement with the Hearings she has been involved in the Children's Panel Chairman's Group research project 'Citizen's Serving Children' and wrote a chapter for the book *Juvenile Justice – Twenty-five Years of the Welfare Approach*, edited by Lockyer and Stone (T&T Clark, 1998). She contributes to teacher training courses at Glasgow and Strathclyde Universities and with the Legal Services Agency. She is involved as a lay member and chair of Yorkhill Hospital, Research Ethics Committee.

Frederick H. Stone is Emeritus Professor of Child and Adolescent Psychiatry, University of Glasgow. He was Secretary-General, International Association for Child Psychiatry, 1962–66; Member, Kilbrandon Committee, 1963–65 and Houghton Committee on Adoption, 1968–71; Chairman, Children's Panel Advisory Committee, Strathclyde, 1988–93; Chairman, Child Protection Committee, University of Dundee, 1994–98. Among his publications are *Child Psychiatry for Students* (with Koupernik, Paris, 1985) and *Juvenile Justice in Scotland* (with Lockyer, 1998). He was awarded an OBE in 1993 for services to children.

Michael Tärnfalk has been a professional social worker since 1990. He has worked mainly with young offenders as a social service officer. Since 2001 he has been a doctoral student at the Department of Social Work, Stockholm University, Sweden. In this work he is studying the role of social welfare law and social work with respect to the criminal process and young offenders. He is an active writer of articles in social work journals.

Lorraine Waterhouse is Head of the School of Social and Political Studies at the University of Edinburgh. She was appointed to the Chair of Social Work in 1994. Her research concentrates on children and families, their health and development. She is a chair of the Complaints Tribunal for the City of Edinburgh Council. She was a member of the Parole Board for Scotland for six years. Educated in Canada, she came to Scotland in 1972 when she worked as a social worker in the Department of Child and Family Psychiatry in the Royal Hospital for Sick Children, Edinburgh. She has written widely on responses to both child abuse and youth crime. Recent articles include: with McGhee and Loucks, 'Disentangling Offenders and Non-Offenders in the Scottish Children's Hearings: A Clear Divide?' *The Howard Journal 43*, 2, May 2004, 164–179; with McGhee, 'Children's Hearings in Scotland: Compulsion and Disadvantage.' *Journal of Social Welfare and Family Law 24*, 3, 2002, 279–296.

Bill Whyte is Senior Lecturer in Social Work at the University of Edinburgh, and Director of the Criminal Justice Social Work Development Centre for Scotland, Universities of Edinburgh and Stirling. Bill teaches on criminal and youth justice social work policy, law, and practice on undergraduate, post-qualifying and postgraduate programmes. He has worked as a social work manager and field social worker in the Lothians, as a residential care worker in a (former) List D residential school and as an independent chair of child protection for a small Scottish Local Authority. He is a member of the National Community Justice Accreditation Panel, and provides advice and consultancy to managers and workers in criminal justice social work, youth social work and to other related professionals. His current research includes Parenting Orders, Community Reparation Orders, National Sex Offenders' Groupwork Programme (CSOGP), Restorative Justice in Glasgow, Young People involved in Sexually Harmful Behaviour, and Evaluation in Youth Justice. Recent publications include, with McGhee and Mellon (eds) *Addressing Deeds: Working with Young People who Offend* (London: NCH, 2004), and 'Responding to Youth Crime in Scotland.' *British Journal of Social Work 34*, 4, 2004, 395–411.

Subject Index

Author Index